BULLIES BASTARDS & Bitches

HOW TO WRITE THE BAD GUYS OF FICTION

Jessica Page Morrell

WRITER'S DIGEST BOOKS
www.writersdigest.com
Cincinnati, Ohio

Published by Writer's Digest Books, an imprint of F+W Publications, Inc., 4700 East Galbraith Road, Cincinnati, Ohio 45236. (800) 289-0963. First edition.

Visit www.writersdigest.com/books for information on resources for writers.

To receive a free weekly e-mail newsletter delivering tips and updates about writing and about Writer's Digest products, register directly at http://newsletters.fwpublications.com.

12 11 10 09 08 5 4 3 2 1

Distributed in Canada by Fraser Direct, 100 Armstrong Avenue, Georgetown, Ontario, Canada L7G 5S4, Tel: (905) 877-4411; Distributed in the U.K. and Europe by David & Charles, Brunel House, Newton Abbot, Devon, TQ12 4PU, England, Tel: (+44) 1626 323200, Fax: (+44) 1626 323319, E-mail: postmaster@davidandcharles.co.uk; Distributed in Australia by Capricorn Link, P.O. Box 704, Windsor, NSW 2756 Australia, Tel: (02) 4577-3555

Library of Congress Cataloging-in-Publication Data

Morrell, Jessica Page

Bullies, bastards & bitches : how to write the bad guys of fiction / by Jessica Page Morrell. -- 1st ed.

p. cm.

ISBN 978-1-58297-484-2 (pbk. : alk. paper)

1. Villains in literature. 2. Characters and characteristics in literature. 3. Fiction--Authorship. I. Title. II. Title: Bullies, bastards and bitches.

PN3383.C4M67 2008

808.3--dc22

2008015526

Designed by Claudean Wheeler
Production coordinated by Mark Griffin

Dedication

To Miss Violet—the children's librarian in my hometown, who years ago recognized the avid reader in me—and to librarians and booksellers everywhere who help keep stories alive.

Acknowledgments

I am especially grateful to the many fiction authors whose books I have read in the past two years while writing this book, with special thanks to George R.R. Martin for creating his Song of Ice and Fire series that stole into my imagination and featured such captivating bad guys. Much gratitude to Stacey, Michele, Marian, Ron, and Clark for listening, and to Stephanie Kip Rostan for watching my back. Thanks are also in line for my editing clients who have taught me so much about what works and doesn't work in fiction. I am especially grateful that, after receiving my lengthy memos, none have hired a hit man. I am also grateful for the brave dears who have been participants in my fiction critique groups and laughed when I pounded the table, shouting, "This scene needs more conflict and about fifty shots of tequila!" And many thanks to the talented and wise Kelly Nickell for her superb editing.

About the Author

Jessica Page Morrell is the author of *The Writer's I Ching: Wisdom for the Creative Life*, *Voices from the Street*, *Between the Lines: Master The Subtle Elements of Fiction Writing*, and *Writing Out the Storm*. Additionally, in 2009 *Dear Bad Writer: A Compassionate Guide for Avoiding the Rejection Pile* will be published by Tarcher-Penguin.

Morrell works as a developmental editor and teaches writers through a series of workshops in the Northwest, at writing conferences throughout North America, and at Evergreen State College in Olympia, Washington. She hosts a Web site at www.writing-life.com, and she's written a monthly column about topics related to writing since 1998 that currently appears in *The Willamette Writer*. She also writes a monthly e-mail newsletter, *The Writing Life*, and a Web log, *The Writing Life Too*. She lives in Portland, where she is surrounded by writers.

Table of Contents

Note to Readers

For exclusive online content, including a glossary with character terms, a worksheet for developing character biographies, and age and formatting charts to help you write villains for younger readers, visit www.writersdigest.com/article/Bullies.

Preface

Between October 2004 and mid-March 2006, I wrote about 350,000 words to complete three nonfiction books. By the time I was finished, I felt anemic and wrung dry, so I began reading to replenish the words, concepts, and images I needed to write this book. Besides Timothy Egan's amazing account of the Dust Bowl days, *The Worst Hard Times*, and Erik Larson's *The Devil in the White City*, I read mostly fiction as a steady diet. I read like I was a lonely recluse while Oregon's spring rains wept down my windows and my flower beds began blooming. I read in the middle of the night, while I should have been editing or writing, in trains and planes and waiting rooms, and most often sprawled on my comfortable, overstuffed sofa.

I traveled far in my literary wanderings, and somewhere in the midst of this reading, a sort of triage for the writer's soul, my weariness subsided. The ragged edges of my brain started mending and were replaced by a galaxy of characters, plots, scenes, and bits that all added up to the particular alchemy that is fiction. And I fell back in love with this part of my life. And then in June 2006, I started writing this book; the ideas I wanted to bring forth, along with the characters who had been occupying my imagination, became my companions during these months of writing.

While I indulged in my reading spree, an important realization was taking shape. I realized that I was going to center this book on the fact that fictional characters are vulnerable.

While musing about this, I went walking in the gala that is Portland's springtime. We're a city of gardeners; everywhere, flowers, ferns, trees, and bushes were awash with color and new life. The air was perfumed and made sweet by blossoms. As sunsets took on a rosy afterglow, I kept walking and teasing at this idea of vulnerability and thinking about how it applied to my life, my relationships, and my sorrows. I cannot speak for your vulnerabilities, but I've been ripped off, lied to, slandered, gossiped about, slapped, falsely accused, and had my truths not believed. I've had my heart broken, had my pride stomped on, witnessed unforgivable acts, and heard words that hurt so much I wished that they would not replay in my head, but they did. In all these moments—some tear-soaked, some life-defining, but all character-building moments—I have felt vulnerable.

And I believe these feelings of vulnerability—when a person feels scared and alone and overwhelmed and pissed off, when the sting of unfairness bites deep—while miserable to live through, are the basis for writing compelling fiction. You see, we don't read fiction to follow the lives of perfect people who float through blissful days. We don't read fiction to applaud from the sidelines as a superhero who never missteps sails to victory. Nor do we read fiction to follow people in the midst of goodness, luck, success, and joy. Instead, we read to wallow in a character's misery and struggles, to plunge into his or her emotional depths, to experience the doubts, worries, and pains.

We worry when characters are vulnerable. And when we worry, we keep reading.

The most vulnerable and interesting characters make the outcome more delicious. The wellspring for these vulnerabilities can often be traced to our memories.

During my walks, memories of my childhood vulnerabilities would strike. When I was in first grade, I visited a friend after school. It was October, and before I left for her house, my mother warned me that daylight saving time was over, and that it would grow dark early. Being six years old, this didn't register. But when I left my classmate's cozy attic bedroom to walk home, the world had turned as black as the inside of a coffin. I didn't know it then, but I have lousy night vision. I could barely grope my way the seven or so blocks home.

The worst of it was walking past the witch's house. Back then, every neighborhood had a witch's house—a place with a sagging porch and peeling paint, where older people with age- and pain-etched faces lived and would yell at kids who trespassed on their property. I stumbled past my neighborhood's witch house as fast as I could, sure that someone or some *thing* would emerge shrieking to snatch me from the sidewalk. With my heart galloping, I felt like I was drowning in the nightmare darkness.

A few months earlier, my parents' friends who lived in the city had made their annual visit. Their two sons were two and three years older than me and, along with my older brother, we were allowed to attend an evening movie. It was a double billing, *The H-Man* and *The Woman Eater*. I remember so clearly the new dress I wore that night: it was blue plaid with a sailor collar, and I loved it.

But I wasn't ready for the movies. The H-Man was a kind of yellow-green slime that crept and oozed over a city, destroying everything in its wake. The Woman Eater was a phallic monster comprised of dozens of writhing snakes, and when a woman was tossed into its embrace, she would die, struggling and screaming in terror. We emerged blinking from this frightfest into the dark for the walk home, which was about two miles. Back then, kids walked the streets of our small northern town without worry. But the boys decided to tease me that night. As a joke, they ditched me to walk alone and would periodically spring from behind trees, screeching and imitating The Woman Eater. Weeping and terrified, I ran home to tattle on the boys, and then was admonished by the adults that I was a crybaby.

Meanwhile, back in my grown-up life, as spring tilted into summer I remembered a summer class that I used to teach for kids in the mid-1990s. It was called *Myths, Monsters, Heroes, and Ghost Stories*. Ten children, ages eight to ten, and I would gather in a classroom at Portland State University and I'd teach techniques for writing fiction. Sometimes they'd read their new stories aloud to the class, and sometimes I'd turn out the lights to read them ghost stories.

With the lights dimmed, we'd talk about nightmares. I told them that I could still remember nightmares from my own childhood, and I recounted a few. I revealed how the flying monkeys in the movie *The Wizard of Oz* terrified me as a girl, and soon after I first watched it, the Wicked Witch arrived in one of my nightmares to bargain with my father for my life. With her bony claw, she clung onto my arm while my father grasped the other, offering her a purple tin box that he stored his mementos in.

Then my students chimed in, describing the usual night horrors, such as being chased by a monster yet being too frozen with terror to scream or run. But there was one girl's nightmare I've never forgotten. She was on a camping trip, and as she looks around the campfire's gleam, she discovers that each of her family members has disappeared to be replaced by a pile of silvery bones, and she's sitting alone within that ghostly circle.

We then listed all our physical reactions to nightmares—having a rapid heart rate, breathing fast, and feeling sweaty, disorientated, and panicked. Our list of symptoms was long. Afterward, we talked about how to transfer our nightmare reactions onto the page. It was my way of trying to teach "show, don't tell," and sometimes it worked.

In fiction, you toss your main characters out on a limb, preferably a limb that dangles off a steep cliff over a raging torrent of sea below, and that sea has bottomless depths. This limb (the frailer the better) can have a thousand permutations, but it is always precarious, with some kind of danger or dreaded outcome possible.

The best means to put your characters at risk is to create characters to torment, threaten, and frighten them. The characters, bad guys in some form, rattle the limb and push the character toward the precipice above raging water. It's with these characters that vulnerability is made visible and conflict boils red hot.

So, in your own life, savor your nightmares and memories of vulnerability, and recall your own cast of bad guys. Their behaviors, though difficult to endure, are valuable fodder for your stories. Play detective in your own life and in the lives of the bad guys you have tangled with. Find the truth of who they are and why they act the way they do. In life, vulnerability hurts; but in fiction writing, exposing these feelings, and the people who cause them, is the essence of powerful storytelling.

INTRODUCTION

Primal Fears

To suffering there is a limit; to fearing, none.

—Francis Bacon

The world is a dangerous place. We're taught this fact as children, when we were warned about stepping into oncoming traffic, playing with matches, accepting candy from strangers, and running with a pointed stick. But children know that bigger dangers loom because monsters, witches, ghosts, and villains all have more fright power than sticks or oncoming traffic. These creatures invaded our nightmares, as they were depicted in movies and Marvel Comics, heard in fairy tales and myths, and told around campfires with the flames crackling and a chorus of night sounds adding an extra shiver to the ghostly tale.

In our childhood, we also first meet real-life bad guys and learn that cruelty is an inescapable reality. These harsh lessons can come in the form of a classroom bully, a sadistic cousin, a teacher who seems to have it in for you, or a creepy stranger. At an early age we learn distrust and unease because life holds dangers, and we discover that it takes resilience and courage to navigate through our days.

This particular legacy of childhood lingers into adulthood, and fiction writers can capitalize on this. In fact, it's a fiction writer's job to remember childhood's hard lessons about vulnerability and dangers, and then to rouse those memories and fears in readers. You see, readers are drawn to vulnerable characters in precarious circumstances. They are the heart of fiction. We enjoy reading about a fictional character threatened by menace since it's safely removed from us, yet we can still enjoy the thrill ride because we're well acquainted with fear and feelings of vulnerability. So, in essence, readers are asking authors to bring on the baddest bad guy, the scariest monster, the freakiest sociopath, the most depraved killer—and they'll flip through the pages with their attention focused on the carnage. Here's how it works.

PRIMAL FEARS

Few other creatures on Earth have such a long period of dependence and vulnerability as the human child, who is born completely helpless and unable to walk until he is almost a year old. Childhood imprints lasting vestiges of vulnerability. In reading fiction, these memories are easily stirred and nothing stirs these memories like a bad guy on the page bringing out the child in all of us, reminding us of times when we were small and not calling the shots, and of times when we were terrified by the monster that lurked in the closet when the lights were turned out.

Children have an intimate and in-depth knowledge of fear. It stalks you on the playground when the oversized seventh-grader demands your lunch money. It lurks in the night shadows when the gloom morphs into creatures and horrors. It happens when you get caught for infractions and worry about the punishment. It can be awakened when nature lashes out of control with a booming thunderstorm, when you walk past a graveyard on a dare, or when the haunted house at the county fair offers up more fright than you bargained for.

However, memories of scary events serve a practical biological function in humans because they allow us to anticipate and avoid future dangers. We all know what fear feels like; it prickles us with an unpleasant sensation of possible risk or danger. As we age, some fears are outgrown like the fear of the dark; some are faced down like the taunts and punches from the classroom bully; and some are bypassed by practical decisions such as wearing a seat belt.

Fear is also a thrill—part fun, part terror—like being poised at the peak of a roller coaster hill before the car plunges down, down, down with reckless speed. It is this thrill-ride aspect of fear that fiction readers seek within the pages of a story.

When a reader is afraid because of what is happening in the story, you're activating neural pathways in the brain that were laid down in childhood by real and imagined dangers. These neural pathways will cause physical and emotional reactions in the reader that will feel much like the torments and real dangers of the world. So, when fiction writers create situations, along with bad guys and creatures most of us want to avoid meeting, the reader will keep turning the pages because he's longing to know the outcome and if the danger will be overcome. But, most important, he keeps reading because he enjoys the arousal and worry that accompanies reading.

THE MECHANICS OF FEAR

The fear response is hard-wired into the human body through a series of mechanisms that evolved from days when our ancestors needed to outrun a charging lioness or avoid a massive grizzly bear lunching in the berry patch. Writers would be wise to understand this instinctual mechanism and how it underlies our experiences of reading fiction and watching films.

Fear is a defense mechanism designed to help us cope with danger and conserve our brains and organs. It is an instinctual, genetic legacy since our ancestors who used fear to their benefit survived to pass along these ingrained reactions. Our ancestors were on a first-name basis with danger, and they were often fleeing, fighting, and hunting for survival. When fear strikes, a blood supply is sent to our muscles to marshal the available energy needed. Called the fight-or-flight response, this energy is aroused by a rush of adrenaline, along with extra minerals and oxygen to the muscles. Often, when a person is afraid, he'll become pale because the blood has been summoned from the skin and stomach to supply the muscles.

The fight-or-flight response sends a cascade of hormones via the nervous system and bloodstream to help the body deal with the threat. Besides the reactions already mentioned, the heart rate and blood pressure increase; the pupils dilate to take in more light; veins constrict to send more blood to major muscles, which is why a chill is often associated with fear; nonessential functions like digestion and the immune system are shut down; blood-glucose levels increase; smooth muscles relax to allow more oxygen into the lungs; major muscles tense because they are pumped up by glucose and adrenaline. The person feeling the danger will have trouble focusing on small details because the brain directs the senses to take in the big picture.

The fear response is created in the brain and happens automatically. It is actually the result of two different response patterns: a simple set of reactions, followed by a more complex reaction. To arouse the fear reactions, you need a setup, followed by a stimulus. Imagine this scenario: It's a proverbial dark and stormy night with lightning flickering across the sky. The wind is slashing at tree branches and sending objects skittering along the street. Sleeping fitfully in the midst of the storm, you're startled awake by a loud banging coming from the direction of the back door. Since it's almost two in the morning, you're sure it cannot be a neighbor or friend, and you wonder what is making the sound. Thus, the knocking is the stimulus, which then alerts the *thalamus* in the brain. The thalamus is a walnut-sized area in the brain's core that serves as a communication center. It cannot immediately judge if the sound is a serial killer or the wind, but it knows you're receiving a danger signal, so it alerts the *amygdala*, which is involved in computing the emotional significance of events. The amygdala receives the neural impulses and then sends a signal to the *hypothalamus*. The hypothalamus is the center for the brain's most powerful hormones that relay information and instruction to all parts of the brain and body. After receiving the cue, the hypothalamus triggers the fight-or-flight response.

There is a more complicated response that is also triggered by the danger signal and helps you judge if there is truly a danger and, if so, what your survival options and reactions will be. When one of your senses perceives danger, it relays this information to the thalamus. The thalamus then sends the data to the *sensory cortex*, where it is interpreted. The sensory cortex determines if there is more than one explanation for the noise and then passes the information along to the *hippocampus*. The hippocampus, which works as the brain's switchboard and is responsible for piecing separate bits of information together, takes in all the information about the storm, perhaps about a possible loose shutter near the door, and keys in to other sounds, such as a branch breaking off and thudding to the ground, which suggests that the wind has increased. When the hippocampus, via the senses, hears the branch fall and the wind increasing a few decibels, it relays a message back to the amygdala that the threat is related to the storm, not an intruder. The amygdala then tells the hypothalamus to shut down the fight-or-flight response.

What's important to know is that the stimulus—the sound in the middle of the night—triggers the simple reaction and the complex reaction at the same time, and it all happens in mere seconds. This means that you'll experience a few moments of terror before you calm down. As a writer, your characters will also experience these reactions, although you won't be spelling them out in clinical terms. Because your reader has been through the fight-or-flight response so many times and memories have laid down the circuitry of what a response to danger feels like, he'll instinctively understand and also *feel* the character's reactions, which lets him vicariously experience the terror and buzz of danger.

WHY WE FEAR

As already mentioned, the fight-or-flight response has been passed down from our more primitive ancestors. It is a survival mechanism found in all animals. However, another function of fear is conditioned and linked to memory. If a child is bitten by a dog when he's four, he can still cower when a dog approaches twenty years later. Or, if he were raised in a household with violence, the sound of raised voices or a vase crashing can send him into a tumult of unpleasant emotions and reactions. Along with fear reactions, powerful emotions can be stirred when an event or threat reminds the person of the past threat.

Fear can also be activated when a person must act in a situation but doesn't have enough information about how to go about things. Let's imagine a second scenario that is occurring during the aforementioned storm. A young couple, Ron and Amelia, are forced to leave the safety of their home in the middle of the night because Amelia is nine months pregnant and her water just broke. So, with Amelia gasping at the pain from the contractions, they venture out into the stormy night replete with booming thunder, fierce winds, and lightning lashing the starless sky. As they drive a few blocks, they discover that the harsh storm has flooded the road ahead and branches are scattered on the roadway. It is the only route to the hospital. Should they turn back and try and call 9-1-1, hoping that an ambulance or rescue vehicle can somehow make it through the road? Will their phone call get through, because they've seen some lines down and they're wondering if phone or power lines are working? Should Ron try to lift some of the branches out of the way?

As Amelia gasps again from a pain that pierces her spine and seems to halve her midsection, Ron reluctantly turns back toward home, not sure he's doing the right thing.

Many of us can look back at crossroads we took at various times in our lives and know with hindsight that the decisions and choices we made were sometimes right, sometimes wrong. These crossroad moments are inherently dramatic because they're laced with uncertainty and linked to fear. This aspect of fear can be helpful for you as a fiction writer as you thrust characters on the horns of dilemmas and beset them with tough choices, or as you force a sympathetic character to face the unknown future.

EMBEDDED IN CULTURE

Worldwide, storytelling evolved for many reasons, but one reason was to help people cope with both real and imagined fears. Sometimes our ancestors were trying to understand how lightning strikes, but also why crops fail, predatory animals attack, babies die, and wells go dry. In fact, daily life offers up countless mysteries, worries, and calamities. But for fiction writers, it's helpful to remember that people the world over have invented, whispered about, and feared monsters and bad guys since the beginning of humankind. Many theories exist about why these monsters and haunts are so embedded in cultures worldwide, but perhaps there are two easy explanations. First, evil *does* exist, and it is easily witnessed every day in acts of violence, cruelty, and exploitation. Second, as modern life becomes increasingly complicated, there is much to be feared because the future is unknown and fate is random and often unexplainable.

Stories exist in many forms, from epic quests to lullabies, to folk tales and fables. You will find tales of dragons, small folks, fairies, and sea monsters. Family feuds, bitter rivalries, betrayals, and jealousies are stock story lines in ancient tales, complete with matricide, fratricide, and regicide; power grabs and turf battles are still found in contemporary stories, as in the television series *The Sopranos*.

Myths are all around us, and the human need for myth and stories will never go away, just as our need to quell our primal fears will never vanish. Humans have always told these timeless exploits. We have always used stories to combat evil and fear by invented heroes and gods who fight for us. Some might argue that the timeless tale of good versus evil is embedded in our DNA, today easily recognized in the success of the Harry Potter series and the Star Wars films. And because both gods and mortal heroes need forces to come up against, there have also always been antagonists and villains—conflict and evil made visible.

BACK TO BAD GUYS

Fear in a reader is a good thing, and it's easy to arouse because it is a biochemical and neurological process. Now comes the next step: creating bad guys who make the reader twist with anxiety, who slip into nightmares.

Because it's so easy to create cookie-cutter bad guys, it's important to invent fresh adversaries, hooligans, and monsters for your characters to meet with. If your vampire brings Dracula to mind, you've failed—just as if your horror story reminds a reader of a Stephen King plot, or your fantasy tale is a copy of the sweeping saga written by George R.R. Martin. Your heroes and bad guys will be shaped by all the stories you've read since childhood, stirred together with long-ago fears, then seasoned with all the creeps, bad bosses, and heartbreakers you've encountered in real life. You bring this rich meld to the task of writing fiction, and you start off by creating characters who are memorable.

Throughout this book, I'm going to keep talking about how flawed and vulnerable characters create empathy in the reader. Sometimes these characters will be protagonists, sometimes they'll be victims in a situation, and at times they'll even be bad guys. Note, too, that while the pronoun "he" is often used in discussions throughout the book, this was done for the sake of simplicity. Almost all character types (except gender-specific ones like bad boys and bitches) can be either male or female. As you read through this book and approach your own writing, it can be enormously helpful to recall the times you felt most afraid, especially noting what your bodily reactions were. These fears and dark moments are treasure troves for creating believable fictional characters.

CHAPTER ONE

Unforgettable

Plot springs from character … I've always sort of believed that these people inside me—these characters—know who they are and what they're about and what happens, and they need me to help get it down on paper because they don't type.

—ANNE LAMOTT

Long after the intricacies of a fictional plot fade from a reader's memory, the characters linger with an almost physical presence, a twinkle of personality, unforgettable actions, and the characters' happy or sad fates. Fictional characters whisper their secrets, allow us to witness their most intimate moments and sorrows, and trust us with their messy emotions, bad decisions, and deepest longings. They penetrate our aloneness, populate our imagination by starring in our inner cinema, and slip their hands in ours and transport us to another place and another time. And while all this is going on, often they teach us what it means to be human, complete with all the troubles, heartaches, and mysteries.

Characters that leave a lasting footprint in our memories can be all types of characters, including stuck-on-themselves divas, difficult drama queens, aging Italian billionaires, lonely singletons, brave knights, and daring spies. It's simple, really: Character, not plot, is what chiefly interests the reader because he translates and feels the character's actions, desires, and passions from his own databank of experiences and emotions.

THINK OUTSIDE THE BOX

Now let's get down to the serious business of creating unforgettable characters—the kind who take up residence in your imagination, who you can't seem to stop thinking about and devising scenarios about when you're writing them, who make an editor sit up and notice when she encounters them in your manuscript.

There are books that teach you how to write likeable or heroic characters, and then there are books that focus almost exclusively on how to create protagonists. This isn't either of them. This is a book about thinking outside the box to create deeply complicated characters that star in all the roles of a drama. As you read this book, I want you to hit the "erase" button on what you've learned about fictional characters, and I want you to travel with me into a realm of characters that create sizzle and leave a lasting impression. These characters are the bad asses. We use bad asses in fiction because readers want to meet story people whom they'll never meet in real life, or, more likely, because they *avoid* these types in real life—especially at an office party, especially in a single's bar, especially in a dark alley. As this book will prove, a bad ass can be a bitchy creature who betrays her friend, as Barbara Covett does in Zoë Heller's *Notes on a Scandal*, an unlikable protagonist, like David Lurie from J.M. Coetzee's *Disgrace*, or a scoundrel, like Black Jack Randall who appears in several books in Diana Gabaldon's Outlander series.

A bad ass can be a protagonist, the main character in the story; an antagonist, the person who opposes the main character; a villain, an antagonist who has evil as part of his personality makeup; or an anti-hero, a protagonist with few or no heroic and likeable traits. A bad ass can also play a supporting role in a story as a secondary or minor character. Thus, a bad ass can star in most any role in the story, and his personality type can have endless variations. But all bad asses share certain characteristics, and we populate our stories with them because a bad ass makes the reader nervous. As writers, we want our readers nervous, if not scared, about what is going to happen next in the story.

Let's now talk about typical characteristics of bad asses, because I'm sure we all have our own definition of a bad ass from real life. This requires that you've still got your erase button depressed, because I want you to explore a whole new definition of what kind of person might star or co-star in your stories. You use a bad ass in fiction because he is going to elicit a complicated set of emotions in the reader, because he will create more complex and intense situations (and often more dangerous situations) than typical likeable or sympathetic characters, and because tension swirls around a bad ass character like leaves in a hurricane.

As in real life, a bad ass in fiction makes a huge impression. While a bad ass can range from a smart aleck to a sociopath, he will *always* be somehow edgy and outside the norm. He will also possess a large and simmering physical presence, with at least one unsavory personality trait. A bad ass draws heat because he will act in unexpected ways in the story. A bad ass might not necessarily be a type that the reader can empathize with since bad asses are often less fearful, less constrained, and have more attitude than the rest of us. In the animal kingdom, bad asses are not the poodles or Persians or even pandas. They're not cuddly or domesticated. Instead, they might be compared to cockroaches, sewer rats, wolves, jackals, and other predators.

Again, while the following chapters will delineate the various types of bad asses you can use in stories, in general, a bad ass takes risks, has chutzpah, and usually is the opposite of a wuss. Sometimes a bad ass has adventures we can only dream about. Sometimes a bad ass can intimidate by merely lifting an eyebrow or giving a cold stare. If a bad ass appears in genre fiction, he is a man (or woman) of action, and he especially acts when most of us would be ducking for cover. In thrillers, the reader might watch a bad ass dig a bullet out of his own leg, ignite a fire with a stick and bow, steal a fortune, save the day, slay vampires, or start a war. But again, a bad ass can appear in any type of story. In the pages of this book, you're going to meet characters who act in ways most of us would avoid and take risks most of us wouldn't dare tackling.

I want to remind you that a bad ass can also be refined—more fox than sewer rat, more ermine than badger. He can possess a great intellect and wit, or quote saints and philosophers. He might also possess a simmering sexuality, look fabulous in a tux, and have admirers or lackeys. Think of the characters played by George Clooney and Brad Pitt in the film *Ocean's Eleven* to imagine this type of bad ass.

A bad ass can be in a position of power or authority, which makes the reader *really* nervous. Perhaps the bottom line is that these characters cannot be typecast, cannot be easily explained, and certainly cannot be easily dismissed. There is always something slightly, or hugely, dangerous about a bad ass, but sometimes this danger can be strangely appealing. We write about bad asses because they fascinate us and linger in our imaginations.

Typically, heroes in fiction and film have also been men and women of action who assert courage to solve a problem in the story. The main difference between heroes and bad asses is their level of morality. While heroes are always sympathetic characters, bad asses are not necessarily sympathetic characters. Heroes bring hope and morality to a situation; bad asses can bring hope to a situation, especially when the chips are down, but it is more likely that they skirt the rules in the process. Another difference is that heroes are always on the side of good, but you cannot say the same for bad asses. Or, possibly, their means of helping for the good are unsavory. Think John Rambo in *Rambo*, Jules Winnfield in *Pulp Fiction*, Harry Callhan of *Dirty Harry*, Buffy the Vampire Slayer kicking butt and taking names.

In genre fiction, a bad ass might be able to survive in the wilderness on sticks and insects, to swim the widest rivers, and to make love for hours. We write about bad asses because they're bigger than life. However, don't be worried that your bad ass characters must all be buff, snarly, and carrying a concealed weapon. A bad ass can be a science teacher, a corporate executive, or a priest. Fiction writers and screenwriters create bad asses because the lives of these characters are messy and complicated and sometimes freaky, and these messes and complications and freakfests make for compelling fiction. It's all about attitude.

Here's one of the first concepts to keep firmly in mind: Your protagonist—the person who will appear in the most scenes, who will be most affected and changed by the story's events—can be likeable, but he doesn't need to be. Or he can be sort of likeable, but rough around the edges. Or he can be a creep, but you cannot help but place him in a starring role because people of his sort fascinate you. That means your protagonist can be quirky, sneaky, nutty, untrustworthy, self-pitying, or delusional. This book will help you create these out-of-the-box types, and well as other characters, such as villains, who star in other roles in the story.

My main purpose for writing this book is to teach you to create characters who live and breathe and astonish and delight and terrify with their particular strain of humanity. I don't know about you, but I love to read a story that is so intricately drawn that it seems like I could step into the story world and walk around. I can smell the place, I can navigate the streets and buildings. I know what kind of car the protagonist drives; I know if he drinks martinis, Cabernet, or Bud, or if he abstains from alcohol; and I know what I'll find when I open his refrigerator or underwear drawer.

If the story has a bad ass antagonist or villain, I'll tiptoe past his lair because I know that he represents trouble (in the case of an antagonist) or danger (in the case of the villain). As I creep along, my heart hammering in my chest, I'll be remembering the inventive torments the bad ass has concocted in previous scenes. If I hear a noise, I'll duck, scared as a six-year-old in a haunted house. I'll be quaking not only because I've witnessed the bad ass in action, but because the writer has imbued the character with complicated yet believable motivations, and has shown him in surprising actions, which stem from influences from his past. In the case of the villain, this is likely a deeply troubled past.

MORAL CONTINUUM

If you're writing about a bad ass—or, for that matter, creating any type of major character—there are two things you need to understand to draw him with accuracy: his moral code and his core personality traits. Let's talk about morality first. In real life, a person's moral code runs the gamut from Mother Teresa to Adolf Hitler. Similarly, all characters in fiction and film can also be placed along a moral continuum; they all need a specific level of integrity, decency, and honesty. As a writer, you'll need to know how moral or immoral your character is, and these crucial decisions will shape your story.

In the real world, we all have codes of morality. Perhaps your moral code is that you never lie, cheat, steal, or commit adultery. Or, perhaps you bend the rules at times, but never break a law. Or, maybe you lie to avoid hurting someone's feelings, as when a friend asks you if you like her new hairstyle. Maybe your moral code is never to harm another person, or maybe your concern extends to all living creatures and, consequently, you are a vegetarian. Your code might include never drinking or smoking or being promiscuous. Perhaps you learned your morals from your family, from your Jesuit schooling, or from a Buddhist monk. The point here is that everyone in real life and in fiction is somehow influenced in childhood and at different stages of life, and these influences are what create a moral code.

It seems to me that in real life, it helps to know what your moral code is. If you know yourself and what you stand for, then when someone tries to steer you into cheating on a test or stealing someone's property, you know where you stand on such acts. Similarly, it's extremely useful to know how far a character will go to get what he wants—if he'll sleep with his best friend's wife, or if he'll rip off his mother. It's also helpful to know how his moral code came about. And if you know if your character is just or vengeful, honest or deceitful, law-abiding or criminal, then these degrees of morality will naturally affect the story and its outcome.

Storytelling is one means by which people come to understand morality and its consequences. For example, the Star Wars movies aren't simply dramas set in space; they're also set against the background of followers of the peace-loving Jedi code and the Force meeting up with enemies from the dark side who possess anger, fear, aggression, and more corrupt values. Likewise, most of Shakespeare's plays are spun around moral issues, as is the Harry Potter series. Throughout human history, storytelling was based on how people made moral decisions. These decisions and actions are at the core of what people think about, so your character's morality and moral decisions need to be meaningful and potent in your stories to keep your reader engaged. With this in mind, take a look at the moral continuum on page 18 to see where some of the major character types described in this book fall.

When you're imagining the morality of a character, you'll want to know how his morality will collide with the moral codes espoused by other characters in the story. It's always helpful to imagine characters in their most private moments and interacting with their closest associates. Perhaps you'll want to reveal a character's moral code by having him

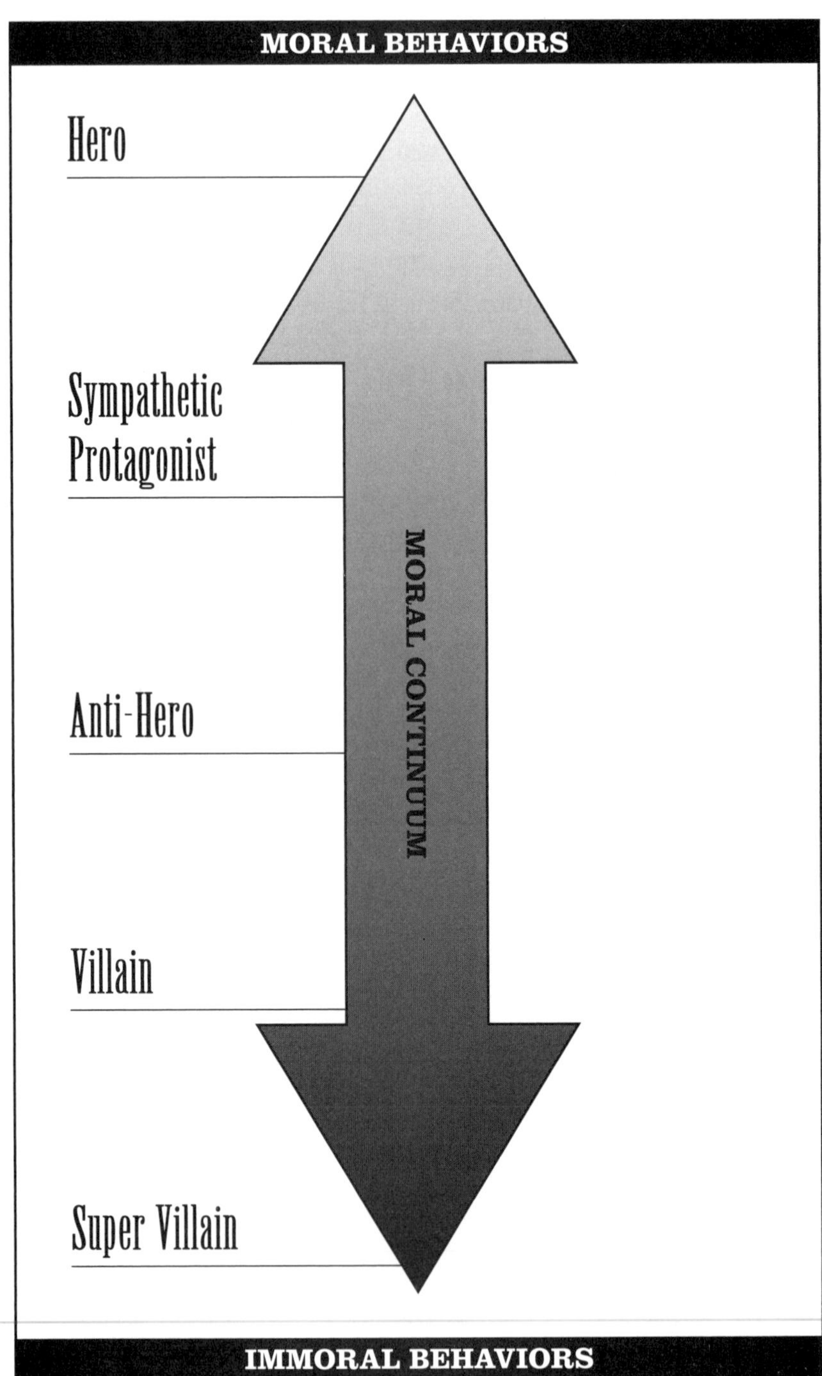
MORAL BEHAVIORS
Hero
Sympathetic Protagonist
Anti-Hero
Villain
Super Villain
MORAL CONTINUUM
IMMORAL BEHAVIORS

interact with children, talk with a shrink, or whisper secrets in a confessional. When devising a character, it's always important to understand how he'll act and react to other vulnerable characters. Is he kind to the wino slumped on the corner, or does he kick him when he walks past?

As in real life, fictional characters can often be most known and defined when the curtains are drawn and they think no one is looking. When a character is alone, is his routine fairly normal with work, meals, hobbies, and rest? Or, in these private moments and behaviors, are the reader's neck hairs starting to prickle? Is their some hint at behaviors that stem from childhood influences or traumas? For example, does the character have an eating disorder or other compulsive behaviors? Does the character harbor an ugly secret? Is the character into kiddy porn on the Internet? Does the politician character have a secret sex fetish? Does the female protagonist pick up strangers in bars and only enjoy anonymous sex? Is the supposedly upstanding character actually cruel to his girlfriend, or controlling with his wife and kids? Are the character's children or mother or dog afraid of him?

If possible, think about your character's private moments and what they reveal. Along those lines, if your character has people in his life that he trusts, think about how he acts around them. Does he never quite let down his guard, but is deeply intimate when in bed with his lover? Also keep in mind that fictional people generally will have traits that the reader both loathes and admires, or perhaps grudgingly admires. However, if you're using a bad ass in your fiction, you will want to know exactly how far he'll go to get what he wants. And, no matter their level of morality, fictional characters generally act in ways we're not allowed to act in real life.

LAYERED TRAITS

A character's single most important job in a story is to stimulate the reader's emotions. This is accomplished by demonstrating character traits, and then giving your character tough choices and excruciating troubles so these traits are dramatized. Before a reader can understand how a major character will react under pressure, he must first understand the character's primary traits. These primary traits will be fully intact and dramatized from the opening moments in the story until the climax. All protagonists and major characters, including antagonists and villains, need a consistent set of three to six primary traits that are introduced early, are the basis for their personalities, and are demonstrated in the story.

It's especially important that your protagonist's primary traits are visible from the moment the reader meets him since readers often, but not always, empathize with the protagonist. These main traits remain consistent throughout the story, are intricately linked to the plot, and are tested by the events of the story. In fact, the plot will always showcase a protagonist's primary traits. When Sherlock Holmes has a tantalizing mystery to solve, his pursuit of the solution will prove that he's analytical, brilliant, curious, observant, and dogged. If the story were about a cooking contest or the dog show world, his traits would not be showcased and the story would fall short. Thus, primary traits are what characters need to accomplish their goals in the story, while also providing the consistency and the foundation that the reader can depend on.

If you look at a character such as Indiana Jones, an archaeology professor and adventurer played by Harrison Ford in the film series, you'll notice that his primary traits are intelligence, adventuresome, curious, and fearless.

I hope that by mentioning Sherlock Holmes and Indiana Jones, you're getting the idea that primary traits can sometimes be an odd mix. For example, Jones is a man of both thought and action. Although he is an academic wearing the tweeds of his era in the classroom, he brandishes a bullwhip as a globe-trotting adventurer, is a two-fisted man of action not afraid to mix it up with villains, and has a lot more swagger than we normally associate with professors.

After the primary traits are established and the reader gets a clear sense of the character's personality, you then add secondary or supportive traits. These add depth to the character without confusing the reader (faithful, lustful, passionate, stubborn, impatient, tender, outspoken, etc.), and flesh out the character. They are also necessary because as your story unfolds, the main characters acquire more and more depth. And since the primary traits are finite, adding secondary traits as the story goes along creates richness and reader interest. The secondary traits can also have consequences in the story. These traits might not be showcased with the regularity of the primary traits, just like secondary characters won't appear in as many scenes as your protagonist.

You also add character tags in this layer of character development—these can be habits such as smoking or a tendency to joke when nervous. Characters can also be heavy drinkers or abstainers, gourmet cooks, or junk food junkies. In the case of Sherlock Holmes, he's a Bohemian, he sometimes uses cocaine and morphine, he smokes a pipe, he's easily bored, he's egotistical, he's an amateur scientist and forensic analyst, he's a master of disguise, and he seems to love going undercover. When you're adding secondary traits, you're keeping in mind that everything the character says and does will fortify the primary traits.

Last, you add a third layer of counter traits that will expose even deeper and more complicated ways in which your character acts in the world. At first glance, some of these counter traits might seem to contradict the primary ones, but in fact they make sense once the reader gets to know the character under a variety of circumstances. These counter traits are demonstrated to the reader after a firm base has been established. They are often demonstrated when the character falls apart under duress, or when he is involved in an extreme or highly emotional situation. The counter traits can also be used to surprise the reader or film viewer and create complications.

In the case of daredevil Indiana Jones, the madcap opening scene in *Raiders of the Lost Ark* follows Jones on an expedition into the teeming jungles of South America, barely escaping with a sacred idol, only to have it stolen by his competitor. Jones leaps onto a seaplane and urges the pilot to make a quick getaway, and he spots the pilot's pet boa constrictor near his feet. Jones jumps out of his seat shouting, "I hate snakes, Jock! I hate 'em!" Thus, we see the tough explorer's highly contrasting trait, and we wonder if he'll encounter snakes in the adventure.

In the case of Sherlock Holmes, while he prides himself on his rationality and self-control, he also can become quite emotional, as when, in "The Adventures of the Three Garridebs," he's upset when he discovers that Watson's been hurt but relieved when he learns that his friend's gunshot wound was superficial. Other stories show a tender side of Holmes that he most often takes great pains to hide, causing readers to wonder why he tries so hard to appear detached.

It's important to keep in mind that your main character's traits are linked to all aspects of the story. Thus, the risk-taking Indiana Jones will always pursue the most treasured items on the globe and face ruthless villains, Nazis, and criminal operations. His ability to make lightning-quick decisions will be shown as he ducks danger, and we'll also hear him quip and banter with women and bad guys. Sherlock Holmes will use his deductive skills to track down master criminals and scoundrels, will detect clues from bicycle tire tracks and cigarette butts, and will use his great mind to make leaps and connections that leave his sidekick Watson gasping in surprise.

An advantage of this character-building technique is that when it's well executed, your reader should continue learning about the characters until the final pages. As you stack secondary and counter traits on top of primary traits, you'll add complexity, emotion, and quirks. Thus, your character is always growing. The reader wants and needs a deep understanding of and relationship with the characters as the story evolves. Using a hierarchy of traits helps you create this relationship.

PRIMARY TRAITS

Three to six traits that are showcased by story events and act as the foundation for a character's personality, overall disposition, and approach to life.

SECONDARY TRAITS

Support a character's primary traits by adding depth and resonance, and include mannerisms, tastes, tags, and habits.

COUNTER/ CONTRASTING TRAITS

Expose a character's deepest layers and vulnerabilities.

As we delve into each of the categories of characters in later chapters, I want you to keep this hierarchy of traits in mind. Not only do they create complicated and knowable characters, but they also provide a foundation of stability.

Also, as will be explained in further chapters, a hero has mostly positive dominant traits, and a villain has none, or perhaps one. An unlikable protagonist will have few positive traits, while a likeable or sympathetic protagonist will have mostly positive traits. Knowing these core traits in your characters, and whether the reader will react to them sympathetically or with revulsion, is the key to creating a bad ass.

In my work, I see lots of problems that doom a fiction manuscript to failure. I most often see writers who don't have an adequate understanding about the underpinnings of structure and scene. After these basic problems, it seems to me that manuscripts that fizzle do so because the writer used cookie-cutter or thinly-drawn characters instead of the types that slip into a reader's imagination and possibly his nightmares.

Writing fiction that catches an editor's attention requires taking risks, especially in writing fascinating characters embroiled in an unbearable situation. When you're creating your main characters, especially when you're creating a bad ass, keep this in mind: While you'll shape characters based on emotions and experiences you understand, your characters will always range much farther than you. They will have more adventures and deeper sorrows, their desires will burn red hot, their desperation will cause them to resort to trickery and deceit, and their failures will bear the mark of doomsday. So, although you'll understand your characters, don't impose your own values, thoughts, and beliefs on your cast. Let them range far from the confines of your own safe world, allow them to surprise you with their antics and desires, and, if possible, give them beliefs and values quite different from your own.

The other thing to keep in mind is that the more time you spend with your cast—the more thought you give to their traits, morality, and desires *before* you begin writing—the easier your task will be. Some people write intuitively, but for all writers, it can be enormously helpful, and also fun, to create biographies of your main characters, to sketch family trees, and to make lists of your characters' loves and hates. This thoughtful approach results in intricately layered fictional people that the reader comes to know and care about.

My aim in writing this book is for you to create fascinating, messed up, rollicking, complicated characters who kick butt and take names. These fascinating, unforgettable types will not always fall neatly into "good guy" and "bad guy" categories. Now, if you're writing for small children you're more likely to create characters who fall more easily into these two broad categories; information on writing for children is found in chapter twelve. For the rest of you, who are writing for adults, I want you to imagine that characters range within a broad moral continuum and can be colored with hundreds of shades of gray.

CHAPTER TWO

The Case of the Unlikeable Protagonist

Writing fiction has developed in me an abiding respect for the unknown in a human lifetime and a sense of where to look for the threads, how to follow, how to connect, find in the thick of the tangle what clear line persists.

—EUDORA WELTY

If your life is anything like mine, the people I have *not* liked—in fact, the ones that gave me a case of indigestion every time we met—are often the most fascinating and complicated people I know. They're the rascals I fret about, struggle to understand, and want to avoid. Since you're a fiction writer, I'm surmising that you also find all kinds of people endlessly fascinating. And while in real life we cannot always understand why people act and think and love as they do, in fiction we can make these people knowable, even when their actions and motives are vastly different from our own.

You see, it's fairly easy to be nice, most of the time. You keep your mouth shut when your best friend is complaining about her husband's drinking for the hundredth time; you say nice things about your friend's children, even though you believe they're spoiled and ill-mannered; and you don't comment when your sister gains twenty pounds in only a few months. You call your mother, recycle, show up for appointments on time, and always signal when you turn. Most of us fall into the good guy category, most of the time. And most of us want to be liked.

Luckily, fictional characters are not much like us. And luckily for the world of fiction, characters exist who *don't* try to be nice; in fact, they sometimes go out of their way to make other characters' lives miserable. Writers who want to add spice and conflict, and who want to push the boundaries of storytelling, will include characters that range from a bit odd, to selfish, to downright evil.

Just a note before we explore this character type: As readers, we are all familiar with unlikeable antagonists and villains. For example, thrillers, suspense, and Westerns often feature a villain, as Larry McMurtry does in his Pulitzer Prize-winning novel *Lonesome Dove* with the sociopathic Blue Duck. When Blue Duck is on the stage, the reader is afraid because whenever he appears, pain, suffering, and death for innocent and vulnerable characters usually follows.

Or, in the case of an antagonist, who is the person opposing the protagonist, he might be a decent sort, or he might be a creep such as an overbearing and demanding boss or a police captain with political motives. However, this chapter is talking about how the person in the starring role is atypical in that he's weird, mean, self-pitying, or dishonest. These qualities are only a few that you might choose if you're dancing out on a limb and writing an unlikeable protagonist. Here's how and why we use these bad asses in leading roles.

LIKEABLE VERSUS UNLIKEABLE PROTAGONISTS

Let's begin by analyzing the qualities of likeability. A likeable character has similar qualities to a real-life likeable person, and these qualities can primarily be identified as the following:

- **He is approachable, someone the reader can understand and come to know.** After all, a person who has secrets and doesn't allow access is difficult to know and trust. If your likeable character *does* have a secret as part of the plot, the story events will reveal it.
- **He is flawed and human.** This doesn't mean that he's a wacky bundle of neuroses, like the sort of characters Woody Allen plays in his films; rather, he is imperfect. His flaws are ones that we can all relate to, such as feelings of inferiority, an easily triggered temper, or an inability to get along with family members.

- **He has mostly redeeming qualities and positive dominant traits.** These qualities could include stoicism, generosity, compassion, and intelligence. Perhaps he takes risks, cares about the environment, tries hard even when he rarely succeeds, is modest, has an even temper, and appreciates the wonders of life. He might have a wicked sense of humor or a brain that whizzes along at the speed of the autobahn. You'll want to create fresh traits for you likeable character from the many possibilities you've observed in real people or conjured in your imagination.

- **He somehow instills hope and belief in the reader so that the reader can take on his cause and goals.** Hope comes in many guises, but it is often present in fiction and speaks about the endurance of the human spirit. Perhaps the character is trying to find love, right a wrong, or understand something important about human nature. Sometimes a character is teaching us to follow our dreams, or to work hard for what we desire, or to know that love is worth the risk.

- **He has a certain toughness and courage.** When the chips are down or the bullets are flying, he somehow fights back, even when the struggle puts him at risk. When trouble lands in his life, he doesn't whine, cower under the bed, call his therapist, or play the blame game. Even when quaking with fear, he takes on the bully, enters the darkened or burning building, and tracks the criminal to his lair. It's never easy, but he does it anyway.

When a likeable protagonist appears in a story, a reader can imagine being him, taking on the problems and complications of the plot. It's no matter if the character drinks beer while you prefer a nice Cabernet. No matter if you don't have the same sense of humor, tastes in lovers, or values, somehow you and other readers can imagine being the character, walking around in his shoes, sleeping in his bed, sitting at his dinner table.

When it comes to unlikeable characters, on the other hand, I believe that although we can sometimes understand their emotions and mindset, we cannot ever imagine being them. Here are the typical qualities of an unlikeable protagonist:

- **He has mostly negative dominant traits.** He might be vain, egoistical, cruel, insensitive, power hungry, devious, promiscuous, or any other traits that most of us like to think we don't possess. If your unlikeable protagonist is going to be redeemed, he will also have at least one positive trait, such as loyalty, intelligence, or ambition.
- **He creates pain for other characters, especially vulnerable characters.** His actions, based on his primary traits and usually somehow linked to his backstory, always cause large ramifications in the story. When vulnerability exists in characters, the reader tunes in.
- **He is his own worst enemy, even though he usually doesn't possess the insight to understand this.** Like people in real life, he might possess the sort of traits that make us avoid people. He might be arrogant, imperious, opinionated, moody, humorless, distrusting, or bullying. He might be immature or untested because life hasn't forced him to face the reality of his personality, or he's gotten away with his jerkiness because he's in a position of power. The trouble is, the clueless unlikeable protagonist cannot understand that he possesses these behaviors or traits until the story's events and other characters slam into his reality.
- **He creates uncomfortable feelings in the reader.** He might elicit feelings of vulnerability, especially if he is someone who the reader can relate to because he's had similar problems with the type in real life. Sometimes this uneasiness with the character is because the character's actions are despicable or shocking; but sometimes it's because the reader just might be afraid to admit that he has similar unlikeable traits, such as being selfish, cold, or ruthless.
- **He draws in the reader.** While the reader might not identify with unlikeable protagonists, he also cannot turn away when the character is on the screen or page. The reasons we read about unlikeable characters are complicated. Mostly it's because, on some level, we're all voyeurs, insatiably curious about how other people live their lives, even when these people exist within the pages of a book.
- **He has complicated reasons for his actions and personality traits.** It's simple: If you don't know the character's backstory, you won't

be able to make him convincing. Maybe he experienced a trauma in his childhood; maybe his parents spoiled him; maybe things have always come too easily; maybe he's never been loved. The trick is that the character's backstory reinforces his current position in the story.

When reading a story or novel with a likeable protagonist, the reader feels as if he's inside the story, living the character's life, and his sympathy is engaged. With an unlikeable protagonist, the reader might feel as if he's watching from the sidelines, or as if he's in a scene or moment, but he's usually watching, not participating or becoming the character. With unlikeable characters, we don't necessarily feel empathy toward them, though at times we might feel sympathy or pity because the person depicts some aspect of humanity. Mostly, we're watching, holding our breaths, perhaps with pulses racing because we're never sure what sort of trouble an unlikeable bad ass is going to stir up next. Often, we'll be shaking our heads in disbelief, as in *I can't believe he just said that/just slapped that child/just cheated on his wife*.

Likeable protagonists can also screw up in their story worlds in all sorts of ways. They marry the wrong person, cannot forgive an injustice, or seek revenge when they should try to wage peace. But with likeable characters, these faults are generally redeemable, understandable, and forgivable, or their good actions somehow outweigh their cruel or thoughtless actions. Often, their character arcs will be about overcoming flaws. With unlikeable protagonists, though, their faults always outweigh their goodness, they are not always redeemable, and they are not so easily related to or accepted. Often, their character arcs are *not* about changing for the better.

For example, a famously unlikeable and unredeemable protagonist is Humbert Humbert of Vladimir Nabokov's *Lolita*. Few readers can relate to becoming obsessed with and falling in love with a twelve-year-old, although in the novel Humbert's obsession with nymphets stems from the death of his first love, Annabel, at thirteen. For the most part, the reader finds his sexual relationship with the girl repulsive, especially since he's masquerading as her stepfather. He's also cruel, subjugating, mad, and ruthless. And although he's also witty and bright and inventive, he's still a sexual deviant.

The reader keeps reading for a complicated set of reasons. First, Humbert's voice is extremely entertaining. Second, Lolita, the antagonist in the story, is not necessarily sympathetic, either. In fact, her presence in the story proves how difficult it can be to judge people in simple, black-and-white terms. In other words, the reader cannot quickly say he's evil and she's innocent—the truth is much more complicated. Humbert and Lolita's relationship is a snake pit of contradictions, obsessions, and bad behavior. Third, since he's writing from prison, the reader is wondering if he's getting his comeuppance, and if he's humbled, repentant, or delusional. Thus, although the reader doesn't empathize with him or secretly long to sleep with a nymphet, the reader keeps reading because the oh-so-edgy and wicked Humbert is utterly captivating, and the situation is as complex as a labyrinth.

Because it can be risky creating an unlikeable protagonist, I would suggest that you try to identify and analyze these sorts of factors when you read stories that depict these types. For example, is the antagonist likeable? Is there a single protagonist in the story? Are the protagonist's motives understandable? Does the ending have a takeaway message about morality or humanity? Then ask yourself if you should emulate these techniques.

Sometimes unlikeable protagonists have redeeming qualities mixed in with their negative qualities, which makes them enormously complex. One such character is Captain Woodrow Call of Larry McMurtry's *Lonesome Dove*. The story focuses on a cattle drive from Texas to Montana, but it's actually about the relationships among a group of men, some of whom are retired Texas Rangers. The two main characters are Captain Woodrow Call and Augustus McCrae, who serves as a foil by contrasting Call's dominant qualities and, as a result, making him better understood. (A foil is a character who sharply contrasts with the protagonist, thus emphasizing both characters' primary traits.) Gus is lazy, loving, loquacious, witty, and happy-go-lucky, whereas Call is all business—grim, close-mouthed, and cold-hearted. Call is a no-nonsense, hard-working taskmaster who tolerates little, and seems to tolerate Gus even less. He especially demonstrates his Grinch-sized heart when, for most of the story, he refuses to acknowledge his son's paternity. However, Call is also an able manager and leader of men, and he's practical and principled as he keeps his promise to Gus and backtracks hundreds of miles to bury his friend's body in Texas. He also acknowledges his son in an offhand way by the story's end, which is a major change in the character arc of a man like Call. In other words, he's enormously complex.

The point is that sometimes unlikeable characters are understandable or redeemable, and sometimes they are such scoundrels that we'd shield our children from them. You have many choices about how dastardly, cranky, odd, subversive, or kinky to make this type of character. Your only constraint is that the character must be compelling, and that if he's redeemable he must possess at least one positive trait.

When you start writing fiction, even if you know a good deal about the story line, you will always begin with characters. You'll want to have a *feel* for the characters and perhaps craft biographies to understand them better. With a character biography, you have a starting point to work from, but you should leave room for flexibility in case your character starts developing in ways that you first didn't imagine.

Start by fashioning several interesting characters, and by the time the first draft is done, you'll know who the protagonist is, who the antagonist is, what the main traits each possess are, what each wants in the story and why, and who is going to succeed or fail. You'll decide if a bad ass will be redeemed, or if the nice guys will finish last. You'll also know which characters your reader will root for and which ones will make him feel queasy or scared.

As you keep refining the story, you make decisions on just how likeable, unlikeable, edgy, or evil your characters will be. For most fiction writers, by the time you've been working with characters for several months, they start taking up residence in your imagination. Sometimes they start whispering suggestions to you, and sometimes they're as difficult to control as a toddler in a supermarket just before naptime. This delightful intimacy with your characters can only come about if you understand their hierarchy of traits, their contrasting traits, their morality, and factors from their backstory that have shaped them.

REASONS FOR USING UNLIKEABLE PROTAGONISTS

There are a number of reasons for using unlikeable characters in fiction, the most common one being that they are often simply much more interesting than nice characters and they create conflict. When a writer can fully depict the inner world of an unlikeable character, the character's thoughts, truths, and dilemmas will resonate. If a character doesn't care if his actions cause pain or discord, then he's bound to bring a lot of friction to the story line. Similarly, if a character is an overbearing, sneaky, duplicitous know-it-all, it's easy to see that he will draw heat. However, there are other compelling reasons for using an unlikeable protagonist:

- **You want the reader to have a complicated emotional and intellectual experience while reading the story.** By using an unlikeable protagonist, you're subverting the normal relationship and empathy that a reader typically feels for characters. In fact, sometimes the reader will feel varying degrees of revulsion toward this character. You must be willing to risk this in order to reveal the shadow sides of the human psyche not often exposed, and to show the fallout that comes from bringing these parts into the light.
- **You want the reader to secretly feel empathy or sympathy for some of the character's traits and weaknesses.** I identify with characters that have trigger-wire tempers, since controlling mine has been a lifetime struggle. You might identify with characters who are snobbish or controlling know-it-alls. However, while the reader might identify with some of the unlikeable protagonist's traits, he still will not feel the sort of total identification as if he slipped into the character's skin, which can happen with a likeable character—especially if that nice character is a taller, slimmer, braver, wittier version of the reader himself.
- **You've written a multiple-viewpoint story or a sprawling epic that requires a large cast.** If one character is a stinker, then other characters can depict other shades of humanity with their more moral and likeable traits.
- **You want to reveal aspects of the human psyche.** People close to us sometimes commit acts that seem unexplainable. A mother of two adorable children gets involved in a tawdry affair; a teen commits suicide; a drunk gets behind the wheel of his car for the hundredth time. In life, many questions go unanswered; in fiction,

you get a chance to explore why people act as they do, and these explorations are deeply satisfying.

- **You have themes in mind that you want to explore and shed light on.** Fiction has remained a dominant art form because it explores important issues and it's instructional. When a reader finishes a novel, he should have a sense of why the author wrote it and what themes and concepts he's expressing or implying via his story. This is where unlikeable protagonists come in. When characters behave or misbehave, we learn. And it seems that misbehaving has lots to teach us, especially when these bad behaviors stem from loneliness, guilt, or other baggage that we're often loathe to admit in our own lives.
- **You want to show that the character can be transformed or become more sympathetic because of the events in your story.** Generally, the protagonist's job in the story is to transform by learning an important lesson or a change in his understanding. In series fiction, though, the character arc takes place over a series of books, not within a single story, so the character can remain unchanged through several stories. But mainstream or literary fiction always requires a character arc, meaning the story events will change some important aspect of the character: his circumstances, status, beliefs, philosophy, or understanding. This development happens whether a character succeeds or fails in the story. If an unlikeable protagonist becomes more sympathetic, this typically ensures the story will have a fairly dramatic character arc, meaning that the ways the character is changed from the opening moments in the story to the closing moments of the story are pronounced. With a positive or upward arc, the character might become happier, stronger, smarter, or more at peace. With a downward arc, the character is likely less happy, less contented, less safe, or less fulfilled. These are only broad outlines of these arcs—like all aspects of fiction, you have endless choices on how to transform your characters.

Most fiction features what can loosely be described as happy endings. If you transform or redeem an unlikeable jerk, then something is affirmed about the human condition. In our modern culture, we like a comeback story. Too often in the real world, it seems that justice fails or people that don't deserve fame or fortune acquire it. Fiction is a chance to tip the scales toward hope.

Not every unlikeable protagonist will transform into a sweetheart by the end of the story, but often the story is written to *pressure* him to change. And if transformation is going to be part of the ending, this outcome must appear impossible or nearly impossible along the way.

Sometimes an unlikeable protagonist is used in a story because he has a lesson to learn or a comeuppance from the other characters and events in the story. The Bible is filled with stories of formerly bad people who mend their ways. One such case is Saul Paulus of Tarsus, who was traveling from Jerusalem to Damascus to arrest followers of Christ. But while he was traveling, he was blinded by a great light. Three days later, his sight was returned; he underwent a conversion, became known as Paul, and began preaching the news of the new religion.

Over the next few pages, we'll look at three of the most common story lines when an author turns to an unlikeable protagonist because he's the best person for the story type: (1) the story is one of redemption, and we all know how much fun it *isn't* to watch a *good* man try to redeem himself; (2) the story is about a character who's *deserving* of a fall—and gets it; or (3) the story is striving to make a statement on the greater human condition, and thus needs an unlikeable protagonist to play in the lead role.

REDEMPTION

As we've just discussed, fiction often features a hopeful ending. This type of ending has existed since the beginning of storytelling. Hope helps us fall asleep at night and get up the next morning to take on the burdens of the day.

A hopeful ending is almost always tied to the protagonist's character arc. For example, in a romance, the hero can start out by being difficult, cold, arrogant, and thin-skinned as he harbors some less-than-noble deeds in his past. By the story's end, he's changed because love has softened or transformed him. He goes from being a real bad ass to a dark good guy. This sort of arc works in other genres, as well as in mainstream fiction. Let's look at an example from mainstream fiction.

Howard Kapostash, the protagonist of Dave King's *The Ha-Ha,* is an example of a complicated and difficult protagonist who is redeemed by the novel's ending. Howard has a brain injury from serving in Vietnam, and he hasn't spoken in thirty years. Scarred both physically and emotionally, he's also unable to read, so he communicates minimally with gestures, facial expressions, and sounds. He has created a lifestyle where he has mostly cut himself off from human ties. He lives in the home he inherited from his parents, and he has little to do with his housemates; in fact, he dislikes two of them, calling them Nit and Nat. He also works as a groundskeeper at a convent, a job that also provides minimal human contact.

Howard has many flaws—he's quick to anger and take offense, and he's embittered, self-pitying, and self involved. He also longs for a relationship with the antagonist, Sylvia, his high-school sweetheart. This relationship shows one of his positive traits, loyalty, since he's loyal to Sylvia, although his loyalty is misplaced. As a drug addict, not only is Sylvia unable to return his feelings, but she has the typical weaknesses of an addict—she uses people, lies, and cheats. When Sylvia is forced into rehab by her family, she asks Howard to care for her twelve-year-old son, Ryan. And that's when Howard's carefully constructed but lonely existence starts cracking.

With Ryan's presence in the household, things start changing and the housemates start acting more like a family and less like strangers sharing a roof. Also woven into the story are Howard's memories of his behavior when he returned from Vietnam and went on a self-destructive binge of drinking, doing drugs, and whoring:

> ... I think of my father's bottles, stowed under the seat of his car or in the tack room, by the privy. That was how I knew he'd given up. I think of a warm night when I was so wrecked I lay on this very lawn, tearing at my thighs and inventing vulgar poems to ward off the explosions above me; I couldn't speak a word of poetry, of course, but I bellowed and screeched at the top of my lungs, and when my mother came out in her nightgown and begged me to stop, I wasn't even sure it was she, not some figment. Even when she took hold of my hands, I swung out, thinking—or maybe that's another occasion. This happened more than I like to admit.

Many of these memories of his twenties are disturbing and paint him in a particularly unsympathetic light. Similarly, if you're writing an unlikeable protagonist into your story, be sure that you expose his misdeeds, especially how he's hurt others.

While Ryan is the vehicle that King uses to redeem and change Howard, his transformation is one step forward, one step back. This too is a lesson that writers should pay attention to. Howard is easily disappointed and frustrated, and each setback sparks off the rage that seems to linger just below the surface. Also stirred into the story are his long-buried longings to be loved and accepted. These feelings make him feel vulnerable, and when he's vulnerable, he reacts in strange ways. If you understand the core vulnerabilities and longings of an unlikeable character you are writing, you too can mine these nuggets.

Because King takes risks as a writer, there are several scenes in the novel where Howard simply flips out. In one scene, he endangers Ryan with his reckless behavior, and as a consequence, he loses his job; in another scene, he ends up in a psych ward because of his actions. But in an even more disturbing scene, Howard brutally attacks Timothy, a homeless vet, after he discovers Sylvia has a new boyfriend:

> I pull to the inside lane so fast that my wheel jumps the curb. Timothy looks up as I climb from the cab, and who knows if her recognizes me? Who knows *what* he sees? He's muttering something and reaching to scratch himself, and then I'm on him, bending low to hit with a shoulder, as we were taught in football, then turning to jab my elbow at his chin. I get a faceful of that chemical scent—metal, filth, urine, war. It's as if I've plumped a particularly nasty pillow. He falls into a shape of impatiens, and I go right after him. Suddenly, I don't mind the stench, and I set my bulk on his thin, stinking chest. His filthy beard brushes my skull, and I give a growl. I'm Howard the bear! A knee to his rib cage, blows to the face—openhanded at first, then punches, with my clenched fist—and I wish I had a tire iron or andiron or a sharpened stick of any size. Something cracks, and there's wetness. Timothy's face is a slippery, sticky mess. Some of the wetness is undoubtedly blood, but some must be saliva, both his and mine, because I'm coughing and drooling and frothing, literally, at the mouth.

You don't need to be Freud to realize that Timothy symbolizes Howard's own frustrations and self-hatred.

Despite this memorable act of violence and other displays of rage, King manages to redeem Howard by the story's end. He emphasizes Howard's character arc by spending lots of time in the backstory exploring Howard's war injury, and then his coma, surgeries, and wildness after returning home.

It's important that Howard's backstory and his many missteps are revealed in the story. If a bad ass suddenly becomes redeemed without the steps that lead to it, the reader will feel cheated. If you're creating a character who is redeemed, you need to depict a believable "before" and "after" in the character arc and also a solid *need* for him to change. In Howard's case, his need to finally connect with people and relate to Ryan is key to his redemption.

COMEUPPANCE

Sometimes an unlikeable protagonist faces a comeuppance in response to his despicable traits and behaviors. Often, the more unlikeable the character is, the harder he falls and the more painful his comeuppance will be. This story type has been around for centuries, as seen in Aesop's Fables, and it satisfies the human need to see justice served.

One such character is the tainted fifty-two-year-old David Lurie in J.M. Coetzee's Nobel Prize-winning novel *Disgrace*. It's set in contemporary South Africa and begins with Lurie's weekly visit to a prostitute, Soraya. This visit helps Lurie get through his week as an assistant professor teaching communications and Romance poets. A former womanizer, his waning appeal at mid-life is difficult to swallow. He imagines Soraya and her colleagues shuddering over him "as one shudders at a cockroach in a washbasin in the middle of the night." He wants more from her than their weekly visits, but when he chances upon her with her sons, it trespasses into her real life and ends their weekly assignations. Lacking these weekly visits, he reflects that "the week is as featureless as a desert."

Coetzee quickly fills the reader in on Lurie's backstory, chiefly focusing on his relationships with women. Twice divorced, Lurie is an uninspiring and uninspired teacher, an author whose books have never really succeeded. As in the case of Howard in *The Ha-Ha*, Lurie's backstory is crucial to the story and, ultimately, his comeuppance. The reader needs the context of his whole life to understand the tidal waves that hit him in the story, and to understand how he's a character who is on a downward arc before the story begins.

As with Howard, Lurie begins the story as being somewhat sympathetic, or at least rather pathetic. After all, the reader can understand what it feels like to be lonely, sexually unfulfilled, and dissatisfied with his job. However, often with unlikeable protagonists in a story, these early feelings of sympathy are erased or diluted as the reader comes to know the character and watch him behave badly as the story unfolds. Because the reader's feelings toward the character change over time, the experience of reading is enriched.

It is when Lurie is isolated, restless, and rudderless that he chances upon Melanie Isaacs, an attractive twenty-year-old student from one of his classes. This is when his real troubles begin and the reader's sympathies at his middle-age losses start to wane because his liaisons with Melanie barely fall short of rape. The affair quickly sours, and she reports him to the college. He is denounced and summoned before a committee of inquiry at the college. While he is willing to admit his guilt, he refuses to yield to pressure to repent and apologize publicly.

Next, Lurie quits his job and flees Cape Town to his daughter Lucy's remote farm. For a while, it seems that he's found a reprieve in the country and that he's rebuilding his relationship with his daughter. But then midway through the novel, a savage attack changes everything and reveals the fault lines in their relationship.

Three men arrive at the farm and Lurie is knocked unconscious and then locked in the lavatory. His feelings of helplessness and being emasculated are complete as his daughter is gang-raped, and he can do nothing to save her:

> He tries to kick at the door, but he is not himself, and the space too cramped anyway, the door too old and solid.
>
> So it has come, the day of testing. Without warning, without fanfare, it is here, and he is in the middle of it. In his chest his heart hammers so hard that it too, in its dumb way, must know. How will they stand up to the testing, he and his heart?
>
> His child is in the hands of strangers. In a minute, in an hour, it will be too late; whatever is happening to her will be set in stone, will belong to the past. But *now* it is not too late. *Now* he must do something.

The men then splash Lurie with methylated spirits and set him on fire. He manages to douse the flames, but before they leave, they kill the dogs, steal household items, and escape in his car. Lurie wants justice, wants the men captured. Lucy reports the attack and thefts, but doesn't report the rapes, which angers Lurie.

Throughout *Disgrace*, Lurie broods on his own aging and mortality, and he reflects on the decay of everything around him and the disarray in the newly configured country. His daughter retreats into herself after the attack, and Lurie feels helpless:

> ... A grey mood is settling on him. It not just that he does not know what to do with himself. The events of yesterday have shocked him to the depths. The trembling, the weakness are only the first and most superficial signs of that shock. He has a sense that, inside him, a vital organ has been bruised, abused—perhaps even his heart. For the first time he has a taste of what it will be like to be an old man, tired to the bone, without hopes, without desires, indifferent to the future. ...

His daughter's rape changes him, and while he apologizes to Melanie's family and reaches other realizations, Lurie isn't rehabilitated and tidied up. In fact, after the attack, he embarks on another affair with a married woman, whom he finds physically repulsive; in another scene, he hires a streetwalker.

As you can see by the example of Lurie's comeuppance, the events are usually dramatic, painful, and altering. Coetzee also illustrates that despite a comeuppance and the pain it causes the protagonist, his core traits are not altered and his essential despair about aging and his country remains. Thus, Coetzee leaves the reader with a rather dismal depiction of the human condition, although the story ending does seem to comment on how humans keep enduring despite the odds.

If, like Coetzee, you want to illustrate inhumanity, despair, wickedness, complacency or other unsavory aspects of humanity, an unlikeable protagonist might be an appropriate vehicle. If you need to set a character against dramatic circumstances, such as a lawless town in the Old West or a country where the new political regimen is incapable of protecting its citizens, then an unlikeable protagonist just might be able to highlight how the world is not a safe or warm place.

Statement

Often, an unlikeable protagonist is used in a story to make a statement about the human condition, the human heart, society's ills, or difficult and raw truths. In *Disgrace*, David Lurie's condition suggests that the human condition is lonely and cruel, with the difficulties of aging, sexuality, mortality, and post-apartheid South Africa as a backdrop. The country and its ills are linked to the story's themes, because it's a bleak place where rape, vandalism, and violence seem almost commonplace.

Sometimes a writer will use a ruthless businessman or politician to comment on greed, power lust, or corruption. A hardhearted or ambitious military commander can portray the senselessness of war. A religious zealot can be used to comment on intolerance. For example, in *Babbitt*, Sinclair Lewis uses George Babbitt, his unlikeable protagonist, a successful realtor, to comment on soulless businessmen, the conformity of the middle class, and the downsides of capitalism. Babbitt is described this way:

> His name was George F. Babbitt. He was forty-six years old now, in April, 1920, and he made nothing in particular, neither butter nor shoes nor poetry, but he was nimble in the calling of selling houses for more than people could afford to pay.

Sometimes an author is highly satirical in his criticisms of society or humanity, such as when Tom Wolfe uses Sherman McCoy, his main character in *The Bonfire of the Vanities*, to explore some difficult realities about American life during the get-rich-quick 1980s. McCoy is a successful bond salesman who lives a sumptuous lifestyle in Manhattan. He's got it all and doesn't know it. Then his life goes to hell when his mistress runs over a young black man while driving McCoy's Mercedes. Tabloids wrongly accuse McCoy of being the driver, and he is brought up on manslaughter charges. McCoy's downfall is used to depict class and racial conflict, and to comment on current journalism practices, hypocritical preachers, the dark side of justice, and the ugly sides of life in New York, among other issues.

When you use an unlikeable protagonist to make a statement, it is absolutely essential that the character be fully humanized—that you lavish the same quirks and details as you do on a likeable protagonist—and that you surround him with a fully developed cast of supporting characters who possess contrasting values and beliefs. This is crucial because you don't want the reader to feel as if your character exists as your human soapbox.

The second trick is to really think through your character's primary traits. Is he going to be subversive, arrogant, or malicious? Is he ordinary, conforming, and dull? No matter what his dominant traits are, they must somehow be showcased in the story line and push at vulnerable characters in the cast. An arrogant character might think he's invulnerable, and the story might prove he's wrong. And, of course, these same traits will also harm the protagonist. Often, the cost of being unlikeable, as demonstrated by David Lurie, is loneliness and isolation.

WHY BACKSTORY COUNTS

As you can see by these examples, backstory is crucial to bringing an unlikeable protagonist to life and depicting his character arc. Let's look at another famous unlikeable protagonist, Ebenezer Scrooge from Charles Dickens's *A Christmas Carol*. Scrooge is so well known that his name has become synonymous with miserliness, and he has a host of negative primary traits. He's a money-grubbing skinflint who is heartless, selfish, and oblivious to people around him. He's also shrewd and symbolizes the wealthy class of Victorian England, who had little care for the poor among them, symbolized in the story by the crippled Tiny Tim Cratchit.

The story is one of redemption as, by story's end, the flint-hearted Scrooge is transformed into someone who cares about others and treasures the spirit of Christmas. But so that the story is believable rather than melodramatic pap, the reader needs to meet Scrooge as a boy via the incarnations of Christmas Past. But first, Scrooge's nephew Fred shows up with his yearly Christmas invitation, which starts jogging Scrooge's memory. This sets the stage for the story since, before the ghosts appear, Scrooge preferred to ignore his memories and, in fact, is not only uninterested in his past, but also is indifferent to the world and people around him.

As the reader meets Scrooge as a boy and learns of his joys and sorrows, his redemption becomes plausible. It is in his boyhood that he was a serious, striving boy, ignored by his father, disliked by his peers. By the time the reader discovers that he was left at school during the Christmas holiday, the reader is beginning to understand reasons that Scrooge is now so cold-hearted. The reader also learns that Scrooge's sister and childhood ally Fran, who was Fred's mother, died young in childbirth, and this was an important loss. In the past, Scrooge is seen enjoying himself at Fezziwig's party, so the reader knows that he's capable of joy and that he was once in love with Belle, but that she broke off their engagement because she grew tired of waiting for him and of his obsession with money and business. It is perhaps in the image of Belle's family that the reader sees most clearly the road Scrooge didn't take and the regrets that he usually ignores:

> … The noise in this room was perfectly tumultuous, for there were more children there, than Scrooge in his agitated state of mind could count; and, unlike the celebrated herd in the poem, they were not forty children conducting themselves like one, but every child was conducting itself like forty. The consequences were uproarious beyond belief; but no one seemed to care; on the contrary, the mother and daughter laughed heartily, and enjoyed it very much; and the latter, soon beginning to mingle in the sports, got pillaged by the young brigands most ruthlessly. …

As Scrooge watches, Belle's husband returns home laden with Christmas gifts and is greeted lovingly by his family amid an uproar.

> And now Scrooge looked on more attentively than ever, when the master of the house, having his daughter leaning fondly on him, sat down with her and her mother at his own fireside; and when he thought that such another creature, quite as graceful and as full of promise, might have called him father, and been a spring-time in the haggard winter of his life, his sight grew very dim indeed.

These scenes from the past are necessary to show how Scrooge became a closed-off miser, and also to prove that there is some hope for his redemption and renewal. Only by revisiting his past could he be nudged toward a much different future.

WALKING A FINE LINE

We've just seen several examples of why we use an unlikeable protagonist in a story. But as you can see in the examples we've discussed, using an unlikeable protagonist calls for walking a fine line. It comes back to the basic fact that a reader wants to be captivated by characters. If a reader is only repelled by your unlikeable protagonist and his situation, he might not be able to finish reading the story. So while some revulsion can be felt by the reader toward an unlikeable protagonist, his feelings should be balanced by also feeling fascinated by the character.

It also comes down to this simple advice: Make certain that you're offering the reader a complete story package. This means that you, as the writer, care about your cast of characters, and somehow this care comes through in your storytelling. The main technique that you'll be using is bringing the reader into the unlikeable character's inner world and past. The reader especially needs access to thoughts and desires, even when they are off-putting. So include introspection as part of your character depiction, even if at times the reader recognizes that the character is not completely truthful. A reader will follow an unlikeable character if his thoughts are well expressed and understandable, if the conflict surrounding the character is compelling, if the situation is inescapable, if the rest of the cast provide contrast to his primary traits and actions, and if the setting is fully described and possibly adding more weight to the conflict, as with the settings in *The Bonfire of the Vanities* and *Disgrace*.

If you look closely at the situations or dilemmas that unlikeable protagonists are cast in, you'll note they're all somehow vulnerable, and often other cast members are vulnerable also. Usually, these situations come about because of the protagonist's misdeeds or arrogance, or they are at least partly responsible for the mess they're in. If David Lurie hadn't had sex with his young student, he wouldn't have lost his job and started the whole chain of events that followed. If Sherman McCoy had been home with his family instead of being with his mistress, he wouldn't have been involved in the muddle that ensued. Both these characters are in a world of trouble, and even if the reader cannot always sympathize with how they act and see the world, the reader can sometimes sympathize with, or at least care about, the mess they've made of their lives.

Often in these stories, the reader will care and worry about other vulnerable characters, such as Lurie's daughter, Lucy. In life, many of us have been affected by difficult people, and have felt vulnerable and possibly even abused by difficult people. Because of our life experiences, we care about other vulnerable characters and can relate to their situations, so we'll keep reading the story to discover how things are resolved. Often (but not always), the unlikeable protagonist finally recognizes the vulnerability of other characters, and sometimes he understands his role in causing harm to other characters.

THE CASE OF THE UNRELIABLE NARRATOR

Let's now consider a subset of the unlikeable protagonist: the unreliable narrator, a literary device that has long been used by authors. I'm including the unreliable narrator in this chapter because the reader often has a complicated relationship with this kind of character, and often wisely cannot trust him and possibly might not like him.

Similarly, a reader often does not trust an unlikeable protagonist because he has unsympathetic traits, but also because he keeps the reader on edge. An unlikeable *and* unreliable narrator is a character who has values and ideas the reader cannot relate to, and whom the reader often finds disturbing. However, unreliable narrators are not necessarily unlikeable, although they *can* be. Back to Nabokov's *Lolita*, Humbert is both unlikeable because of his actions and unreliable because he's so obsessive and dishonest.

Typically, characters are unreliable because they cannot face the truth of who they are or what the reality of their situation is, and their denial is often central to the telling. In Humbert's case, he is implying that he's in charge of the situation between him and Lolita, but the reader sees that Lolita is the one who actually holds the power in the relationship. When the reader is forced to analyze the *real* dynamics of a situation, rather than the narrator's version of things, it makes the experience of the story more personal.

ROGUE'S GALLERY

Unlikeable protagonists are more common in fiction than you might suppose. If you're using one in your story, it can be enormously helpful to analyze how published authors have brought them to life and imbued them with complexity. Here are some examples:

- Rhoda, *Household Words* by Joan Silber
- Rebecca, *Back When We Were Grownups* by Anne Tyler
- Mother, *Loverboy* by Victoria Redel
- Becky Sharp, *Vanity Fair* by William Thackeray
- Don Vito Corleone, *The Godfather* by Mario Puzo
- Captain Queeg, *The Caine Mutiny* by Herman Wouk
- Emma Bovary, *Madame Bovary* by Gustave Flaubert
- Charles Coker, *A Man in Full* by Tom Wolfe
- Julia Lambert, *Theatre* by W. Somerset Maugham
- Hugo Whittier, *The Epicure's Lament* by Kate Christensen
- Charles Blakely, *The Man in the Basement* by Walter Mosley

In real life, people tell white lies, bold lies, and whoppers, and, in fact, some people live a life of lies, as when they marry people they don't love, hide their pasts, or masquerade as people they are not. In fiction, when an unreliable narrator fronts a story, his lies are often complicated and mesmerizing. An unreliable narrator can be speaking in first or third person, and his unreliability can exist in varying degrees—some narrators are completely unreliable, while some just have certain blind spots.

There are two main reasons for creating an unreliable narrator, or one who cannot be trusted. First, unreliable narrators mimic real life in that we constantly encounter cads and liars, and we are often faced with the difficult task of separating fact from fancy in these encounters. Second, unreliable narrators naturally cause lots of tension in a story because the reader will be caught off guard, and he will be playing detective, comparing the narrator's report with the facts of the story. While trying to sort fact from fancy, the reader will become more involved, and what usually results is a certain amount of pathos, along with an unforgettable glimpse into the human soul.

When you're creating an unreliable narrator, begin by asking yourself what the character doesn't know, or refuses to admit, about himself. This is an exercise that can be useful in creating any main character, but often with unreliable narrators there is a specific lack of self-knowledge along with reasons for denial.

Reasons for a lack of candor can stem from mental disabilities, as seen in Benjy from William Faulkner's *The Sound and the Fury*; a compelling bias, as when Big Chief tells the story in Ken Kesey's *One Flew Over the Cuckoo's Nest*; youthfulness or a lack of knowledge, as when a story is told by Mark Twain's Huck Finn; a case of naïveté, such as Nick Carraway reporting on Gatsby in F. Scott Fitzgerald's *The Great Gatsby*. Sometimes there is a combination of reasons for unreliability, as with Holden Caulfield in J.D. Salinger's *The Catcher in the Rye*, who is both young and troubled by mental health issues. And then there are narrators who deliberately attempt to deceive or mislead readers for more nefarious reasons.

SUPPLYING A MOTIVE

An unreliable narrator can be delusional, eccentric, self-serving, or not too bright. The key to creating a realistic yet unreliable narrator of this sort lies in knowing his motives. As already mentioned, sometimes an unreliable narrator is also unlikeable, but more often, he is sympathetic, as with Huck Finn and Holden Caulfield. The reader not only relates to the character, but also enjoys his company and worries over his sorrows and troubles. This type of narrator is often in a denial of sorts, unable to acknowledge his unfavorable qualities or admit to weaknesses.

One of the most arresting examples of a narrator whose unreliability stems from his avoidance of the truth is found in Kazuo Ishiguro's *The Remains of the Day*. The character is Stevens, the butler at Darlington Hall. Stevens's motives lie in the strict English class system, and in his notions of loyalty, duty, and propriety. He appears to be a man who holds himself with the strictest self-discipline; these qualities especially are shown in a scene where his elderly father dies, and Stevens carries on his duties with a stiff upper lip. The story is a tragedy because Stevens turns a blind eye to his master's true nature and his involvement with the Nazis. But even more tragically, Stevens fools himself about his own needs for intimacy and his romantic feelings for the housekeeper until it is far too late. In fact, Ishiguro's novel is a terrific example of how a series of missed cues can be central to creating a story based on an unreliable narrator. It also shows how, although a character has blind spots, the reader still somehow sympathizes with him, particularly in light of the social milieu he lives in.

Anita Shreve's *All He Ever Wanted* is told mostly in first person through the view of Nicholas Van Tassel, who is an example of an unreliable narrator who is also unlikeable. The story begins in December 1899 when a fire breaks out in a hotel kitchen, and dining room guests are forced out into a New England winter evening. In the melee that follows, Nicholas spots a woman in the crowd, and his fate is sealed:

> The woman had almond-shaped eyes and an abundance of dark brown lashes. Her nostrils and her cheekbones were prominent, as if there were a foreign element to her blood. Her acorn-colored hair, I guessed, would unwind to her waist. She was holding a child in her arms, which I took to be her own. My desire for this unknown woman was so immediate and keen and inappropriate that it quite startled me; and I have often wondered if that punishing desire, that sense of fire within the body, that craven need to touch the skin, was not simply the result of the heightened circumstances of the fire itself. Would I have been so ravished had I seen Etna Bliss across the dining room, or turned and noted her standing behind me on a street corner? I answer myself, as I invariably do, with the knowledge that it would not have mattered in what place or on what date I first saw the woman—my reaction would have been just as swift and as terrifying.

Thus begins Nicholas's obsession with Etna. This obsession is the key to his unreliability because he cannot view her objectively, and his obsession allows him to justify his every action. This meeting is followed by a courtship, marriage, and children, but he knows that he hasn't won her complete love or affection. Although they have two children, their nightly intimacies reveal her lack of passion for their marriage bed.

He lays the blame for this on Etna because he learns she's not a virgin on their wedding night; although true to the times, they never discuss this fact. Then, as the story goes along, his true nature emerges, and the reader discovers that he's obsessive, to the point of ruthlessness, as well as jealous, self-righteous, racist, and scheming. But, of course, he never comes out and admits to these faults, and the reader must discover what he's withholding. As is the case of most unreliable narrators, what is *not* said matters greatly.

UNMASKING THE UNRELIABLE NARRATOR

It is often necessary in a story that contains an unlikeable protagonist, an unreliable narrator, or a villain to unmask him by the story's end. Often, at first, these bad asses are walking among other characters in the story world seemingly benign or decent sorts, but actually disguised because the reader doesn't know much about their inner worlds. This wolf in sheep's clothing approach often works well, because then, when the character is unmasked as being ruthless, untrustworthy, or evil, he's even more dangerous because he managed to hide among the rest of the cast.

This unmasking of a character, showing the reality beneath the civilized veneer, can be extremely satisfying to the reader. It's a sort of hide-and-seek game played between the writer and reader. The reader's satisfaction is increased when a writer foreshadows some of these qualities but doesn't give away too much too soon.

Don't be afraid to be drawn to difficult characters, complicated types, and odd viewpoints. Our task as fiction writers is to reveal the mysteries of human behavior in all their permutations. It can be compelling to show characters who are like us, and especially those that are not like us. Remember, too, that a character doesn't need to be likeable, but he does need to be understandable.

Like people in the real world, unlikeable protagonists are enormously complicated. Sometimes they have something to hide, and sometimes they cannot seem to help themselves—they are liars, cheats, or just downright delusional. As a fiction writer, it's important to concoct characters who are imperfect in all the roles of your stories. In fact, one of the biggest mistakes a writer can make is to create perfect characters because this robs the story of credibility and diminishes the reader's embroilment in the story.

But herein lies one of the big dilemmas of writing fiction. Earlier in this chapter, I wrote that when an unlikeable character is in a story, the reader usually cannot fully identify with him in any role he plays in the story. To succeed in making an unlikeable protagonist believable, then, you need to inhabit him, or at the least possess a deep understanding of him, and listen closely as he whispers his darkest thoughts and secrets. You cannot stand back and wave a magic wand or merely craft words on the page as the author. You might need to *become* this less-than-lovely human. You need to know what he knows, feel what he feels, and want what he wants; this likely won't be comfortable, especially if he behaves immorally. But if you can slip into his skin, feeling his vulnerabilities and desires, no matter if dwelling within this character makes you feel a bit queasy, you'll be able to write a provocative story.

CHAPTER THREE

Bastards: Anti-Heroes

The cave you fear to enter holds the treasure you seek.

—Joseph Campbell

If you dare to write about less-than-charming characters, you don't need to redeem them with an ending in which they see the error of their ways, mend their faults, and allow their flinty hearts to be transformed into a choir loft of goodness. You see, Hollywood movies have greatly influenced audience expectations to such a degree that bad people are expected to become good, endings are expected to be tidy and hopeful, and outcomes are expected to be laced with sunshine. Fiction can, and should, mimic life, with all its messes and discomfort and disquiet. Fiction should also prove just how complicated and troubled many people are.

In fiction, sometimes it's difficult to categorize the various character types, especially when the characters' morality cannot be easily defined. This chapter is about a kind of protagonist—meaning he's the focus character in the story—who sometimes has the morality we've traditionally come to associate with bad guys, which is where the term *anti-hero* comes from. An anti-hero is a protagonist who is as flawed or more flawed than most characters; he is someone who disturbs the reader with his weaknesses yet is sympathetically portrayed, and who magnifies the frailties of humanity.

In days of old, especially in the eighteenth century, protagonists were often heroes and antagonists were usually villains, and they were often depicted in stories as either good or evil, clearly delineated as black and white. My hope is that this chapter, and the book as a whole, will prove that, as in real life, characters come in many shades and types. An anti-hero is a protagonist who typically lacks the traditional traits and qualities of a hero, such as trustworthiness, courage, and honesty. If he were assigned a color, it would be gray.

Often, an anti-hero is unorthodox and might flaunt laws or act in ways contrary to society's standards. In fact, and this is important, an anti-hero often reflects society's confusion and ambivalence about morality, and thus he can be used for social or political comment. While an anti-hero cannot slip into a white hat, he will always:

- have the reader's sympathies, although sometimes his methods will make this difficult.
- have easily identified imperfections.
- be made understandable by the story events, meaning that the reader will come to know his motivations and likely will be privy to his inner demons.
- have a starring role in the story.

An anti-hero is often a bad ass, a maverick, or a screw-up. You might want to picture Paul Newman playing the title character in the film *Cool Hand Luke*, Clint Eastwood as Harry Callahan in *Dirty Harry*, or Bruce Willis playing John McClane in *Die Hard*—slightly scruffy and worn, sometimes moral, but sometimes not. If the character is a woman, perhaps her slip is showing and her lipstick is smeared, she sleeps with men she doesn't know well, and she often cannot fit into traditional women's roles.

An anti-hero can also play the part of an outsider or loner—a "little man." This kind of anti-hero often possesses a fragile self-esteem, has often failed at love, and is sometimes estranged from people from his past. Perhaps the best-known anti-hero of our time is Tony Soprano of the television series *The Sopranos*. Bridget Jones of Helen Fielding's *Bridget Jones's Diary*, Sam Spade of Dashiell Hammett's *The Maltese Falcon*, Philip Marlow in Raymond Chandler's stories, Gulliver of Jonathan Swift's *Gulliver's Travels*, and Randall McMurphy of Ken Kesey's *One Flew Over the Cuckoo's Nest* are also well-known anti-heroes. The reader loves these characters because they are realistic and relatable—just like the people in the reader's life, they're imperfect and roiling with contradictions.

Anti-heroes can be rebels in search of freedom or justice, and they're usually willing to take the law into their own hands. They often occupy a gray area between good guy and bad guy—John D. MacDonald's Travis McGee comes to mind, as does Jack Sparrow in the *Pirates of the Caribbean* films. Robin Hood was an anti-hero, as was Wolf Larsen in Jack London's *The Sea-Wolf*. Of course, there have always been real-life anti-heroes, such as Butch Cassidy and the Sundance Kid, Wild Bill Hickock, Calamity Jane, and Bonnie and Clyde. Sometimes fast living, sometimes an outcast, and never superhuman, this character type provides you with lots of latitude in exploring themes and issues, often amid a true-to-life environment.

Anti-heroes can be obnoxious, pitiful, or charming, but they are always failed heroes or deeply flawed. Often riddled with paradoxical traits and qualities, they resemble real people more than any other type of fictional characters do, and they are increasingly popular these days in fiction, film, and television.

One of the most important qualities to remember is that anti-heroes rarely, if ever, reflect society's higher values—or what we like to think of as our society's values; their thinking and values are often antithetical to those of the norm. For example, the sort of traits valued by most members of society—such as honesty, strength, integrity, and compassion—will not always be exhibited by an anti-hero in a story. Or, he might have a character arc where he grudgingly adopts some of these traits. Traditional depictions of fictional characters meant that main players were good guys with traits that we all want to emulate. Anti-heroes turn that assumption upside down.

And here is the trick to creating anti-heroes: They always possess an underlying pathos. Most characters come with flaws, neuroses, and "issues." But with an anti-hero, these problems are more noticeable and troublesome, and they sometimes get in the way of forming intimate attachments. There is always something that is screwing up the anti-hero's plan, and that something is usually from his past. A story with an anti-hero in a starring role might depict how a person cannot easily escape from the past, particularly deep losses.

CHARACTERISTICS OF AN ANTI-HERO

It takes a fine hand to draw an anti-hero because this character requires a great deal of nuance to arouse complicated reactions in the reader. As we've just discussed, an anti-hero is a character that the reader roots for, despite his flaws and the bad things he's done or how he justifies these misdeeds. Sometimes the anti-hero is able to toe the line between good and evil, but often he's a danger to himself and others. Sometimes an anti-hero also has remarkable ability to compartmentalize. Perhaps he kills an enemy or a bad guy, then in the next scene shows up at a kid's birthday party, apparently unruffled by his recent grisly task.

Like all main characters, understanding an anti-hero's character arc is crucial in designating his role in your story. After all, you'll need to know if his good behavior is accidental, or if he is redeemed by the story's events. One trick to creating an anti-hero is to fashion his primary traits so that his essential nature and personality are clear to you as you craft each scene he appears in. Then you need to know the *why* of these traits and beliefs—in essence, how he came to be. If your character is lawless, rebellious, or obnoxious, it is likely that your character will somehow justify these behaviors.

An anti-hero is not simply a bad ass who cannot follow the rules. The *reasons* for why he acts as he does, along with his self-concept, are important to the story. Another trick to creating a complicated anti-hero is to shape his less-than-moral traits and acts into a profound statement about humanity. As you create anti-hero characters, consider that they:

- are not role models, although we secretly would like to kick ass like they do.
- can be selfish and essentially bad people who occasionally are good.
- are sometimes unglamorous and unattractive in character as well as in appearance.
- can be motivated by self-interest and self-preservation, but there is usually a line anti-heroes won't cross, which sets them apart from villains.

ANTI-HEROES AS LITERARY LEGACIES

If you're interested in using anti-heroes in your story, it's helpful to understand their roles in literature throughout time, and how they are changing in modern times. In ancient times, Achilles is an anti-hero in Greek mythology, and Satan is an anti-hero in John Milton's *Paradise Lost*; Geoffrey Chaucer's Pardoner and William Shakespeare's Macbeth could also be classified as such.

The title character from Gustave Flaubert's *Madame Bovary*, published in 1856, was a shocking departure from the literary characters of the time with her adulterous behavior, sad fate, and deep hungers and dissatisfactions. In the 1930s and 1940s, the rise of American authors in the suspense genre brought more anti-heroes into the fore, and included mostly grizzled, hard-drinking detectives like Hammett's Sam Spade and Chandler's Philip Marlowe who walked the mean streets of urban America. After the atomic bomb exploded to end World War II, there was an upsurge of anti-heroes as main characters, as if to give voice to the cynicism and angst of the post-nuclear age. Harry "Rabbit" Angstrom in John Updike's Pulitzer Prize-winning series is a famous example of a subcategory of anti-heroes, the flawed everyman. Rabbit embodies many unpleasant truths about humanity. He is bigoted, selfish, and self-pitying; he frequently complains that his life, his job, and his family are not good enough for him. When things get tough, he runs, abandoning his responsibilities for an easier path, only to get dragged back into his fate. He embodies the sometimes insignificance of the individual, especially since he is a has-been, having peaked in high school when he was a basketball star.

In today's literary marketplace, graphic novels and comic books are fueling the rise of anti-heroes as a type of main character. Anti-heroes are not only a vital offshoot in literature, reflecting humanity and social ills, these days they are also becoming more the norm than the exception. Perhaps it's because the world has grown so complicated, and the many shades of dark, light, and shadow are simply more realistic than the black-and-white depictions of old, or than the unambiguous setup of good versus evil. Perhaps today's anti-heroes reflect an outcome that's more like the not-quite-bad guy versus the bad guy. The bottom line is that these main characters possess their own unique moral code, are unpredictable, and are fun to write. And, let's never forget, readers sometimes see themselves and their neighbors when anti-heroes are at the helm of a story.

- often have motives that are complicated and range from revenge to honor.
- forced to choose between right and wrong, will sometimes choose wrong because it's easier.
- can play both sides with good guys and bad guys, profiting from both.
- can sometimes be coerced to help underdogs, children, or weaker characters, and they sometimes do so voluntarily.
- can embody unattractive traits and behaviors, such as sexist and racist attitudes, and violent reactions when wronged.
- can show little or no remorse for bad behaviors.
- are usually a mess of contradictions.

HEROES VERSUS ANTI-HEROES: IDENTIFYING THE DIFFERENCES

The role of a hero as the main player who drives the story has been around for centuries. Heroes somehow embody the forces of good and overcome great odds to succeed in the story. In classical stories, a hero was always extraordinary, might have divine ancestry, and was more of a demi-god than human. Hercules is this type of hero.

Over time, the term *hero* came to be no longer associated with god-like types, but instead came to mean an extraordinary man or woman who overcame great obstacles, who often sacrificed him- or herself for a cause, who displayed courage when facing the story's problems, and who held moral and exemplary traits. Heroes appeared in myths, epic poems, operas, fairy tales, and, in fact, most story types.

But so the story contains suspense, heroes are never perfect; in fact, in the tradition of Aristotle, they possess a fatal flaw that can be their undoing. But because they are heroes, part of their quest is to rise above this flaw so that their grace, perseverance, and greatness of spirit can inspire and uplift readers. Heroes in fiction are also designed to learn from their mistakes; often they rise from the ashes to defeat the bad guys.

In many of the character types discussed in this book, there are no absolutes, as in "a villain will always be 100 percent evil" or "a hero will 100 percent good." If there were absolute truths about every character type, it would make our jobs as writers easier, but we'd also end up with parodies or caricatures of the human condition. Likewise, anti-heroes can be difficult to classify because they vary so broadly, and there are few absolute traits shared by every type. You'll know an anti-hero is in story because he's in the starring role though his morals and motives are questionable, and despite his moral traits, or lack thereof, you will still sympathize with him. Here are some general differences that I hope will clarify on which side of morality you'll find an anti-hero, and how an anti-hero is the antithesis of a traditional hero:

HERO	ANTI-HERO
A hero is an idealist.	An anti-hero is a realist.
A hero has a conventional moral code.	An anti-hero has a moral code that is quirky and individual.
A hero is somehow extraordinary.	An anti-hero can be ordinary.
A hero is always proactive.	An anti-hero can be passive.
A hero is often decisive.	An anti-hero can be indecisive or pushed into action against his will.
A hero is a modern version of a knight in shining armor.	An anti-hero can be a tarnished knight, and sometimes a criminal.
A hero succeeds at his ultimate goals, unless the story is a tragedy.	An anti-hero might fail in a tragedy, but in other stories he might be redeemed by the story's events, or he might remain largely unchanged, including being immoral.

A hero is motivated by virtues, morals, a higher calling, pure intentions, and love for a specific person or humanity.	An anti-hero can be motivated by a primitive, lower nature, including greed or lust, through much of the story, but he can sometimes be redeemed and answer a higher calling near the end.
A hero is motivated to overcome flaws and fears, and to reach a higher level. This higher level might be about self-improvement, a deeper spiritual connection, or trying to save humankind from extinction. His motivation and usually altruistic nature lends courage and creativity to his cause. Often, a hero makes sacrifices in the story for the better of others.	An anti-hero, while possibly motivated by love or compassion at times, is most often propelled by self-interest.
A hero (usually when he is the star of the story in genre fiction, such as Westerns) concludes the story on an upward arc, meaning he's overcome something from within or has learned a valuable lesson in the story.	An anti-hero can appear in mainstream or genre fiction, and the conclusion will not always find him changed, especially if he's a character in a series.
A hero always faces monstrous opposition, which essentially makes him heroic in the first place. As he's standing up to the bad guys and troubles the world hurls at him, he will take tremendous risks and sometimes battle an authority. His stance is always based on principles.	An anti-hero also battles authority and sometimes go up against tremendous odds, but not always because of principles. His motives can be selfish, criminal, or rebellious.

A hero is a good guy, the type of character the reader was taught to cheer for since childhood.	An anti-hero can be a bad guy in manner and speech. He can cuss, drink to excess, talk down to others, and back up his threats with fists or a gun, yet the reader somehow sympathizes with or genuinely likes him and cheer him on.
A hero can be complex, but he is generally unambivalent; an anti-hero is a complicated character who reflects the ambivalence of many real people.	An anti-hero's actions and ways of thinking demand that the reader think about issues and ask difficult questions.

ROLES FOR ANTI-HEROES

The roles for anti-heroes in contemporary fiction seem endless, as society is coming to terms with the notion that morality is not always absolute. Here are some roles that you might consider for your anti-hero character.

EVERYMAN: Picture this category of anti-hero as the opposite of Superman. Not only does an everyman anti-hero not possess supernatural talents or abilities, but he also might have a lackluster appearance and come with a beer gut, a bad back, and a bald spot. When you create an everyman type for a story, you'll be featuring a story character that the reader can easily identify with, because the real world is populated with these types. Often a person of humble origins, the everyman is never elite, exceptional, or even charismatic. The everyman is ordinary—the grocer, the baker, the candlestick maker. Writers use everyman characters so that the reader can imagine himself amid the story events. Because this type of character isn't extraordinarily brave or talented, he'll react realistically to story events and often won't rush in to save the day or solve the story problem. In fact, often he is dragged kicking and screaming into a fight and likewise often only changes under duress.

As mentioned earlier, Updike's Rabbit Angstrom is a famous example of this category of anti-hero, as are the unnamed lead character in Philip Roth's *Everyman*, Richard Ford's everyman character Frank Bascombe, who's featured in three novels, *The Sportswriter*, *Independence Day*, and *The Lay of the Land*, and Saul Bellow's Tommy Wilhelm in *Seize the Day*.

The everyman character is usually in some way bumbling, inept, or in over his head. Sometimes the character is seriously adrift; sometimes he is thrust into a position of danger where his lack of bravery or talents will make his situation tenuous and dangerous. An everyman will always possess at least several unsympathetic, or even despicable, traits. Sometimes this character is an optimist, sometimes he is a cynic, but he is always a realistic depiction of humanity.

VIGILANTE OR TARNISHED KNIGHT: A vigilante is a person with his own moral code who takes the law into his own hands, as in the days of the Old West. In many ways, this anti-hero type is closest to heroes in literature because of his *aims* in the story. The aforementioned Dirty Harry Callahan played by Clint Eastwood in the film series exemplifies this type. While a vigilante still might be part of the system, he is often an ex-cop or ex-military man, and he has often left his previous position because of a mistake or because he simply cannot play by the rules. Often self-employed, he may work as a private investigator, security professional, or bodyguard. A vigilante often takes on the dangers of the role with excess relish or dispassion.

In George Pelecanos's *The Night Gardener*, Dan "Doc" Holiday exemplifies this type. He left the police force because of his drinking and shady dealings, but he now doesn't have much to live for. After sleeping off a drinking binge he stumbles onto a body in a community garden and is pulled back into unsolved cases from early in his career. The story uses a cast of good and bad cops, and it shows that the police often operate in a moral limbo; right and wrong are not always simple, and playing it straight isn't always the way to solve a case.

CHARMING CRIMINAL: The suave Cary Grant as John Robie in the film *To Catch a Thief* as a good example of this type. Readers and film audiences know crime is bad, but they just cannot help but like, or at least sympathize, with this likeable rogue. He's not made for the nine-to-five

HEROES AND ANTI-HEROES: A BREAKDOWN

Here is a side-by-side comparison of heroes and anti-heroes that should make their differences apparent.

Hero: Clarice Starling from Thomas Harris's *The Silence of the Lambs*	**Anti-hero:** Kathy Mallory from Carol O'Connell's suspense series
Starling is tough, fragile, determined, and on the side or upholding the law and defending the weak. Her back-story—she's an orphan who once tried to save a lamb from slaughter to stop the screaming—makes her more compelling. She overcomes her lack of experience and, showing unusual courage, destroys the serial killer and rescues his latest victim.	Mallory is an NYPD detective who goes up against the city's most desperate and dangerous criminals. She's streetwise and tough; she has demons from her past, seems to believe that a conscience is a hindrance, and is seen by most characters around her as driven and heartless. Mallory will do anything to solve a case, including endangering or ruining the lives of others.
Hero: Ma Joad from John Steinbeck's *Grapes of Wrath*	**Anti-hero:** Isadora Wing from Erica Jong's *Fear of Flying*
Joad holds her family together despite horrible odds and extreme trials. She's wise, strong, and selfless, and she depicts leadership qualities. The story especially illustrates that, in a crisis, a hero will rise to meet the difficulties. Joad's calm and fearless presence during the harshest moments of the family's plight—including death, hunger, and bereavement—lends courage to her family members, who might collapse without her strength to rely on.	In one of the first post-feminist novels of the 1970s, Wing shocks the reader with her sexually liberated antics, her fierce honesty about her sexuality, her selfish drive for pleasure and freedom, and her seeming lack of conscience. Like Ma Joad, she strives to be the author of her own destiny, but her goals—such as wanting anonymous sex—and self-definition place her firmly in the anti-hero category of characters.

Hero: Jem Finch from Harper Lee's *To Kill a Mockingbird*	**Anti-hero:** Huck Finn from Mark Twain's *The Adventures of Huckleberry Finn*
Like the best heroes, Jem shows grit and moral qualities that can be emulated. Jem learns harsh realities about his small town and human nature throughout the story; he discovers the meaning of true courage, as when his father faces down a rabid dog, and when a neighbor fights addiction and finds his moral compass. In the story's climatic scene, despite the odds, he fights a villain to defend his younger sister.	Huck is a complicated character whom Twain uses to reveal many of the chilling truths about the old South, particularly the racism that was rampant and dehumanizing. An uncivilized outsider, and the sort of boy parents don't want their children to associate with, Huck's quest is for freedom. In the beginning of the story, Huck believes that slavery simply is the way of the world, but as the story progresses, he begins to see the humanity in everyone, black and white.

routine, so he skirts the law, usually by stealing or scamming. Professional gamblers might fall under this type also. With a charming criminal at the helm, these stories usually feature nonstop action and witty dialogue, with the reader or film viewer enjoying being in the know as the plans are laid for the heist or scam.

While charming criminals tend to rip off companies or banks, Red, the convicted murderer in Stephen King's "Rita Hayworth and the Shawshank Redemption," is an exception. Although Red murdered his wife, he's aware of the depravity of this crime. In fact, he claims he's the only guilty man serving in Shawshank, and at the story's end, he is paroled to a new life. Sometimes an author places this more likeable type amid less savory characters, as Elmore Leonard does with his character Ernest Stickley, Jr. in *Stick* and *Swag*. When the charming criminal is the lesser evil in a story, his humanity is emphasized. Often, a story will center on a complicated scam or heist, as in the film *Ocean's Eleven*, where Brad Pitt and George Clooney play characters who are part of an ensemble cast of likeable thieves.

DARK HERO: Dark heroes, also called Byronic heroes, are angst-ridden, and are often misunderstood loners. Picture James Dean as Jim Stark in the film *Rebel Without a Cause* and Clint Eastwood as William Munny in *Unforgiven* to understand this type. Also picture this dark hero character dressed in black. This tradition of a dark hero has been around since John Milton wrote *Paradise Lost,* but it was firmly in place with characters in Gothic novels of the eighteenth century and is, in fact, the precursor to the anti-hero as a character type. Typically, this character is a young and attractive male with attitude and a lousy reputation, although the Ellen Ripley character, played by Sigourney Weaver, in the film *Aliens* also falls under this category.

BAD BOY: Bad boys are anti-authority and cannot handle conventional morality; they instead possess a personal moral code that is sometimes disturbing to others. While they have many bad habits, they are often portrayed sympathetically, even if the reader cannot identify with them. Bad boys might be guns-for-hire or assassins. They are most often found in comics, Westerns, action films, thrillers, vampire novels, sci-fi, and Gothics. Sometimes their quest can ennoble them. Bad boys typically bring a lot of fire, defiance, and eroticism to a story, along with a sense of danger. Lestat de Lioncourt of Anne Rice's *Interview With the Vampire* and *The Vampire Lestat* is an extreme example of this character type. A more typical example of a bad boy is Paul Newman as the title character in *Cool Hand Luke* and as "Fast" Eddie Felson in *The Hustler*.

RELUCTANT HERO: A reluctant hero is a tarnished or ordinary man with several faults or a troubled past, and he is pulled reluctantly into the story, or into heroic acts. During the story, he rises to the occasion, sometimes even vanquishing a mighty foe, sometimes avenging a wrong. But he questions whether he's cut out for the hero business. His doubts, misgivings, and mistakes add a satisfying layer of tension to a story. Han Solo, the smart-aleck smuggler of the Star Wars series, is an example of the type. Like many anti-heroes, the reluctant hero character is a loner, selfish, and self-serving, and he reluctantly puts aside his own interests for the good of humankind. Sometimes this character has also experienced a fall from grace, and can be a disgraced or dishonorably discharged military person, cop, or, in the case of Solo, part of the Imperial Starfleet.

Ezekiel "Easy" Rawlins, Walter Mosley's series character, is another example of the reluctant hero. In the series, which takes place over several decades beginning in the 1940s, Rawlins is an unwilling detective in the Watts section of Los Angeles. He's usually pulled into the puzzle at the heart of a story by a friend, often because it seems that black people won't achieve justice without his help. Rawlins walks a crooked line between the established order and his own code of honor, and his street smarts and underground contacts are often what help him solve the case. Like many anti-heroes, at the reluctant hero character's core is pain and rage—emotions that make his actions endlessly fascinating.

LOSER: This type of anti-hero has traits similar to the everyman, but the loser usually begins the story at a low ebb in his life. For example, Quoyle of E. Annie Proulx's *The Shipping News* is a quintessential loser. Unattractive, lumpy, and sometimes dim-witted, it seems like he can barely muddle his way through daily life. After his ill-fated marriage, the reader is especially worried that someone so clueless is not going to be able to survive, much less raise two daughters on his own. A loser is known for a terrible ineptness, bad luck, especially troubling flaws, and qualities that make him seem especially ill-suited for the task at hand. This sort of ineptness keeps the story teetering at the edge of disaster. Willie Loman of Arthur Miller's *Death of a Salesman* is another good example of a loser character. Loman's identity is so tied to his worth as a salesperson and as someone pursuing the American Dream that when he fails to produce, he fails to feel any worth.

OUTCAST: This category of anti-heroes includes characters who often accept or even glory in their roles as social outcasts. They often defy conventions of society, behavior, or morality, but the reasons for why they are outside society are many. They are not interested in the trappings of middle-class life, so most outcasts won't be homeowners with a wife, two children, a Golden Retriever, and an SUV. Their roles in the story will always shine a light on beliefs or systems that most of us take for granted or give little thought to. In Joseph Heller's *Catch-22*, Captain John Yossarian is a classic example of an outcast. The book has many themes, including the idiocy of a military bureaucracy, the senselessness of war, and the impossibility of living by the rules of a greater society. Mark Twain's Huck Finn is an outcast because of his social status, but when he takes off with Jim, a runaway slave, it solidifies his position as outcast.

SCREWBALL: Screwball characters are usually depicted in the midst of a fairly complex situation, such as a mystery with romance, lots of sexual tension, and a series of complications factored into the story. Usually, the character is strong-willed, unpredictable, and sometimes zany, such as Joan Wilder in the film *Romancing the Stone* and Stephanie Plum in Janet Evanovich's suspense series. These characters are used for hilarity and for surprising plot twists. Stories with screwball characters are fast-paced, veer toward absurdity, and feature lots of laughs amid the characters' antics. Carl Hiaasen is especially known for creating screwball characters in his novels, as are Elmore Leonard and Pete Hautman.

DISGRACED HERO: A disgraced anti-hero might have once been a true hero, but he was somehow undone by his own demons; so he cannot assume that role now, although at times his actions can be heroic. Like a vigilante, a disgraced hero is more closely aligned with heroes than other anti-types, such as outcasts. Robert B. Parker's Jesse Stone is a good example of this highly flawed type of character. After drinking himself out of a job in Los Angeles, Stone takes a job as small-town sheriff in Massachusetts. The underlying question in each story is: Can Stone overcome his personal demons so that he can handle his job? Disgraced heroes are kin to dark heroes, and they are often leading the helm of mysteries and thrillers. They are always scarred by something in their pasts, such as a mistake that cost another person his or her life, the death of a loved one, a childhood trauma, or a military stint. This type of character is often a loner and will always be haunted by the past and have self-destructive behaviors.

ODDBALL: An oddball character can be a nerdy geek who wears a pocket protector or an autistic savant, among many other types of people. The point is, they just don't fit in, and because of their oddities, they are often ridiculed or avoided by others. Their presence in a story creates extreme sympathy along with tension because oddballs can range in nature from explosive to outlandish. Sometimes an oddball will only have a few char-

CREATING YOUR ANTI-HERO: AN EXERCISE

Here's a great exercise for creating an anti-hero. Reflecting on people you've met over the years, slip into your most judgmental state of mind and make a list of the many habits, addictions, and behaviors that drive you crazy. If you're allergic to smoke, add chain smoking to your list. If you're uncomfortable with people who drink too much, add that trait. If people who never exercise get on your nerves, or people with poor hygiene drive you up the wall, add those traits, too. These habits can be large flaws, such as lying, or smaller ones, such as slathering on too much aftershave. Considering the people you have met, do you especially dislike liars, racists, or adulterers? Do stingy people drive you crazy? How about people who are financially irresponsible, or who brag too much? How about people who are always late, who are slobs, who are too strict with their children? From this list, you'll have a resource of flaws to build your anti-heroes from because anti-heroes are highly flawed and often make people uncomfortable.

acters in the story who can see beyond his strangeness. Such is the case of the Dean Koontz series character who is boldly named Odd Thomas.

Odd is a short-order cook by trade, but his particular psychic skills bring him into the company of the dead and newly murdered citizens of his town, along with other wandering dead, such as Elvis. Besides being able to commune with the dead, Odd is also able to see other depraved spirit creatures, bodachs, so that he knows when violence or carnage is forthcoming. Odd seems to signify that the world is not safe and the dead are restless.

In *The History of Love*, Nicole Krauss's characters are mostly oddballs, including Leo Gursky, the lonely octogenarian who nurses the loss of his true love, as well as his estrangement with his only son—a famous writer—and his own great manuscript. Krauss seems to use all her cast to make the reader think about aloneness and estrangement. The novel focuses mainly on the slowly converging stories of Leo Gursky and Alma Singer. Leo is an eighty-year-old retired locksmith in New York, a survivor of a Nazi massacre in the Polish village where he grew up sixty years before the novel opens. Alma is a fourteen-year-old girl whose father has recently died, whose mother shields herself from loneliness by working nonstop as a literary translator, and whose nine-year-old brother, Bird (over whom she vigilantly watches), thinks he might be the Messiah. Leo and Alma—and all the many other characters in this slender, densely woven novel—are connected across time and space by the impact on their lives of an almost-forgotten novel called *The History of Love.* The key to using oddballs in a story is that they're sympathetically and intricately drawn; you must find fresh quirks and eccentricities that make them endearing to the reader, although perhaps not so to their fellow cast members.

REBEL: Although many anti-heroes have a rebellious nature, sometimes an anti-hero exists almost solely as a rebel with a cause. This character type will fight or resist the status quo, and their reasons for rebelling often fuel the plot and place them in direct opposition with other characters. Rebels can be tragic, or they can succeed at their cause; they can be loners, or they can be part of a group. A rebel steps outside the norm to create a new artistic form or new culture, such as the beatniks and hippies of the 1960s and 1970s. Like outcasts, rebels serve the plot to shine a light on some aspect of society that they believe needs to be changed. Often, they question authority and demand that society is not dehumanizing or corrupt. Randall McMurphy in Ken Kesey's *One Flew Over the Cuckoo's Nest* is a good example of a tragic rebel anti-hero because he loses to the evil Nurse Ratched, and the lobotomy that makes him a placid patient also robs him of his humanity.

CREATING ANTI-HEROES BASED ON OPPOSING TRAITS

Most people possess a paradoxical nature or a jumble of traits that don't quite seem to jibe. When a character has opposing traits, the reader will have a deeper and more profound relationship with him because people in real life are complex and textured, and fictional characters who possess these same dichotomies are relatable. Also, because characters who are strictly one-dimensional are predictable and dull, the reader wants characters to possess contradictory or oppositional traits. After all, in real life, we can change moment to moment or day to day. We experience varying moods, sometimes we ride a high cycle of success, sometimes we plummet to the depths of despair during periods of loss or disappointment. Sometimes people become cynical after a series of failures, sometimes people are corrupted by success. And sometimes people are simply a roiling blend of traits that seem to be a mishmash of characters.

Mario Puzo's blood saga *The Godfather* is one of the best-selling novels of all time, and it is the basis for three films. In the tale, the godfather, Don Vito Corleone, struggles among the underworld bosses for power while the story line depicts how family values and criminal traits are transferred from one generation to the next.

Many of the characters are sympathetically drawn and built from a complex set of traits. Puzo humanizes the members of the crime family by showing them in intimate moments, such as gathering for Sunday dinner and dancing at a wedding, and somewhere between the cannoli and the spaghetti and the guns, the reader tends to think of them as people first and criminals second. So, oddly, the reader finds himself siding with the family, although common sense dictates that they are ruthless criminals.

The central character, Don Corleone, is an icon of American fiction and an anti-hero, as described in the book:

> But great men are not born great, they grow great, and so it was with Vito Corleone. ... It did not happen in a day, it did not happen in a year, but by the end of the Prohibition period and the start of the Great Depression, Vito Corleone had become the Godfather, the Don, Don Corleone.

One of the reasons Corleone is so memorable is because he's so paradoxical, and thus fascinating. He's a sentimental father seen weeping over his son's corpse, an astute businessman, and a ruthless scourge, whose olive oil business is a front for a far-reaching crime syndicate. He is pro-family and anti-social. He is compassionate, yet he will slit your throat if you cross him. He appears benevolent, but he is a despot who stops at nothing, including bribing politicians and officials to hold on to power. He is a prince of justice helping out other Italians who have been victimized, but he is also a blackmailer, murderer, thief, and tyrant.

Corleone is also a realist:

> ... [Corleone] had long ago learned that society imposes insults that must be borne, comforted by the knowledge that in this world there comes a time when the most humble of men, if he keeps his eyes open, can take his revenge on the most powerful. ...

And because he's a realist, he's also paranoid; "Keep your friends close, but keep your enemies closer" is one of his mottos.

Corleone is a man of few words, but he can be amazing eloquent, as when he says, "I made him an offer he couldn't refuse." He demands ultimate loyalty and friendship, and when he's crossed, he dispenses fierce justice. Shrewd and always in charge, his son Michael says of him, "It's all personal, every bit of business ... He takes everything personal. Like God."

Keeping Corleone in mind, let's consider how some of the uglier traits in an anti-hero can also be tempered with a positive side, thus creating a character who is endlessly complicated.

Negative Trait	Positive Trait
Controlling	Efficient, great managerial abilities
Hot-tempered	Passionate
Manipulating	Able to see the big picture
Overbearing	Charismatic
Scheming	Capable, competent
Selfish	Focused
Greedy	Generous to family, works hard to provide their comforts
Ruthless	Ambitious, tender with children and elderly mother
Dishonest in business dealings	Honest with wife, children
Intolerant, insensitive	Perceptive
Brusque	Forceful, decisive

You have many choices when it comes to creating the central traits for your anti-hero, and sometimes these traits will be similar to those ordinarily bestowed on heroes or likeable protagonists. Your anti-hero can be courageous, truthful, analytical, charismatic, independent, quick-thinking, and resourceful. On the other hand, he could be ruthless, cynical, aloof, selfish, and controlling. These traits need to be demonstrated in scenes and via the character's thoughts, especially when he's making tough choices. You always want to demonstrate the fallout of a character's negative traits. If he has a hair-trigger temper, then his spouse and children might suffer. If he's impetuous and mouthy, he creates enemies. If he relies too much on logic and analysis, maybe he misses out on love and laughter.

And here is another trick to creating an interesting anti-hero (or villain): Make his central traits also his downfall or curse. Thus, his strengths and core traits also get him into trouble. Corleone—because he was assured, powerful, and at the top of his game—feels safe in his world. His enemies think otherwise, and, in a bid for power, they attempt to assassinate him. This assassination attempt changes everything in the story, including who becomes the next Don.

If your character is a loner, make certain that this quality dooms him to a showdown or tight spot where he's outclassed, outgunned, and sorely in need of allies. If he's truthful, make certain that this leads to hurt feelings and misunderstandings. If he's highly self-sufficient, mark certain that this trait, too, comes with a cost.

FACE-OFF

If you think giving one character opposing or paradoxical traits creates fascinating fiction, try pairing up two or more characters with complementary and opposing traits in a story. A terrific example of a complicated cast of characters can be found in Colin Harrison's thriller *Afterburn*. While there are three main characters in the story, the story line focuses on two of them, both anti-heroes. The story is a lesson on how two central characters with contradictory and similar traits and opposing agendas generate layers of conflict and suspense.

Afterburn is an ugly tale because it graphically depicts torture and its darker themes. It's the troubling tale of a Vietnam War pilot, Charlie Ravich, who survived capture and torture by the Viet Cong and went on to become a successful business tycoon. At midlife, he's been married for years, and he is busy crafting major deals, traveling inter-

ROGUE'S GALLERY

Here are some anti-heroes who have memorable roles and traits, such as rebelliousness, arrogance, ruthlessness, and sneakiness:

- Bettina Balser, *Diary of a Mad Housewife* by Sue Kaufman
- Archie Bunker, *All in the Family* television series
- Al Swearengen, *Deadwood* television series
- Roland Deschain, The Dark Tower series by Stephen King
- Gregory House, *House* television series
- Burke Devore, *The Ax* by Donald E. Westlake
- Alexander Portnoy, *Portnoy's Complaint* by Philip Roth
- Mickey Sabbath, *Sabbath's Theater* by Philip Roth
- Adrian Monk, *Monk* television series
- Vic Mackey, *The Shield* television series
- Narrator, *Notes From the Underground* by Fyodor Dostoevsky
- Joseph K., *The Trial* by Franz Kafka
- Narrator, *Woodcutters* by Thomas Bernhard
- Jay Gatsby, *The Great Gatsby* by F. Scott Fitzgerald
- Parker, the series by Donald E. Westlake, writing as Richard Stark
- Achilles, Greek mythology
- Mike Hammer, the series by Mickey Spillane

nationally, and building dreams. But not only has the nightmare incarceration during the war left scars and permanent wounds, he's also scarred by the death of his beloved son from leukemia, it looks like his daughter might not be able to have children, and his wife is acting increasingly odd and forgetful and insists that they move to a staid and expensive retirement community. But Charlie isn't ready for golf and a rocking chair. He loves the world of high-powered deals, but he wants something more. He wants to leave a legacy behind, another child to carry on his genes.

So, without his wife's knowledge, he starts looking for a woman to bear his child, and it's clear he will follow through with his plan no matter what it takes. This brings him into contact with Christina Welles, a recent parolee who is brilliant, attractive, and seductive, and who has a complicated and dangerous past that she might not be able to outrun.

Charlie and Christina are both enormously complicated, yet they are alike in many ways. The parallels between the two characters pile up, but so do their differences. As he suffered and then survived his captors, she also suffered and survived a terrible trauma. Both are haunted and secretive, both are sentimental about family. Both have endured loss, including the deaths of loved ones. Both have been betrayed, and both are fighters. They are equally ruthless and brilliant in business, with her dealings falling into criminal activities and his sometimes barely skirting legality. He's middle-aged and ailing; she's young and strong. He's feeling the decline of his sexual powers; she's sexually insatiable. He's a hard-hearted executive; she's a hard-hearted math whiz and grifter. He was a prisoner in Vietnam; she was a prisoner in a women's correctional facility, taking the fall for a scam operation.

It is perhaps both Charlie's and Christina's desperation that sets them on a collision course. He wants a child, while she wants to outwit the criminals she once worked for and start fresh. But as mentioned before, it is often the anti-hero's methods that separate him from society. In the business world, most tycoons don't murder their competition as the Corleone family does, although sometimes the law is skirted in boardrooms and during stock deals.

Anti-heroes like Charlie and Christina make the reader wonder where morality and immorality begin or end. For example, in an early scene, Charlie sees Chinese billionaire Sir Henry Lai choking to death in the men's room and, knowing that stock in Lai's company will plunge, calls his broker, causing his net worth to increase by $8 million.

Taking a cue from Harrison, try to pair up anti-heroes against antagonists, villains, or other anti-heroes if there is more than one in a story. If the characters possess a complicated meld of similar and dissimilar traits, as well as opposing agendas, desires, and motivations, the results just might be combustible. Now, it's more likely that you'll be exposing similar and opposing traits in a hero versus villain, or in a protagonist versus antagonist. Whether these oppositional pairs come from the same background or from vastly different worlds, as Christina and Charlie do, it's important that the reader believes that they can meet in a story. Thus, you'll need a device or situation that draws them together, and, as *Afterburn* shows, this often is a character's agenda or desire.

Whenever possible, give major characters in your stories secrets and plausible reasons for not revealing them, and then release these secrets at the last possible moment. Sometimes a story will require that the reader will be in the know, as in *Afterburn* when the reader is aware that the mob is after Christina, but other stories will require that the secrets be kept from the reader. Giving characters secrets, especially ones that are dangerous and place several characters in the line of fire, creates tremendous suspense for the reader.

An anti-hero can be a guy living an ordinary or undistinguished life. He can also be a character who is at the bottom of his downward character arc, or one who is on his way to greatness. He can be as vain as a peacock, or he can possess a fragile sense of self-worth. While anti-heroes are necessarily complex, beware of making them too angst-ridden or too wacky to be understood or sympathetic. Unlike a villain, an anti-hero can have a character arc in which he is redeemed or transformed by the end of the story; in fact, he can become heroic. The most important thing to remember when crafting an anti-hero as your main character is that he is the antithesis of the ultra-competent hero.

CHAPTER FOUR

Dark Heroes and Bad Boys

The test of any good fiction is that you should care something for the characters; the good to succeed, the bad to fail. The trouble with most fiction is that you want them all to land in hell, together, as quickly as possible.

—MARK TWAIN

Let's face it: We're fascinated by the rowdies and ruffians of film and literature. Now let's talk about two types of anti-heroes mentioned in the previous chapter that add pizzazz to a story because they're hot, unpredictable, and sometimes mysterious. I'm talking about bad boys and dark heroes, and writers use them in fiction because they are typically outsiders in society, and they are often misunderstood. As outsider types, they are sometimes in need of redemption; sometimes they're not bad men, they just don't play by the rules.

Dark heroes inhabit the dark side of life. This means they often have a sinister, brooding, or gloomy nature. It does not mean they need to be evil like villains do, although they can certainly have a range of less-than-desirable traits. They often have secrets, and they often have been wronged in the past. Understanding their backstories is crucial for you to unlock their potential as you write them. The stories they appear in are often about how their faith and humanity needs to be restored. This character arc should compel you to keep pushing them onward, challenging their cracked beliefs and shell-shocked souls.

Bad boys tend to be a lighter sort—although certainly not light enough to be considered cheery, optimistic, or in any way traditional. Bad boys, known for rule-breaking and sass, might also come with a swagger and a knowing grin. They might wear leather jackets and jeans and ride motorcycles, or they might drive their sports cars way too fast. On the other hand, when a bad boy wears a suit or tuxedo, the appeal is incendiary.

There is something dangerous, sexy, irresistible, and macho about a bad boy. A bad boy is often defined by his job or social role, and you'll find him in a variety of gigs—he might be a cop with an attitude, a pirate, or a mercenary. He might be a high-born and rakish nobleman starring in a romance story, or he might be a private investigator from the wrong side of the tracks in a suspense story. The key is that a bad boy is a primal type with a simmering sexuality and pronounced attitude, along with a flair for rule-breaking that will always spell jeopardy for someone in the story.

Certainly both dark heroes and bad boys make for fascinating fiction, often proving just as entertaining to the writer as to the reader. At their core, these character types have some kind of decency or humanity, although it can be buried or needs to be reformed. Also, though we'll thoroughly explore villains in chapter six, I just want to pause here and make sure it's clear why bad boys and dark heroes do *not* fall into the villain camp. While it's difficult to paint any character type with broad strokes because there are so many variations, and because these days writers are breaking the boundaries with character types, bad boys and dark heroes always differ from villains in that villains are oppositional characters who exist to thwart and torment the protagonist.

Villains have an agenda that will deliberately cause pain to the protagonist, and in traditional depictions, these characters will never have a complete character arc. Thus, villains usually, even when they change in the course of the story or are defeated, are just as evil in the beginning of the story as they are at the end. When you look at a villain's core traits, he's not a good guy with a bad agenda. He's a bad guy with a bad agenda. Bad boys or dark heroes are most often good guys at heart, who have a slight or pronounced darkness and an unusual agenda.

Bad boys and dark heroes can star as anti-heroes, meaning they're the protagonists in the story, but they can *also* thwart the protagonist as antagonists in a story, as I'll demonstrate in chapter five. Still, just to reiterate, they don't exist to intentionally cause pain, and thus they are dramatically different from villains.

DISTINGUISHING BETWEEN A BAD BOY AND A DARK HERO

Bad boys and dark heroes are fascinating types of fictional characters and can have many uses in a story. But don't start thinking that these two character types are synonymous. They're not. In fact, there are some crucial differences between the two, as well as between the types of stories they inhabit. You might initially want to lump them together because both types are popular in genre fiction, often starring in pirate flicks and in romance and erotica novels; they brood on Gothic moors, swashbuckle through thrillers, shoot it out in Westerns. And, again, while it's difficult to proclaim broad generalizations since there will always be exceptions, these days, dark heroes most often appear in Gothics, romances that typically take place in earlier eras, thrillers, comic books, and graphic novels, while bad boys most likely appear in contemporary romance, thrillers, and suspense novels.

Both types are flawed; they're risk-takers, and they're impossible. We're afraid of them, we sometimes love them, and if other characters need them, might despise themselves for their need, or at least in the beginning of the story.

They are usually alpha males—but they're the sort of men that women are attracted to despite their mothers' warnings. They're often rebellious and charismatic, sort of like human heat-seeking missiles. Despite all they have in common, though, there are some very specific differences between these two anti-hero subsets.

Bad boys, as exemplified by the Ranger character in Janet Evanovich's Stephanie Plum series, bring sizzle and tension to a story and are often particularly helpful to writers who want a quirky character who acts in surprising ways. Bad boys sometimes have an element of criminality or violence about them, which is ultimately used to create an air of unease in a story because the reader keeps wondering about their pasts and true nature. These characters also are likely to come from the wrong side of the tracks and hate authority, yet they are often honest and even principled.

They also tend to be extremely physical, extremely sexual, and extremely sensual. When you're writing bad boys, remember that they're always fiery, never hypocritical, and always brimming with sexual tension.

Dark heroes, as exemplified by the brooding and angst-ridden Heathcliff of Emily Brontë's *Wuthering Heights* and Mr. Rochester of Charlotte Brontë's *Jane Eyre,* often were once considered by their fellow characters to be "good" but were forced by life, circumstances, or an enemy into a less positive role. These characters have often undergone some kind of trauma that created their seemingly impenetrable shell, and therefore they often lash out when they feel threatened. Sometimes dark heroes are also lost souls, meaning that they might never fit back into their former lives or society. In this case, the reader might see dark heroes struggle to change, only to discover—and see them discover—that they simply aren't capable of it. To keep things interesting, they can also display occasional hidden sensitivities or positive qualities. As opposed to true heroes, dark heroes are hard-edged and imperfect. Because of this, they serve to reflect society's brutal realities. In fact, sometimes they are so dastardly they take your breath away. But—and this is what ultimately sets them apart from other, less redeemable characters—they can also be sympathetic, meaning a reader will feel a range of emotions for these characters.

But here's an important reminder: While bad boys and dark heroes are not spun from cotton candy, they can be as tough and strong as classical heroes, act in heroic ways to save the day, and even be self-sacrificing at times. Before we go on to explore these character types in extended individual profiles, let's take a quick look at some of the common characteristics of dark heroes, bad boys, and traditional heroes just to make sure we've got their subtle differences straight.

DARK HEROES

These characters are somehow tormented and usually have not reconciled their needs for love or community. In fact, they typically have a hard time admitting any vulnerabilities. A dark hero is usually:

- an alpha character (we'll discuss alphas in greater detail in chapter eight).
- an outsider or from the wrong side of the tracks. If he's of noble birth, he often rejects some aspects of his family's values.

- angry, cynical, aloof, and self-serving.
- marked by a traumatic past event or childhood abuse.
- hiding behind a gruff or cold façade, but beneath is not as bad as he tries to act.
- not living up to his best self.
- wearing a serious or pained demeanor.
- exhibiting some kind of inner conflict.
- living outside of the moral and legal codes of the time.
- tarnished by the evil he goes up against.
- willing to adopt a vigilante approach to problem-solving.
- guided by ambiguous morals and unresolved emotions.

BAD BOYS

Writers most often use bad boys because they bring an extra layer of tension to a story. Like dark heroes, they are often shaped by their circumstances and pasts. Perhaps they fell in with the wrong types at a tender age, or were wrongly accused of something. Perhaps someone or something taught them to bend the rules—at least a bit. In addition, a bad boy is usually:

- an alpha character.
- interested in freedom and adventure over security and safety.
- the black sheep of the family.
- a rebellious pleasure-seeker.
- unconstrained and untamed.
- promiscuous.
- unapologetic about the things he does.
- daring and risk-taking.
- suave without being too polished.

- extremely self-sufficient and highly independent.
- cocky, forthright, and extremely self-assured.
- not interested in maintaining a certain reputation.
- able to use humor in situations.

TRADITIONAL HEROES

Traditional heroes in fiction are usually men of action who are the masters of their own destinies. Jamie Fraser of Diana Gabaldon's Outlander series personifies a traditional hero. He can be hard-edged or suave, but he's always an alpha or dominant male who takes huge risks to protect those he loves, along with risking all to defend his beliefs, his country, or his property. He is always formidable, intelligent, and brave. Readers admire his boldness and willingness to sacrifice. A traditional hero is usually:

- an alpha character.
- taught honor in childhood.
- the product of a relatively normal childhood.
- haunted by something he has overcome in his past.
- law-abiding (or trying to be and has plausible reasons for breaking rules).
- a leader of mankind.
- controlled, at least most of the time.
- faithful with the right woman.
- sometimes easy-going in demeanor, but is always going to have a grave purpose.

THE KEY COMMONALITY: THE SYMPATHY FACTOR

As mentioned in the previous chapter on anti-heroes, a reader's sympathies are always somehow stirred by bad boys and dark heroes. The reasons for this sympathy are complex—it can stem from our tendency to root for underdogs, our belief in the goodness in most humans, even those who appear most flawed, or because when trouble comes wrapped in human clothes, we just cannot resist the pull. It might be because we sense these characters' vulnerabilities that they're loath to admit. Recent psychological studies also imply that because we grow up mirroring other people's emotions and reading their nonverbal cues, we then translate these behaviors into reading fiction.

Besides sympathy, the reader may come to *empathize* with characters, although typically the reader tends to empathize with bad boys more so than with dark heroes. Empathy and sympathy are not the same thing. Sympathy leads to empathy. Sympathy means the reader understands a character's human qualities; empathy means the reader projects himself into the story and the character's situation.

As a writer, you must always empathize with your characters; otherwise, you won't be able to write them with the proper depth and nuance. But empathy toward your characters doesn't mean you get to ease up on them, because your job is to rake them over the coals of hell. Instead, it means you have an intimate knowledge of what makes them tick. When a reader empathizes with a character, it comes from an understanding and a willingness to suspend judgment and to take on the character's cause or dilemma.

Bad boys and dark heroes are less-than-noble characters; they are not as civilized, as housebroken, or as under control as a true-blue good guy. They'll swig down that fourth shot of tequila, slap a woman, not to mention mess with her head, and they might seek revenge.

The thing is, even when bad boys and dark heroes are breaking hearts and shedding blood, the reader still empathizes with them and is fascinated by the mayhem that trails them. Often what makes bad boys and dark heroes sympathetic is that the reader gets the chance to closely observe their tarnished humanity, something not always possible in real life. The reader wants to follow these rascals up close and personal, while in real life, he would recognize their dangers and might even avoid them.

If dirty work needs doing in a story—an Old West town that needs cleaning up or a villain who needs to be tracked to his lair—a dark hero or bad boy, like a tarnished knight, is often well suited for the job. Fiction has always cast characters to take on tasks we cannot accomplish in day-to-day life.

Sympathetic characters of this nature can be found in the old "spaghetti Westerns" made from about 1960 to 1975. These low-budget minimalist films came out of Europe and were named so because they were often helmed by Italian directors. The trend came about because Europeans loved American Westerns, but American filmmakers were rarely making Westerns any more. Perhaps the best known of these films were the three that Clint Eastwood starred in for director Sergio Leone: *A Fistful of Dollars, For a Few Dollars More,* and *The Good, the Bad and the Ugly,* in which he played a gunslinger or bounty hunter wandering the countryside and settling scores for a price. Eastwood's character took the law into his own hands, but he was essentially on the side of good and order.

While Eastwood's character, a dark hero type, employed unusual means to bring about justice, viewers found him irresistible because he was inscrutable, macho, and capable. While his motives were questionable, he brings his own kind of order out of chaos—actions that readers and film viewers always appreciate. In fact, he was a man of action, was extremely self-reliant, and just didn't give a damn—all qualities that have universal appeal. His character's darkness was a departure from the usual heroes starring in traditional Westerns, and this stirred the viewers' imaginations.

PROFILE OF A DARK HERO

Dark heroes are tricky to cast in your story because, while as a writer you want them to be mysterious and slightly twisted, or perhaps even beastly, the reader needs a window into his soul to glimpse his humanity. This is especially true if he's the tall, dark, and silent type, and if he is going to be redeemed or have a pronounced character arc. Edward Rochester of *Jane Eyre* is a good example of dark hero, as he is moody and odd, sometimes cold, sometimes charismatic, and at times unreadable. When he is about to marry Jane, she discovers that his dark past is twined to the madwoman locked in his attic.

A typical dark hero is somehow tortured, and he is often a loner. In stories set in previous centuries, he is usually a patriarchal male—dominant and likely overbearing, yet still aloof. He's also typically scarred emotionally, and sometimes physically, because dreadful, probably even traumatic, events happened to him in the past. Or, perhaps he once did terrible things or has been wronged or wrongly accused. These past events ultimately set him apart and turn him away from society, love, or the rules of civilization. Thus, a complicated backstory providing reasons for his behaviors and traits is vital to creating a dark hero character.

He's often a smoldering type, secretive, and a bit—or downright—sinister. On the other hand, a dark hero can be charismatic, as seen with Rochester. Dark heroes often seem at first glance to be beyond redemption. But if you dig deeper, the best written dark heroes are complicated and nuanced types. Mr. Darcy in Jane Austen's *Pride and Prejudice* is a good example of dark hero; he even describes himself as "selfish and overbearing." Mr. Darcy is the picture of a sexy, brooding, and seemingly unattainable dark hero. In Austen's story, as in romances that feature this type of character, the heroine falls for him, and—despite serious misgivings and the fact that he is so mysterious and baffling—the reader falls for him, too. Sometimes the dark hero will insult or rebuff the heroine, or he is deliberately cold or dangerously violent.

In the case of Mr. Darcy, the backdrop of the Regency period in England is necessary to set the scene. In that society, women wielded little power, and the sexes were generally kept separate, which meant there weren't a lot of opportunities to truly know the person you were attracted to or were courting.

In several social situations, Mr. Darcy appears rude, arrogant, and moody, comparing unfavorably to his more charming friend, Mr. Bingley. When the heroine and dark hero first meet in a story, they usually dislike each other; this dislike is often based on false evidence or blunders, as is the case with Elizabeth Bennet and Mr. Darcy. As the story unfolds, the reader comes to know that some of Mr. Darcy's prickliness is because, as a true gentleman, he's in a tough situation when the rake Mr. Wickham is on the scene.

In stories that feature a dark hero, as *Pride and Prejudice* does, there is an underlying concept that there exists only one woman in the world who can unlock or salvage the dark hero's tortured or troubled soul, thus setting free his hidden passions and goodness. In Mr. Darcy's case, it is Elizabeth. Mr. Darcy is also redeemed by his relationship with his sister and his actions on behalf of the younger Bennet daughter Lydia. While Lydia's virtue cannot be salvaged when she runs off with Mr. Wickham, Mr. Darcy manages to save her reputation by arranging a marriage. As Austen demonstrates, it's important that all the facts of the situation are brought to light so that the reader can judge the dark hero on all his merits.

Take the case of Emily Brontë's dark hero, Heathcliff, in *Wuthering Heights*. Heathcliff is a complicated man who is capable of bitterness, rage, and jealousy that turns into a vendetta. In fact, his dark emotions are what drive the story.

What you can learn from Heathcliff and Mr. Darcy is that a dark hero always suffers from some kind of torment. In Heathcliff's case, it is his love then loss of Catherine; this torment is especially dramatized in the scene where, after her death, he beats himself against a tree. Scenes like this are necessary in a story with a dark hero, because the reader needs some proof of his humanity, so as you write, be sure to reveal the cracks in the façade that hide the more vulnerable person beneath it.

A dark hero in fiction generally has somehow been wronged, but he often doesn't want to admit the extent of his pain. A big element of the dark hero is his mysteriousness, and although common sense would dictate otherwise, many female characters and readers fall for mysterious men. Typically, a dark hero's torment is not always revealed in the opening chapters, which create a compelling question in the story. A dark hero, especially one in a romance, also often has extreme emotions, such as loving deeply, and the reader usually has the sense that a better man lies beneath the gruff exterior. This type of character, like a villain, is usually somehow shaped by his environment or past, particularly a loss or trauma. However, with a dark hero, this loss or trauma can sometimes be recovered from, while with a villain, it usually inflicts permanent damage.

Why are dark heroes featured so often in stories, particularly in romances? Because they draw heat. Because they're not easily known. Because they're often misunderstood, and we can relate to the unfairness of this. Because many women fantasize about passion with these types (women like a challenge). Because although they often show a mask to the world, within lurks the real person. This last reason is one that you need to key into, because your job as the writer is to reveal the person beneath the haughty and proud exterior. And this unmasking often lies beneath every story a dark hero appears in.

Heroines who fall madly in love with dark heroes are destined to suffer greatly, and they often find that loving a dark hero is nearly impossible or requires great sacrifice. In real life, most women will not marry this type of man. After all, he's not the sort to rise groggily with the baby in the middle of the night or clean out the cat box. But in a story, the reader can easily imagine his skin against hers and the sort of lovemaking that comes after capitulation.

More than that, though, the reader needs to experience a story's emotional pitfalls, shifting landscape, and drama that rises, falls, and zigzags. Dark heroes all but guarantee the ride will be a wild one. The unpredictable nature of the Mr. Darcys of the world makes these sorts of structural delights possible. And let's not forget that redemption is one of the most powerful themes in literature. When a dark hero is redeemed, it is often because he allows love or understanding into his life that was previously somehow closed off.

DARK HEROES IN THRILLERS

When a dark hero stars in a thriller, readers, particularly male readers, can imagine this take-no-prisoners approach to life and be swept along in the vicarious thrills and adventures. He'll play the anti-hero role to the hilt and will be complicated, but principled, although these principles are generally not the ones we teach our children. He's often a man of action *and* intellect, utterly self-reliant.

Thriller is a loose term that refers to many subgenres of fiction and film where intrigue and action bring lots of excitement to the story. With a thriller, the reader is identifying with the protagonist's struggle to survive and feels his fear, thus the thrills of these story types. Typically, these stories are page-turners, so they're super fast-paced with a high ratio of realistic action, surprises, and high stakes, usually a life-or-death situation. There is typically a crime and criminal at the heart of the thriller and examples are Tom Clancy's *The Hunt for Red October* and Frederick Forsyth's *The Day of the Jackal.*

In Mickey Spillane's *One Lonely Night,* private investigator Mike Hammer stumbles onto a mystery while out walking late one cold night. He spots a terrorized woman and a man pursuing her. Both end up dead, and Hammer is left to wonder what has just happened and who is involved. The plot revolves around a Communist takeover of the free world. As the story opens, Hammer muses on his fate:

> ... I used to be able to look at myself and grin without giving a damn about how ugly it made me look. Now I was looking at myself the same way those people did back there. I was looking at a big guy with an ugly reputation, a guy who had no earthly reason for existing in a decent, normal society. That's what the judge had said.
>
> I was sweating and cold at the same time. Maybe it did happen to me over there. Maybe I did have a taste for death. Maybe I liked it too much to taste anything else. Maybe I was twisted and rotted inside. Maybe I would be washed down the sewer with the rest of all the rottenness sometime. What was stopping it from happening now? Why was I me with some kind of lucky charm around my neck that kept me going when I was better off dead?
>
> That's why I parked the car and started walking in the rain. I didn't want to look in that damn mirror any more. So I walked and smoked and climbed to the hump in the bridge where the boats in the river made faces and spoke to me until I had to bury my face in my hands until everything straightened itself out again.
>
> *I was a killer. I was a murderer, legalized. I had no reason for living.*

This bit of self-revelation summarizes why a dark hero can provide writers with so much latitude and possibility. Hammer lies at one end of the extreme for dark heroes (Mr. Darcy would lie at the other end) and operates with a take-no-prisoners code of justice, which means nothing or no one stands in his way. In fact, in this story, Hammer takes on a liberal judge who condemns his methods.

A key to creating an extreme dark hero is to hone his cynicism and motivation. With Hammer, he's usually after vengeance, pure and simple. Hammer doesn't have much patience with the tedious process of the law—he serves justice with a gun or fist. Living in a world of perversion and corruption, he can never be called an errant knight, since his means are too blood-thirsty.

Spillane wrote thirteen Mike Hammer books, so readers have plenty of time to get to know him. Like other dark heroes, another key to understanding Hammer is knowing his past. In *I, The Jury*, the first book in Spillane's series, a murder victim is Hammer's friend; this death starts the story, which, in fact, starts the series. At the crime scene, Hammer vows to find the killer and punish him, no matter what the cost. Thus his vigilant approach is born. In *I, The Jury*, Hammer also shoots the woman he loves, an act that haunts him for life.

Stir In Redemption

Another example of a thriller with a dark hero is Robert Ludlum's *The Bourne Identity*. The story begins as a man is plucked from the waters of the Mediterranean with gunshot wounds and amnesia. After being nursed back to health, the man begins to search for his identity. He discovers a Swiss bank account with millions of dollars in it, and the man takes on one of his aliases, Jason Bourne. As hit squads try to end his life, his past is revealed in tantalizing bits. He begins to remember strange memories of a secretive black ops unit during the Vietnam War, and these memories stir difficult, hidden emotions. The reader learns that Bourne was part of a botched CIA plan to bring down an assassin, and thus, a deadly puzzle begins unraveling.

Writers can learn many tricks from Ludlum and this story. First, he makes Bourne sympathetic. This sympathy begins when the reader watches Bourne being shot then toppling into the Mediterranean. He's then pulled out of the water nearly lifeless, and the reader observes the seriousness of the gunshot wounds, his efforts to get better, and then his struggle with recovering from amnesia.

In the second paragraph of the book, the reader hears gunshots and watches a man lunge from the cabin of a trawler, clutching his stomach. A second man follows him and shoots again, and, with a fifth gunshot, the first man plunges into the darkness below:

> He felt rushing cold water envelop him, swallowing him, sucking him under, and twisting him in circles, then propelling him up to the surface—only to gasp a single breath of air. A gasp and he was under again.
>
> And there was heat, a strange moist heat at this temple that seared through the freezing water that kept swallowing him, a fire where no fire should burn. There was ice, too; an icelike throbbing in his stomach and his legs and his chest, oddly warmed by the cold sea around him. He felt these things, acknowledging his own panic as he felt them. He could see his own body turning and twisting, arms and feet working frantically against the pressures of the whirlpool. He could feel, think, see, perceive panic and struggle—yet strangely there was peace. It was the calm of the observer, the uninvolved observer, separated from the events, knowing of them but not essentially involved.

> Then another form of panic spread through him, surging through the heat and the ice and the uninvolved recognition. He could not submit to peace! Not yet! …

With this exciting opening, the reader cannot help but turn the page, worried over the unnamed character's survival. So, whenever possible, slip several sympathy-provoking details about your protagonist—in this case, a dark hero—onto the page the first time you introduce the character. Your character can be injured or ugly or lonely, but there should always be something about him that stirs the reader's emotions, that makes him care from the get-go.

Note, too, that although Bourne is a trained and ruthless killer responsible for many deaths, the reader cannot help but be on his side. Ludlum does this by suggesting that Bourne works on the side of the good, and that the people he's taken out are dangers to society.

Sympathy also comes into play via a subplot where Bourne falls for Marie St. Jacques, thus showing that he's capable of caring. Then the reader learns that at one time Bourne had a Thai wife and two children. They were killed during the Vietnam War in a bombing. And his family's deaths are a big factor in making him a dark hero, since this apparently is a psychological wound he cannot recover from. After they die, he trains to be part of the top-secret unit and seek revenge for his family's death.

Ludlum also shows that Bourne's past has tarnished his soul. The reader cannot help but fret over a character who has somehow lost his humanity. When Bourne first begins recovering, the reader learns that he's had plastic surgery on his face, and the reader begins wondering why Bourne needs to alter his appearance. This hints at the high price he's paid to be a professional assassin, which becomes underlined in the story by how he can trust no one, not even so-called friends from his past or the agency he works for.

And this is where the redemption comes in. The gunshot wounds and amnesia give him an opportunity to live differently and question his own morals and values. His memories of his past disturb him, as do the stirrings of his conscience. In fact, he's stuck with a moral dilemma, asking himself what kind of man he has become and if he's doomed to remain that same sort of man. Ludlum also uses the Maria St. Jacques character to motivate him toward a more moral path. When Bourne is in Zurich recovering his bank account, he takes St. Jacques as a hostage to escape a slippery situation. However, he realizes that he has placed her in danger, and he risks his own life to prevent her from being executed. This act starts him on the road to redemption, making him more than a killing machine. In fact, in the sequel, *The Bourne Supremacy*, the story opens with him married to St. Jacques and teaching at a university.

When a dark hero appears in a story, the tale is often influenced by Gothic, noir, or horror traditions. Thus, often the setting has a nightmarish cast to it, with dungeons, caves, dimly lit manors, and gardens that are more likely visited under the half-moon of midnight than on a summer's day. Or it can take place amid a city's underbelly and criminal element, as in Mike Hammer's milieu, or in the shadowy world of international espionage, as in Ludlum's stories. A story with a dark hero can also take place at sea, as in stories like Herman Melville's *Moby-Dick*, because its endless unfathomable depths are also a dark and dangerous landscape.

Here's an example from the opening of *The Bourne Identity* of how this powerful effect of setting can emphasize that the story has a dark hero:

> The trawler plunged into the angry swells of the dark, furious sea like an awkward animal trying desperately to break out of an impenetrable swamp. The waves rose to goliathan heights, crashing into the hull with the power of raw tonnage; the white sprays caught in the night sky cascaded downward over the deck under the force of the night wind. Everywhere there were the sounds of inanimate pain, wood straining against wood, ropes twisting, stretched to the breaking point. The animal was dying.

With each carefully chosen word of Ludlum's story, the reader is being pulled into a world of intrigue and darkness.

PROFILE OF A BAD BOY

Bad boys, like dark heroes, aren't your run-of-the-mill men. They're always alpha types—imagine James Bond, Daniel Cleaver from Helen Fielding's *Bridget Jones's Diary*, Brad Pitt's character in the film *Thelma & Louise*, and Russell Crowe in real life. Bad boys are more fun than dark heroes. Often boyish no matter their age, these naughty characters take themselves less seriously, and they are often the sexiest of all the character types.

Besides a simmering sensuality, these characters also possess an intense physical presence—part primal, part male lion, with a big dose of testosterone stirred in. They're the sort of men women most want to sleep with. The problem is, they're likely to be in bed with someone else.

A bigger-than-life bad boy exists in Janet Evanovich's suspense series, which features Stephanie Plum as a screwball heroine, laugh-out-loud dialogue, a realistic sense of places, villains who range from miscreants to sociopaths, and a cast of secondary character so quirky and fun and real you expect them to walk in the door while you're reading. Then there is Ranger, or Ricardo Carlos Manoso, who is the sort of bad boy readers find so irresistible. With the sort of steamy sexuality that turns women weak in the knees, a body that could stop a clock, and a mysterious past, Ranger exemplifies a bad boy. If you return to all the bad boy qualities listed earlier, Ranger has them all, in spades.

With each book, Evanovich reveals a bit more about him, such as that he was once in the Special Forces, his security business is a legitimate enterprise, and he has a daughter. As an overall strategy, Evanovich uses Ranger to create personal complications for the protagonist, especially a too-close-for-comfort wedge between her and her on-again, off-again boyfriend, Joe Morrelli. In his youth, Morrelli was a budding bad boy, but he's reformed these days and works as a Trenton cop.

Meanwhile, Ranger often bails Plum out of tight spots and helps her apprehend criminals who are beyond her capabilities, and he also employs her for computer work at his firm.

When a bad boy is in the story, he can serve as a temptation, while creating inner conflict and the sizzle factor, as Plum illustrates in *Hard Eight*:

> Ranger is more associate than friend, although I guess friendship is mixed in there somehow, too. Plus a scary sexual attraction. A few months ago we made a deal that has haunted me. Another one of those jumping-off-the-garage-roof things, except this deal involved my bedroom. Ranger is Cuban-American with skin the color of a mocha latte, heavy on the mocha, and a body that can best be described as *yum*. He's got a big-time stock portfolio, an endless, inexplicable supply of expensive black cars, and skills that make Rambo look like an amateur. I'm pretty sure he only kills bad guys, and I think he might be able to fly like Superman, although the flying part has never

been confirmed. Ranger works in bond enforcement, among other things. And Ranger always gets his man.

Later in the story, a scene between Ranger and Plum is used to slow the pace before the climax, and it illustrates how, when a bad boy is in the story, there are opportunities for sexy repartee:

"Where do you get all these cars from?"

"You don't actually want to know, do you?"

I took a beat to think about it. "No," I said. "I don't suppose I do. If I knew, you'd have to kill me, right?"

"Something like that."

He stopped in front of my parents' house, and we both looked at the door. My mother and my grandmother were standing there, watching us.

"I'm not sure I feel comfortable about the way your grandma looks at me," Ranger said.

"She wants to see you naked."

"I wish you hadn't told me that, babe."

"Everybody I know wants to see you naked."

"And you?"

"Never crossed my mind." I held my breath when I said it, and I hoped God wouldn't strike me down dead for lying. I hopped out of the car and ran inside.

Notice how Evanovich is able to plumb the depths of this character. In the case of Ranger, she's revealing him over the course of the series like a prolonged and tantalizing striptease. For instance, the reader meets his associates, learns that he has at least one safe house, and knows that he eats mostly health food and that his condo is elegant and beautifully appointed. And while the story line suggests that Ranger might be guilty of at least one homicide, the reader also sees the special tenderness and protectiveness he has toward his daughter and Plum.

Following Evanovich's lead, there are several tricks to make these character types more than boy toys. First, like a dark hero, make sure the best bad boy has something mysterious about him, possibly something in his past or present that he's hiding. Second, to make this character believable, give him an interesting profession or a special skill that distinguishes him from other people and character types. Think gunslinger, not accountant. Third, create a means so that a bad boy is an inescapable factor in the story. He needs to have complicated ties to other characters, and preferably several reasons why other characters need him and are entwined with him. Finally, this type appears in stories when the writer wants to emphasize physicality and a dangerous sex appeal.

DARK HEROES AS ROGUES

Rogues are stock characters in fiction and are almost always a type of dark hero, with modern origins in hard-boiled detective stories, such as those found in *Black Mask* magazine, and in the novels of Dashiel Hammett, Raymond Chandler, James M. Cain, and Horace McCoy. These authors are not afraid to feature tough-guy anti-heroes who not only broke the rules but don't give a damn about what anyone thinks of them. A rogue, which is short for *troubled rogue male*, is the baddest of the bad asses, the darkest of the dark heroes. If you imagine the moral continuum mentioned in the introduction, picture this type at a low moral ebb, just above villains. Besides hard-boiled detective fiction, rogue characters often appear in thrillers, comic books, and graphic novels. Their situations often provide commentary on realties of modern life. This type of character is usually:

- an alpha-alpha.
- a loner, and often an outcast.
- someone who has been injured, wronged, or traumatized.
- an extremely physical, tough-guy type who is sometimes unsophisticated.
- not likely to be redeemed by story events.
- not loveable.
- devoid of emotions (except extreme emotions, such as rage).
- someone who can operate on both sides of the law, but can resort to crime to achieve goals.
- working a low-status job or has an unusual means of survival (a computer hacker, for instance).

The *troubled rogue male* is exemplified in the character of John James Rambo in *First Blood* by David Morrell. A Vietnam War vet and former member of the elite Special Forces, Rambo is having problems adjusting to civilian life, and is a drifter when the story opens. He is also suffering from post-traumatic stress disorder from time spent as a POW. The story conflict starts brewing when he locks horns with a small-town police chief and fights his own version of the Vietnam War. When the story was adapted into a movie starring Sylvester Stallone, *First Blood* became an instant success—spawning a series of blockbuster feature films—and Rambo became an American icon. The book opens with this first glimpse of the rogue dark hero:

> His name was Rambo, and he was just some nothing kid for all anybody knew, standing by the pump of a gas station at the outskirts of Madison, Kentucky. He had a long heavy beard, and his hair was hanging down over his ears to his neck, and he had his hand out trying to thumb a ride from a car that was stopped at the pump. To see him there, leaning on one hip, a Coke bottle in his hand and a rolled-up sleeping bag near his boots on the tar pavement, you could never have guessed that on Tuesday, a day later, most of the police in Basalt County would be hunting him down. Certainly you could not have guessed that by Thursday he would be running from the Kentucky National Guard and the police of six counties and a good many private citizens who liked to shoot. But then from just seeing him there ragged and dusty by the pump of the gas station, you could never have figured the kind of kid Rambo was, or what was about to make it all begin.
>
> Rambo knew there was going to be trouble, though. Big trouble, if somebody didn't watch out. The car he was trying to thumb a ride with nearly ran him over when it left the pump. The station attendant crammed a charge slip and a book of trade stamps into his pocket and grinned at the tire marks on the hot tar close to Rambo's feet. Then the police car pulled out of traffic toward him and he recognized the start of the pattern again and stiffened. "No, by God. Not this time. This time I won't be pushed."

Rambo possesses many of the qualities found in dark heroes, including rage, self-sufficiency, and physical presence.

Rambo is later arrested for vagrancy and carrying a concealed weapon, which creates the inciting incident for the story, as a deputy beats Rambo during his arrest, causing flashbacks of his captivity in Vietnam. He, in turn, assaults the deputy, steals a motorcycle, and takes off with law officials, and eventually the National Guard, in hot pursuit. Like Morrell, create a compelling, believable backstory for your dark hero so his past shapes his psyche and taints the front story.

A writer uses a troubled rogue in a story to create lots of danger, adventure, and some ass-kicking. This type of character often appears like the tip of an iceberg: what we can see looks dangerous, but we don't know how dangerous, because there are hidden depths. A rogue's backstory is obviously important, but if the writer only provides glimpses of it here and there, it keeps the reader on edge and wondering just how far the character will go to get what he wants. So don't provide the reader big backstory dumps; instead, deliver it in bits and pieces. The longer you can keep the reader guessing about the character, the more suspense the story generates.

And while the troubled rogue is dangerous, like many of the anti-hero types we've been discussing, they cannot be easily labeled. In fact, a wise writer will make certain that they lack the black-and-white shadings of self-righteousness, vigilante-style zeal, or unalloyed evil.

When you write a story with this character type, it's helpful to know your themes and intentions. For example, a story with a rogue male character has a chance to show what displacement or alienation can do to a person. Or, as with *First Blood*, you might want to use a rogue to show how war damages the men who fight.

Most stories start off by introducing a threatening change to the protagonist's circumstances. With a rogue male, this threat might be the last straw, it might be his only chance to find his place in society, or it might place him on a collision course with society. The key to making the incident start off the plot is making the rogue's reaction somehow atypical. With a rogue dark hero, you want the reader especially off balance since the character is capable of surprising behaviors and reactions.

DARK HEROES IN A SERIES

At first glace, it might seem like a dark hero is an odd choice for a series character, but a series gives writers a chance to really plumb the depths of a character and to show the reader that sometimes people are thrust into their lots in life.

When you create a series with a dark hero, it's helpful to know his long-term character arc. Will he be redeemed by love or a heroic deed? Will he be able to escape or overcome the demons from his past? It's also important that in the opening of the first book in the series, the reader understands the dark hero's morality. In *The Bourne Identity*, for example, the reader witnesses the title character being shot repeatedly, and the reader understands that he plays for high stakes with the most ruthless people, and that he's not exactly a choir boy.

Some authors choose to start a series with their dark heroes demonstrating more integrity, then take him on a downward arc. You might call these protagonists dark heroes in the making. Such is the case with Henry "Hank" Thompson, the contemporary dark hero of Charlie Huston's noir trilogy. No matter where the dark hero's morality lies in the opening of a series, at some point, he must be stripped of, or nearly stripped of, his humanity.

Huston's trilogy begins with *Caught Stealing*, where, on page one, Hank wakes up with a mega hangover and serious injuries. When the story opens, Hank is in his thirties, he's tending bar in New York, and while he isn't exactly setting the world on fire, he's getting by, and he's basically a decent sort. But Hank is classified as a dark hero because of his past, and because the story yanks him into a downward spiral:

> You live in New York, but you always act like a guy from a small town in California. You help winos out of the gutter, you call an ambulance when you see someone hurt, you loan money to friends who need it and don't ask for it back, you let folks flop at your pad and you help the blind across the street. One night you go to break up a fight in the bar and get knocked around pretty good, so the next day you start taking boxing classes. You drink too much, but your parents don't know that.
>
> You're a good guy, you're tough and you have a reputation in your neighborhood for helping people out. It's nice. It's not the life you expected, but it's nice enough for you. You feel useful, you have friends and your parents love you. Ten years pass.
>
> One day the guy who lives across the hall from you knocks on your door. He needs a big favor. That's when life really changes.

Hank's neighbor, Russ, asks him to take care his cat while he's out of town for a few days. This is where the story takes on a Hitchcockian twist, as when an innocent bystander is pulled into a dangerous situation. Within days of taking on the cat, a seemingly benign gesture of friendship, two Russians show up at the bar and beat Hank so badly that he ends up losing one of his kidneys. Then more bad guys start appearing like rats scuttling off a ship. He sees two brothers knock on his neighbor's door, then a crooked cop and his minions appear at Hank's apartment and start torturing him by tearing out the staples from his surgery. They're looking for something, but he doesn't know what. And that's only the beginning of his troubles, because it turns out that all these bad guys are looking for what is missing—a huge sum of money. Then things start getting really ugly.

All through *Caught Stealing,* Hank is trying to protect his friends from these criminals. His efforts don't work, because when greed and villainy go hand-in-hand, no one is safe.

Early in the book, the reader learns Hank's backstory, and like all dark heroes, his backstory is crucial to the front story. When Hank was a kid, he was a superstar baseball player, on this way to the pros, when an injury knocked him out of the game. Soon after, he was driving in the country with his best friend, and when he swerved to avoid a calf in the road, the car crashed and his friend was killed.

Near the end of *Caught Stealing,* after Hank has been chased, threatened, and beaten, and a trail of death stretches out behind him, he reflects on his situation:

> The past is over. My life will never be what it was. And considering what I've made of my life so far, that may not be such a bad thing after all. It's time to stop hoping things are going to work out and start giving myself a chance to get out of this alive. …

By the end of the story, Hank's girlfriend, boss, friends, and a slew of criminals are all dead. Plus, he's on the run with the money, feeling haunted by the string of events, and wanted for murder—he's become a true dark hero.

In the second book in the trilogy, *Six Bad Things,* Hank is a refugee living on a beach in Mexico. His life isn't too bad now, except for the nightmare images of his dead friends. Then the nephew of a Russian mobster finds him, and quicker than you can look over your shoulder, Hank's back on the run, but this time, he needs to protect his parents from the Russian mob that's after him and the money. Like in the first book, Hank leaves a trail of mayhem and dead bodies behind him, and he becomes harder and more tormented by his role in life.

In the final book in trilogy, *A Dangerous Man*, Hank is living in Las Vegas and working as an assassin for the Russian mobster in exchange for his parents' safety. He's undergone plastic surgery and his character arc is at its lowest ebb. No longer in shape, he's a pill-popping zombie because he cannot live with the horrors of his evil deeds.

Then he's ordered to act as a bodyguard for a young, minor-league ballplayer with a gambling jones. In Miguel Arenas, Hank sees his own wasted youth and promise. Then Arenas gets drafted by the Mets, and Henry must return to New York, where this whole mess began. Again, the story has a chase plot, and again, bodies are falling like leaves in autumn. But in his relationship with Arenas, and by saving Anna, the mother of the young Russian he killed, Hank sees his final chance for redemption.

As the story winds down, the reader feels the anguish of all Hank's darkness as he talks with Anna, who has just shot him twice. Naturally, he's not in good shape when he confesses his nightmares about killing her son:

> ... I dream about him sometimes, too. Like you. I. I dream about all of them sometimes. And. If I could. Anna, if I could change. I was. When I was young, when I was a kid. I was driving and I, I hit this, this tree. And if. My friend was in the car and he died, you know. It was. And I thought, sometimes, I thought I wished it had been me. But I really didn't. When I was honest, honest to myself, I was thanking God that it was him and not me. But now. Now I wish, God, every day I wish it had been me. All the lives, Anna. You have no idea. All the lives that could have been saved.

Not all dark heroes are pulled into the story with such devastating abruptness, but, if like Huston, you're using a dark hero in a series, the roots of the story must begin in his past and a trauma, accident, or wrong fork in the road that sends him down a crooked or dangerous path. You want your reader to wonder what might have become of the character without that past trauma or bad fork in the road. Would Hank have had a normal life if he hadn't been injured, and then was responsible for his friend's

ROGUE'S GALLERY

Here are more dark heroes and bad boys to add to your repertoire and understanding:

DARK HEROES

- Christopher Moltisanti, played by Michael Imperioli in the *The Sopranos* television series
- Beast, *Beauty and the Beast* animated film
- Wulfric Bedwyn, *Slightly Dangerous* by Mary Balogh
- Jake LaMotta, played by Robert DeNiro in the film *Raging Bull*
- Shane, played by Alan Ladd in the film *Shane*
- Billie Bob Holland, James Burke series
- Port Moresby, *The Sheltering Sky* by Paul Bowles
- Pinkie Brown, *Brighton Rock* by Graham Greene
- Jack McEvoy, *The Poet* by Michael Connelly
- Harry Bosch, Michael Connelly series
- Robert "Roy" MacGregor, played by Liam Neeson in the film *Rob Roy*

BAD BOYS

- Count Alexei Kirillovich Vronsky, *Anna Karenina* by Leo Tolstoy
- Llewelyn Moss, *No Country for Old Men* by Cormac McCarthy
- Billy Lynch, *Charming Billy* by Alice McDermott
- Gray Rouillard, *After the Night* by Linda Howard
- Jack Boudreux, *Cry Wolf* by Tami Hoag
- Ben Lewis, *Heart of Fire* by Linda Howard
- Luke Callahan, *Honest Illusions* by Nora Roberts
- Mr. Big, played by Chris Noth in the *Sex and the City* television series

death? The series shows how guilt and love can be hugely motivating, and how a decent type can be pulled into a life of crime. Just as Huston did by making Hank loyal and generous, give your dark hero some redeeming or sympathetic qualities, and make him as complicated as possible.

Anti-heroes in all their roles and formats have amazing potential for fiction writers. We hate them, we love them, they scare the heck out of us. And while many fictional characters will surprise readers with their antics and go-for-the-jugular oomph, bad boys and dark heroes can be especially capable of surprising and even shocking readers. What can be better for a writer?

CHAPTER FIVE

Antagonists: Bullies and Mischief Makers

Surely all art is the result of one's having been in danger, of having gone through an experience all the way to the end, where no one can go any further.

—RAINER MARIA RILKE

Within the world of fiction, there are people who oppose the goals and desires of the protagonist or hero, and these characters are the antagonists. They are the co-stars in the story, who provide opposition and interject complications and challenges into the protagonist's situation. Antagonists always have an agenda, and they force protagonists into places they'd rather not go.

Opposition from characters can range from fairly benign to the malevolent "run-for-your-life!" type. This chapter is going to cover the qualities and roles for the lower-level antagonists, those that are not out to destroy a protagonist (as a villain would), but rather are out to cause him trouble, heartache, and growth.

First, let's clarify an important point: While a villain is always an antagonist, an antagonist is not necessarily a villain. Both character types are adversaries or opponents of the protagonist—both are designed to thwart, test, and torment—but villains have wickedness or evil as part of their makeup, they have mostly or all negative primary traits, and their presence in the story always puts the protagonist or hero in extreme danger. Antagonists, on the other hand, don't need a sinister agenda or component of evil. Nor do they need to be malicious, and they won't necessarily wish the protagonist harm, as a true villain would. That doesn't mean that all antagonists are innocents; some can be real stinkers. But their main purpose in fiction is simply to have an opposing agenda and to be agents of change. They always will clash with the protagonist, create suspense by their actions, and have a mission and the will to pull it off.

It's also important to understand that the antagonist doesn't need to be the antithesis of the protagonist; however, when the two characters in these roles are significantly different, these differences create tension. Likewise, when an antagonist and protagonist are similar, especially when they cannot see their similarities, it can stir up trouble. For example, if the two characters are equally driven, stubborn, or obsessive, and they are after the same prize, things will start to sizzle. Think of an antagonist as a sort of human roadblock, competitor, or nuisance who ultimately—and sometimes unintentionally—nudges the protagonist in the right direction.

Also keep in mind that antagonists always have powerful roles in the story because their potency will be directly linked to the potency of the story. An impotent or wimpy antagonist will cause the plot to fizzle—after all, why worry when the character doesn't have the backbone to really stir up trouble? So stories are only as good as their antagonists.

Sometimes writers withhold information from the reader to create suspense, but if the reader never comes to know and understand the antagonist, if the antagonist is never on stage with the protagonist in scenes, so that the reader is up close and worrying over the antagonist's ploys, then your story is in trouble. The closer the proximity between the protagonist and antagonist is, the more tension you create in the story world. For example, if your story features a grizzly bear waking up from its hibernation in a secluded valley in Montana, that causes a threat in the story because any time a grizzly is around, there could be danger. But the threat is still remote. However, if the grizzly is hungry and smells the garbage or food odors emanating from a cabin and it ambles down to investigate, then things start getting interesting and the threat is more ominous. If the grizzly cannot break into the garbage, so it breaks down a door and thunders into the cabin where the protagonist is sleeping, then the situation is truly threatening—especially if the protagonist has left his rifle out in his truck and has only a frying pan to defend himself with. The point is that the closer and more knowable the threat from an antagonist is, the more effective the story will be.

JOB DESCRIPTION FOR ANTAGONIST

The antagonist's job is to stand in the way of the protagonist's desires and goals, thus forcing him to change. In the end of the story, the protagonist can overcome the obstacles set forth by the antagonist, be destroyed by them, or become stuck in a state of constant conflict. (There is one exception to this job description, and it's seen in literary fiction where the protagonist himself is solely what stands in the way of his happiness or goals. This is generally exemplified by inner conflict or opposing desires.)

Essentially, the antagonist's role in fiction is to reveal as much about the protagonist as possible, showcasing the protagonist's primary traits in events that force him to act in specific ways. A good antagonist:

- provides complications and difficulties that elicit sympathy for the protagonist;
- creates the basic situation or dilemma of the story;
- reveals how the protagonist deals with adversity;
- forces the protagonist into new physical or emotional territory; and
- threatens the protagonist by inflicting physical or emotional pain.

The antics of the antagonist reveal the protagonist's flaws and weaknesses as well as his strengths. Over the course of story, these antics spark the events that serve as the story's catalyst, which is what reshapes the protagonist's self-concept. The antagonist also exists as a contrast to the protagonist, to provide an opposing—or at least different—viewpoint and set of moral values. When an antagonist starts messing with the main character, questions arise: *Will the protagonist rise to the occasion, or muddle through despite doubts and misgivings? Will he falter? Will he succeed despite flaws and fears?*

As noted at the start of this chapter, it is not necessary for the protagonist to hate the antagonist, or that any ill will be involved. In fact, the antagonist might very well respect or admire the protagonist. That said, the antagonist should still get on the protagonist's very last nerve, so when you're writing your antagonist, adjust the *scale* of his annoying behaviors to the needs of the story, and make these behaviors push your protagonist's buttons. If your protagonist takes himself too seriously, perhaps the antagonist is carefree and laughs at your protagonist's stuffiness. If the protagonist is sexually adventuresome, the antagonist is not only monogamous, but only prefers the missionary position. Or vice versa. If your protagonist is a timid type and stuck in a dead-end job, the antagonist jumps from airplanes and cliffs and bails out of jobs that bore him.

Like a protagonist, a well-written antagonist will be unforgettable or indelible. However, unlike the protagonist, you have choices about how much stage time to allot your antagonist. Some authors will need him in almost every scene. Sometimes, he'll only appear from time to time, but he still will exert a lot of pressure. For example, in a mystery, an antagonist might be the police captain who is pressuring the detective to pin the murder on an innocent man. The detective knows the real killer is still out there. But meanwhile, the captain, who is thinking of running for political office, wants the case closed and doesn't care if the evidence is circumstantial or trumped up. The captain likely will only appear in a few scenes because most of the story will focus on the detective chasing down the killer, but his influence and agenda will be felt throughout the story.

CASTING YOUR ANTAGONIST

If you read one hundred novels and started categorizing the various roles that the antagonist is cast in, you'd notice that there is a variety of parts that an antagonist can play. You'd also realize that antagonists can display a wide range of morality. Some antagonists believe they only want what is best for the protagonist; some have a cold-hearted agenda. But all of them reveal the vagaries of the human family—how we run the gamut from fundamentalist preachers to con artists to prostitutes to suburban moms.

Somewhere in that continuum, you fit your antagonist with her traits and morality that will cause trouble, stirring up tension and conflict. Antagonists can also display less-than-admirable behaviors. These people can be backstabbers, liars, cheats, flirts, or thieves. On the other hand, an antagonist can be the voice of conscience in the story, or be so cheerful and Pollyannaish that she cannot be trusted because she's simply too naive and childlike.

Within the larger category of antagonists, there are endless possibilities for the difficulties they cause protagonists. Here are some examples of roles you might want to cast your antagonist in:

ADULTERER: Adultery is usually an act that causes pain. Although sometimes an adulterer tries to justify her actions, this intimate betrayal can cause layers of complications in a plot. Adulterers have been around since the beginning of literature, and famous ones include Daisy Buchanan and Jay Gatsby in F. Scott Fitzgerald's *The Great Gatsby*, Lara and Yuri Zhivago in Boris Pasternak's *Doctor Zhivago*, and femme fatale Cora in James M. Cain's *The Postman Always Rings Twice*.

BAD BOSS: The role of the bad boss works best when other characters need the job. If your protagonist is independently wealthy, a bad boss won't have much leverage in her life. Often lurking beneath a bad boss's exterior is insecurity, a need for power or control, or other motivations that are best hidden. In John Grisham's *The Firm*, the protagonist Mitchell McDeere discovers that the partners of his law firm are the ultimate bad bosses.

In fact, the firm is actually a front for a white-collar crime family, and anyone who gets in their way are in serious danger.

BETRAYER: The closer the person, the worse the betrayal and pain. Betrayal is a classic plot complication because the reader can relate to being betrayed and the pain it causes.

In *Lord of the Flies*, William Golding's tale about how civilization can dissolve when English schoolboys are stranded on a remote island, Sam and Eric are twins who are inseparable. At first seemingly loyal to Ralph, who represents order, they capitulate and join Jack's tribe—their first betrayal. Jack has given in to his primal drives and as the story progresses becomes Ralph's enemy. In one of the final scenes, the twins reveal Ralph's hiding spot to Jack, a dangerous betrayal.

BULLY: A bully is someone who likes to torment other people through physical attacks, emotional abuse, threats, or coercion. This person usually got away with harmful behaviors in her childhood, so as an adult, she continues to humiliate, exploit, and hurt vulnerable characters. Women bullies often are playing more of a psychological game and often don't know more acceptable means of acquiring power. While children's stories sometimes show the young protagonist facing up to a bully, they create a lot of emotions in readers, no matter their age. In Charles Dickens's *Bleak House*, the scheming lawyer Mr. Tulkinghorn is trying to profit when he learns of Esther Summerson's secret past, an illegitimate birth.

CAD: A cad is a timeless character type who is long on charm and is considered dashing and sexy, all traits that conceal his dishonorable and predatory nature. Shallow types who use women for pleasure, and sometimes for money, cause a lot of heat in a story. Mr. Wickham, who runs off with the teenager Lydia Bennet in Jane Austen's *Pride and Prejudice*, is a famous cad. Besides ruining Lydia's reputation, Mr. Wickham also has resigned his commission to evade gambling debts and seems to have no inclination for honest work. Daniel Cleaver, Bridget Jones's boss in *Bridget Jones's Diary*, is another cad, as he starts a sexual relationship with Bridget that is based more on convenience than on real feelings.

CONTROL FREAK: Some people have the mistaken idea that they were born to control other people. This might mean a parent who cannot let go of control over her children's affairs after they're grown, an insecure husband, or a corporate tycoon who demands absolute loyalty. Control freaks are often deluded about their importance in other people's lives and are actually motivated by insecurity. Jane Fonda playing the character Viola Fields in the film *Monster-in-Law* is an example of a control freak. Fields, who recently lost her job to a younger woman, is out to stop her son from marrying his girlfriend.

When a control freak lies on the extreme end of the spectrum, he might also be a batterer, as illustrated by Bobby Benedetto, the husband of protagonist Fran in Anna Quindlen's *Black and Blue*. Benedetto is also a good example of how sometimes a control freak can fool his victim in the early days of their relationship, as when Benedetto first comes off as passionate and alluring, and Fran is swept away by his charm.

DADDY/MOMMY DEAREST: When a parent is an abuser, the situation is always fraught with conflict since the parent usually has the upper hand and the abuse can leave a lasting impact on the child. Pap, the town drunk and ne'er-do-well in Mark Twain's *The Adventures of Huckleberry Finn,* is a famous example of lousy parent, especially when he demands that he shares in the gold that Huck and Tom Sawyer found.

FEMME FATALE: This female character is irresistibly attractive and sexual, but somehow dangerously so. Her role often is to lead the protagonist or hero into danger as she needs rescuing or she's conning him. Femme fatale characters are often found in hard-boiled detective stories and noir movies, such as Brigid O'Shaughnessy in Dashiell Hammett's *The Maltese Falcon.* These days, James Ellroy often includes this type in his stories, such as in Lynn Bracken in his novel *L.A. Confidential.*

GOSSIP: A gossip talks about everyone, rarely cares about the truth of what is said, and often has an underlying or ugly motive. Mrs. Bennet of Jane Austen's *Pride and Prejudice* is a famous gossip, and she has other not-so-attractive traits, as she's querulous, shallow, and manipulative in her attempts to see her daughters married to men of wealth.

LIAR: When a lie is set in motion in a plot, it can cause lots of complications. Lies can be fibs or whoppers, and the person who spreads the lie can be someone incapable of honesty, or she can be someone with higher morals, perhaps trying to protect another character with the falsehood. Often, a lie can set a plot in motion and provide a wider context for the reader to come to know the story world, as in E.M. Forster's *A Passage to India.* In Harper Lee's *To Kill a Mockingbird,* Mayella Ewell falsely accuses Tom Robinson, a black man, of rape, which sets the plot in motion and reveals the racial attitudes of the town.

LOVE INTEREST: When an antagonist is used as a love interest in a story, the author has a choice to culminate or destroy the relationship. In Kazuo Ishiguro's *The Remains of the Day,* the protagonist is the loyal English butler James Stevens who puts his duties to his boss, Lord Darlington, above everything, including his conscience. Miss Kenton, the housekeeper, is in love with Stevens, but he does not see this until she eventually marries someone else. The story is about Stevens finally understanding what he has lost by refusing love and choosing duty.

MENTALLY ILL: As in real life, when a character in a story is mentally ill, this factor can provide all sorts of problems for the people around him, especially if the illness is serious, such as schizophrenia or severe depression. A mentally ill antagonist could be a spouse, child, sibling, boss, or any other central figure in the protagonist's life. An antagonist with mental illness might threaten suicide or display dangerous rage. The bottom line is that when mental illness is present, the protagonist and antagonist will have vastly different coping skills and versions of reality.

In Roxana Robinson's *Sweetwater*, protagonist Isabel Green is immediately swept away by the allure and larger-than-life personality of Michael, the antagonist. However, within months of knowing him, she discovers his dark side, including a mental illness so debilitating that at times he must be hospitalized, and she comes to feel like a prisoner of his illness.

NARCISSIST: As in real life, narcissistic characters are so self-involved that they cannot see things through the protagonist's viewpoint, and they don't possess much empathy for anyone besides themselves. Hit man and thug Vincent Vega, played by John Travolta in the film *Pulp Fiction*, is a prime example of a narcissistic character who creates a lot of trouble and tension because of his self-absorption.

POWER HUNGRY: Some people will never be content to play a small role in life. No matter what their realm is, they want to be on top. This type of character could be a parent who is overbearing and rules the home with an iron hand, a boss who wants his employees to be afraid of him, or a minister who wants his flock to obey him. The need for power will always stir up conflict and will likely mean that someone in the story will not want to be a follower. In Isabel Allende's *The House of the Spirits*, Esteban Trueba is a character who exemplifies where an extreme need for power can lead. Gordon Gekko, played by Michael Douglas in the film *Wall Street*, famous for his "greed is good" speech, is another good example of a power-hungry, über-aggressive type, especially when paired against the naive protagonist who is new to Wall Street.

PSEUDO-FRIEND: In the beginning of a story, the pseudo-friend character is often posing as the protagonist's friend. However, as the story progresses, the pseudo-friend is unmasked, and the reader discovers he has ulterior motives or a vastly different agenda than first imagined. Donna Tartt's *The Secret History* is a modern-day Greek tragedy about a group of students who conspire to kill a member of their group. (If your school chums are plotting your murder, it's clear that they're not real friends, and you best run. Fast.)

SNOOP: Advice for this character might be: "get a life." Traditionally a neighbor or family member, a snoop or busybody stirs up trouble by spying on people or taking too much interest in other people's lives. Often, what she discovers has bigger ramifications than first imagined. A snoop is particularly effective in stories set in small towns, and if she has an agenda or grudge, such as Miss Ruth in Augusta Trobaugh's *Sophie and the Rising Sun*.

USER: There are people who get by in life by using other people for money, influence, or friendship, but their real motive is getting ahead on another person's efforts. Users are often motivated by greed and laziness, and they know how to manipulate others to achieve their ends. The character Jack, played by Thomas Haden Church in the film *Sideways*, is a blatant example of a user. Since he and his friend Miles are heading off on a road trip before Jack's wedding, Miles assumes that they're going to spend time playing golf and drinking wine. But Jack is out for a sexual fling before marriage and doesn't care about the price others pay for his pleasure-seeking.

WEAKLING: It seems counter-intuitive to include a weakling as an antagonist, but a weakling can have lots of permutations in life and fiction. Because he needs protection, lacks self-awareness, or is somehow self-destructive, he can have many uses in a story. A weakling might be a character who can be led or coerced into mischief, crime, or violence. One example is Lennie Small in John Steinbeck's *Of Mice and Men*, who, because he's childlike and at the same time physically powerful, wreaks havoc for his friend George Milton, who longs for a better life but is brought down by Lennie's behaviors.

EXPLORING THE DYNAMICS BETWEEN ANTAGONIST AND PROTAGONIST

An antagonist is a threatening force and somehow makes the protagonist feel bad—shaky, unsure, worried, unworthy, unattractive, unlovable, you name it. When an antagonist appears in a story, he weakens the protagonist's position—physically or emotionally—and keeps doing so until their differences are resolved. His role is to stand in the way of what your protagonist wants and needs, he must do this effectively, convincingly, and often *intimately.*

If that threat is in human form, you might want to analyze your antagonist after reading this list, making certain the dynamic between your characters is stirring up enough trouble. While the following points can work as a checklist to measure this dynamic, not every story and antagonist will fit all these qualities. However, the goal here is that your story dynamics fulfill most of the criteria.

- **The antagonist is a worthy opponent.** The qualities and strengths between the antagonist and protagonist should be well matched. Think of the scales of justice, with the protagonist and antagonist possessing traits that balance out each other. If your antagonist is cunning, your protagonist is wise or street smart. If your antagonist uses charm and flattery to get what he wants, the protagonist will see through these wiles, or at least will not be vulnerable to these efforts throughout the story. If the antagonist has power in his world, the protagonist also has a sphere of influence where he is respected and valued.

- **The antagonist is chosen to show how the protagonist deals with adversity.** This includes how the protagonist rises to the occasion, falters, and succeeds or fails. It's also extremely instructive to show how a protagonist picks himself up and returns to the game after stumbles or defeats.

- **The dustup between the antagonist and protagonist is harrowing.** This doesn't mean that every story features fisticuffs or a shoot-up at sunrise, but somehow the situation will cause a threat that makes the reader lean in with worry and apprehension. In fiction, a protagonist's happiness and well-being is always at risk. Sometimes the protagonist is also protecting or defending other vulnerable characters. The antagonist is the vehicle to create the risk; he is the person designed to tilt the outcome toward misery or happiness. The trick here is making sure that the reader can identify what is at stake in the story and can empathize with the protagonist's vulnerability in the situation.

- **The relationship between the protagonist and antagonist has some kind of intimacy, proximity, or kinship.** The antagonist is not merely a bystander or a disinterested party. If the protagonist and antagonist share a history, then the situation is particularly suspenseful and emotional.
- **The confrontation between the antagonist and protagonist brings up intense emotions in the protagonist, such as contempt, rage, compassion, or respect.** It's simple, really; if there's no emotions in the characters, there will be no emotions in the reader. The reader must also witness a character being buffeted by circumstances that are beyond the norm. Fiction is written about the most exciting, dangerous, rollicking moments of the protagonist's life. The more intense the situation and powerful the antagonist is, the more powerful the emotions will be.
- **The antagonist exposes the protagonist's Achilles' heel.** An Achilles' heel might be the protagonist's self-doubts or feelings of unworthiness, his inability to trust or believe in love, his need to prove himself in his family, or his fear of the dark. A protagonist's weakness creates an extra dose of suspense because it makes a successful outcome look doubtful.
- **The struggle between the antagonist and protagonist is somehow debilitating to the protagonist so the protagonist's victory can be all the sweeter.** If your protagonist is not somehow battered by the story's events, you don't have enough conflict. Remember, characters suffer because the reader doesn't want to.
- **The protagonist is brought down by humility or humbling.** Again, since characters suffer more than we do in real life, protagonists often must be humiliated or learn a painful lesson to arrive at a new way of seeing the world or being in the world. And that road is never easy.
- **The protagonist takes his struggle personally.** The struggle is not something the protagonist can easily brush off; it usually as-

sumes the central conflict in the story, and his identity or reputation is tied to it.

- **There is a lot at stake, and the stakes increase as the struggle continues.** This keeps the suspense boiling throughout the story.
- **There is obsession on the part of the protagonist.** Because the outcome matters so much, the protagonist focuses intently on it, and often this focus causes negative ramifications in his life. Many stories feature opening scenes where the protagonist is not yet obsessed with, or aware of, a goal or bringing down an antagonist. However, as the story moves along and the protagonist's motivations deepen, he needs something, and he needs it badly. And that something is often to beat out the antagonist.
- **The protagonist has something to prove.** This often is revealed during the defining moments of a protagonist's life, when he is most exposed.
- **The protagonist bets everything on his last hand.** There is usually an all-or-nothing quality to a protagonist's last gambit, and because he's been weakened by the events of the story, this wager causes the outcome to be especially doubtful and suspenseful. If the story features a direct final confrontation with the antagonist, suspense is amplified when the protagonist seems to be running on empty and is outgunned.
- **There is a witness besides the reader to ensure that the struggle has major ramifications.** If there is not a direct witness, then other characters must learn of the outcome.
- **The climatic scenes, which might include a confrontation, bring about complicated and sometimes conflicting emotions in the protagonist, and sometimes in the antagonist.** In your story, your protagonist might be feeling attacks of conscience or doubts about the rightness of his acts, and he worries about the ramifications of his actions, thus increasing the reader's emotional involvement.
- **The dustup between the protagonist and antagonist reflects timeless themes, patterns, and lessons learned.** If nothing is learned or

proven about human nature in fiction, particularly in the climatic scenes, it is a sign that your story is thin, and the reader will feel cheated and let down.

THE ANTAGONIST IS PERFECT FOR HIS ROLE

Your antagonist should possess the perfect qualities for his role and be a perfect counterpoint to your protagonist. You also want your antagonist's behaviors to hit your protagonist's flaws like an arrow hits a bull's-eye, thwarting your protagonist's desires with deadly accuracy and pushing him toward change. If your protagonist really needs the promotion, the antagonist, also vying for the job, will have better or showier skills and weasel her way into the good graces of the boss. If your protagonist, who is not exactly a George Clooney double and is rather unsure of himself, is desperately in love with a woman in his office, then the antagonist is also vying for her heart, and he is not only a handsome devil, but is also debonair and assured.

Or, if your protagonist, Justin, is a captain of troops in battle, the antagonist, Robert, might be his First Lieutenant who, at first glance, seems like more of an alpha male because he's brawnier and faster, can shoot with legendary accuracy, can drink everyone in the platoon under the table, and is more gung-ho when it comes to dashing into battle. His role in the story might be to prove that Justin has the real courage and brains to lead other men. This might be accomplished by Justin saving Robert's life when he's gunned down—Justin crawls along under a deadly barrage of enemy fire and drags him back to his foxhole and staunches his wounds.

Or, Robert might be in the story to show that real leadership isn't about dashing into gunfire or getting revenge for the death of a platoon member, but rather about keeping the safety of his men first. Justin might prove that keeping calm in a crisis or using strategy, not brawn, is what wins battles. But he needs Robert in the story to provide an opposite take on things, and maybe to whisper behind Justin's back that he's the real man of the outfit, further fueling suspense and tension.

Keep in mind that an antagonist should carry weight in the story, even though he's usually not in most scenes. The antagonist's presence should always be a threat, but it should be a threat with just the right proportions a story needs. In the previous example, the macho and reckless Robert is doubly dangerous because it's war time and his sort of antics can get innocent men killed. In a less violent role, such as in a story set in a family or business, an antagonist might be using cunning, manipulation, or behind-the-scenes tactics to thwart the protagonist. No matter what the story type or exact role is, the antagonist has the perfect arsenal of character traits and tactics to wreak the maximum damage for the protagonist.

A terrific example of an antagonist who is perfect for the job because of his emotional ties and influence on the protagonist comes in Matt Haig's *The Dead Fathers Club*. This story opens when the ghost of Philip's father, who was killed in a car accident, appears soon after his own funeral. This appearance happens in the Castle and Falcon, the pub Philip's family owns, and then the story flashes back to the moment the family learned of the death. This flashback creates a nice dose of emotion that colors all that follows:

> Dad died because his car crashed into a bridge outside of Kelham which is a village near Newark. ...
>
> Before we saw the news there was a policeman who came to the back door and I knew the policeman because he had been into the Pub before talking to Dad. The policeman had a face like an empty plate and he opened and closed his mouth for a long time with nothing coming out but air.
>
> I was watching from the top of the stairs and they couldnt see me and I couldnt hear them properly but I knew something was wrong from the way the policeman had his hat on his chest.
>
> And then they went into the office and shut the door and I could hear nothing for ages and then I heard Mum. She was howling like a WOLF and the noise hurt my stomach and I closed my eyes to try and hear the policeman and all he was saying was Im sorry and he kept on saying it
>
> Im sorry
>
> Im sorry
>
> Im sorry
>
> and I knew that he hadnt done anything wrong because he was a policeman and policemen only say sorry if something very bad has happened. So I knew right then what the pain in my stomach was. And I saw the policeman leave and the hat was in his hand but not on his chest any more like the Bad News had been in there and set free. And I saw Mum and she saw me but didnt see me properly and she

> went to the corner of the hall by the radiator and sat down in a ball and cried and shook her head in her hands and said No no no no no and everywhere round us looked the same but bigger and I wanted to go and tell her it was OK but that would have been a lie and so I just sat there and did nothing.

Sometimes it can be helpful to use a scene like this to show how the characters are off balance and weakened by the inciting incident. When people are grief-stricken, they are not always rational, not always at their best. This sort of insight into the characters' states of mind, like other factors in the story, increases tension and suspense.

So, still numb with grief from his father's death, eleven-year-old Philip learns about the Dead Fathers Club, the club whose members were all murdered, and his father's claims that his brother Alan, a mechanic, tampered with his car and was responsible for his death. When Philip realizes that Uncle Alan is moving in on his mom and has plans for the pub, and with goading from his father's ghost, Philip decides that something must be done. He must avenge his father's death or his dad will be part of the Dead Fathers Club forever.

But, of course, things in fiction are never simple, and plans never go smoothly. In fact, the more Philip wants to help his father, the more trouble

NOT ALWAYS HUMAN

Not all antagonists are humans. Nonhuman antagonists can be tracked back to Jonah and the whale in the Bible; they can occur in any genre, and they can range widely. For example, the whale in Herman Melville's *Moby-Dick*, the shark in Peter Benchley's *Jaws*, and a disease in Stephen King's *The Stand* all serve as antagonists.

Sometimes antagonists are a force or societal flaw, such as the bigotry in James A. Michener's *South Pacific*, Harper Lee's *To Kill a Mockingbird*, and Mark Twain's *The Adventures of Huckleberry Finn*; injustice and sadism in Stephen King's *The Green Mile* and Big Brother in George Orwell's *1984*; and racism and economic fallout from the U.S. government interring Japanese-American citizens during World War II in David Guterson's *Snow Falling on Cedars*. In Ernest Hemingway's short story "The Snows of Kilimanjaro," Harry, the protagonist, is in a face-off with death, the ultimate antagonist.

he gets into. Torn between his loyalty to his father and his concerns for the living, Philip needs to figure out if more violence is the solution. Because of the emotional hold Philip's father has on him (their bond is proven through a series of recollections), he's perfect for the role as the antagonist—particularly because he seems to be really suffering in the afterlife and keeps insisting that Philip murder Alan. The best antagonists exert continual pressure.

The Dead Fathers Club is also an example of how an antagonist pushes the protagonist to do things he would never have done without the antagonist's influence. Philip's father is stirring up a boatload of trouble for Philip as he wrestles with his grief and other complicated emotions, along with his notions of right or wrong. Philip starts committing a series of crimes of increasing seriousness until his revenge murder plot goes terribly awry and creates a chain reaction of more complications and grief. This story also illustrates how an antagonist who stirs the deepest emotions in the protagonist has a particularly potent role to play, and how deep changes can happen in the protagonist's outlook by the story's end.

THE ANTAGONIST AS AN AGENT OF CHANGE

Protagonists are rarely static characters; they usually change in some way because of the events of the story. Even in series fiction, the protagonist exhibits a change by the end of the story—the only difference is that such a character changes in smaller increments throughout each installment of the series. With an antagonist, you also have a choice whether to make him static or give him a character arc. Some antagonists will be forced to change because they're defeated, some will skate off, unfazed by the story's events, some will be scarred by events of the story, and some will be redeemed. While the protagonist will almost always change, antagonists change or remain the same depending on the needs of the story.

Generally, if an antagonist falls along the lower end of the morality continuum, then you, as the author, must make tough choices about whether he, too, will learn from the story's events. Sometimes he needs to be utterly defeated by the protagonist, sometimes he needs to get a comeuppance by the story's events, sometimes he must declare a truce with the protagonist, and sometimes he will lose, but only to return another day. Thus, the story's ending will seriously impact the antagonist. It might make him itch for retribution, it might force him leave town, or it might make him graciously accede that the protagonist deserves the hand of his beloved because he's better suited to marry her. Sometimes stories in which the antagonist is unchanged can seem cliché or simplistic, while stories where both the antagonist and protagonist change have more richness and depth.

But let's talk more about the protagonist changing, because this character arc is essential to so many stories. As in real life, characters in stories don't change unless they have a good reason to, and antagonists provide those reasons. *The Dead Fathers Club* provides a terrific illustration of how this works in fiction. In most stories, a protagonist changes his outlook, values, and personality for the better; in the case of a tragedy, though, he might change for the worse or be destroyed by the story's events.

Another example of the antagonist as an agent of change can be found in Anna Quindlen's novel *Rise and Shine.* It's the story of two sisters living in New York. The older sister, Meghan, is the megastar of a television talk show and acts as the story's antagonist. Bridget, the protagonist, is younger and works as a social worker at a woman's shelter. The inciting incident of the story happens when Meghan utters a profanity on the air; nothing is the same afterward.

Although the sisters are close, the relationship is pricklier than Bridget cares to admit and is perhaps based more on Bridget's longing for closeness than on reality. In the first pages, their dynamic is established as they jog in Central Park and recall how they both attended the same dinner party the previous evening. Bridget had arrived at the party carrying a bunch of anemones:

> "God, flowers, Bridget?" my sister said, running around a stroller-size class of new mothers trying to trim their baby bodies. "I couldn't believe you brought flowers to a dinner party. That's the worst. With everything else you have to do when people are showing up, you have to stop to find a vase and fill a vase and cut the stems and then find a place for them and if they're blue, Jesus, I never know where to put them in our apartment, and then—"
>
> "How is it possible that you can make bringing someone flowers sound like the Stations of the Cross?"

> "Sometimes I just leave them on the kitchen counter and toss them with the leftovers." I knew this was exactly true; Meghan had long had staff to toss the leftovers and the people from Feeding Our People, the big society starvation charity, sent over a van to pick up the excess from her larger dinner parties. "Just bring wine ..."

On the surface, it looks like Meghan has everything and Bridget has little, but the story proves that there is a deeper truth to their situations. The novel explores the nature of fame in contemporary society, the gap between rich and poor, how sisters relate to each over time, and how people navigate big changes.

Birth order and family dynamics are set into play early in childhood, and when these roles shift, it can be profound. In *Rise and Shine*, it's not only Meghan's job crisis that causes Bridget to change, but also a tragedy in the third act of the story that forever changes everyone and redefines the sisters' relationship. By the story's end, both sisters lead lives that are vastly different from the ones they pursued in the opening, and their relationship is deeper and more honest. Quindlen's story is also a good example of how both the protagonist and antagonist must change in order to become more fulfilled.

Sometimes the protagonist refuses to change, signaling an intellectual or moral failure. However, this failure is ultimately exactly what the story needs to create the most logical ending. In real life, when we meet a huge challenge or temptation, we try to muster all our resources, but still we sometimes fail. Similarly, to make fiction realistic, a protagonist might fail or find the going just too difficult. Sometimes this means he's a static character, with this inability to change reflecting the harsher realities of life.

THE ANTAGONIST AS AN INTIMATE ASSOCIATE

You don't need to be a fan of *The Jerry Springer Show* to know that the people who can cause the most hurt in another person's life are those who are closest—spouses, lovers, siblings, parents, neighbors, and friends. In fact, the more intimate the relationship is, the sharper the pain will be. When people who care about us stab us in the heart, the hurt is much more difficult to manage than if a stranger had wounded us.

Elizabeth Berg's novel *Say When* proves that proximity can create excruciating conflict and a painful collision of wills. The story revolves around a married couple, Griffin (the protagonist) and Ellen (the antagonist). The first paragraph sets up their conflict:

> Of course he knew she was seeing someone. He knew who it was, too. Six months ago, saying she needed a new direction in her life, saying she was tired of feeling helpless around anything mechanical, that she had no idea how to even change a tire, Ellen had taken a course in basic auto mechanics—"Know Your Car," it was called. She'd come back the first night saying it was amazing, she's had the admittedly elitist idea that mechanics were illiterate, but this one was so well-*spoken*, and he'd walked into the classroom carrying a pile of *books* he'd just bought—hardback! Mostly new fiction, she'd said. But also Balzac, because he's never read him.

Ellen's infatuation soon becomes more serious, and the conflict heats up:

> Week after week, he'd watched Ellen dress for class, each time paying more attention to herself: fresh eyeliner just before she left one week, a more deliberate hairstyle the next, a lingering scent of perfume in the bedroom the night she'd gotten ready for the last class—the ridiculously expensive perfume Griffin had given her for her last birthday, for the record. He felt helpless against her drift toward another man, felt as though he were standing around stirring change in his pocket when he should be waging an earth-pawing kind of war. But the truth was that from the time he'd married her ten years ago, he'd been waiting for something like this to happen. She was always just beyond his grasp, in one way or another. He supposed, actually, that her cool reserve was one of the things that attracted him to her.

Thus, in the first few pages, the situation is established and the reader also soon learns that Griffin had never met anyone who appealed to him more than his wife, and that they have an eight-year-old daughter, Zoe. By page five, on a Sunday morning, as Griffin's going downstairs to cook hash browns and eggs, Ellen confesses to being in love with the mechanic and asks for a divorce.

This is when things get really interesting because, after Ellen's confession and Griffin's answer, he informs her that he's not going to make her

ROGUE'S GALLERY

Antagonists come in all sizes and shapes, and their proximity to the protagonist varies. Some are relatively benign, some are downright stinkers, but all are agents of change. Here are some examples:

- Heartbreaker: Ashley Wilkes, *Gone With the Wind* by Margaret Mitchell
- Bully: Mrs. Danvers, *Rebecca* by Daphne du Maurier
- Control Freak: Jenny Fields, *The World According to Garp* by John Irving
- Flirt: Curley's wife, *Of Mice and Men* by John Steinbeck
- Pursuer: Javert, *Les Misérables* by Victor Hugo
- Betrayer and liar: Mayella Ewell, *To Kill a Mockingbird* by Harper Lee
- Adulterer: Sula Peace, *Sula* by Toni Morrison
- Bully: Professor Snape, Harry Potter series by J.K. Rowling

situation easy. She mentions how their daughter needs stability, and since she's a stay-at-home mom, he should move out:

> ... He said quietly, "I'm not going anywhere."
>
> "Pardon?"
>
> "I said, I'm not *going* anywhere. I'm not moving."
>
> She nodded. "I see. Well, *I* can't. I have to be here to take care of Zoe."
>
> Griffin pictured his daughter, a redheaded tomboy who would grow up to be a redheaded beauty who would knock the stuffing out of any man who crossed her. "All right, you can stay, too," he told Ellen.
>
> "Griffin. One of us has to go."
>
> He picked up his mug, took a sip. "Well, let's see now. It isn't going to be me. You try to figure out the rest, Ellen. And from now on, call me Frank. I don't want you to call me Griffin. That's what my friends call me."

The chapter ends with Ellen leaving the house, and the story is set in motion with both characters on a collision course of pain. You can see how the battle lines are drawn and how her affair and desertion have an enormous capacity to wound. The conflict is especially difficult because the reader learns that Griffin is still deeply in love with her, and he knows her intimately and thoroughly. The reader, who has already sympathized with his situation, is now thoroughly in his corner.

But because Ellen is the antagonist, she has something to teach him. Berg, a clever writer, plays with the reader's emotions by establishing Griffin's flaws in the marriage, and although they don't seem equal to Ellen's in the beginning of the novel, by the end of the story, the reader understands Ellen's despair in the marriage and her reasons for leaving. Berg also portrays Griffin as a basically decent person who still has a huge capacity to hurt and misunderstand his wife, who took her for granted, and who didn't work hard enough at the marriage.

All this works because of their proximity, since they begin their separation by living together and because they are both responsible for their daughter. In fiction, there often is a simple delineation: the protagonist is the good guy, the antagonist is the bad guy. But if you follow Berg's example and choose to imbue both protagonist and antagonist with a mix of positive qualities and faults, the story can be doubly engaging and realistic.

You have lots of options when creating an antagonist for your story, since this type of character can range in morality and capacity to make trouble. If you introduce an antagonist as a passive or low-key sort of person, make certain that you somehow hint at or foreshadow his potential for causing trouble for your protagonist. Generally, an antagonist is in motion throughout the story, causing the protagonist to react. As when the protagonist is first introduced, when the antagonist walks into the story, make certain he arrives on the scene with his primary traits intact and makes a strong first impression.

CHAPTER SIX

Bad to the Bone: Villains

Evil men have no songs.

—Friedrich Nietzsche

There's a sadist in every reader, and when your character is in the most harrowing danger, the reader most enjoys the story. And harrowing danger usually occurs when a story features the wickedest of the bad asses: the villain. Villains make the hero, and the reader, squirm in anguish. They creep into the story from the land of nightmares, and they always have surprises and special talents and torments up their proverbial sleeves. Villains are identified by their values—not the stuff of Sunday school teachings, but rather of something perverse and complicated and frightening. They are also identified by their traits, usually ones that are dark and ruthless, and by their motives, which are usually for power, revenge, or profit.

This chapter and the three that follow are going to look at specific qualities of villainy, the degrees of villainy—including when and how a villain might be sympathetic or criminally inclined—and how protagonists, especially heroes, match wits with villains. Let's get started in creating this oh-so-potent character type.

EVIL AS THE SOURCE CODE

Evil is the source code of writing a villain, and you want to understand its ramifications in all your characters' lives. In the most general terms, evil is the absence of good. But there are many shadings of evil, and you'll want to choose an exact shade of evil to paint your villain with. For example, you might want to use deception as a pale shade of evil for your villain, but his behaviors might be sketched in coal black tints because not only does he torture characters, he also relishes the task.

Your villain's motives will match his traits; often, the more depraved the motives are, such as to create terror in a large population, the blacker his traits will be. So a villain with far-reaching plans to harm many people might be merciless, ruthless, calculating, and a natural leader, although the types he leads wouldn't qualify for a citizen's merit badge, either.

Along those lines, depicting a character that is purely evil can be tricky; just as when you create a protagonist who is wholly good, the reader starts yawning, when you create a villain that is wholly wicked, the reader grows restless. If your villain revels in the pain of others, you might be creating melodrama, just as if your hero is a pure-hearted do-gooder. (But then sometimes it's appropriate that a villain loves to induce pain, or doesn't care if he causes pain, especially in the case of the super villain or sociopath, who will be discussed in chapter seven.)

To depict a villain who is not melodramatic or thinly drawn, start by understanding the nature of his evil and deciding the darkness of his soul, just how far he'll go to achieve his aims, and why he does what he does.

Besides being the opposite of goodness, evil will always create vulnerability in its victims. Evil comes from acts that oppress, harm, manipulate, and torment people. Evil always causes emotional duress and leaves a legacy of trauma. Evil cannot exist unless the person performing the evil act intends to harm someone by his acts. People who act in these ways have limited access to their own goodness and humanity, and they are constricted and twisted.

Evil—and its components of greed, corruption, domination, and deviancy—holds timeless appeal for readers. Wickedness in fiction fascinates and horrifies us because the rogues of fiction represent our shadow side, our denial, and our hidden desires. Carl Jung, the famous Swiss psychiatrist, had a unique approach to explaining the human psyche. According to Jung, one important aspect of the psyche, which he called the *shadow*, is the opposite of the conscious self, and it often holds all the negative tendencies a person usually denies. The shadow is often on display in our dreams. For example, a person who believes he is a good-hearted person might in reality harbor a shadow side that he hides from the world. This shadow might be greedy, dishonest, envious, or somehow corrupt. In his *Collected Works, Volume 11*, Jung says, "Unfortunately there can be no doubt that man is, on the whole, less good than he imagines himself or wants to be. Everyone carries a Shadow, and the less it is embodied in the individual's conscious life, the blacker and denser it is."

We project the shadow, and we see dark tendencies in others that we cannot see it in ourselves. Thus, a villain with all his scelerous tendencies can actually be a reflection of our hidden selves. It's simply more comfortable to boo and hiss at a villain's actions than confront our own weaknesses and dark tendencies.

CHARACTERISTICS OF EVIL

In ancient cultures, gods and goddesses sat in judgment of humans, making decisions about which actions were evil, and which mortals deserved punishment for their deeds. Today, we have judicial systems in place to pass judgment, but the realities of evil are still profound. Again, the more you refine your notions of evil and how evil will affect your characters, the more impact your villain will have on the reader. Here is a list of some general characteristics of evil that should start your creative juices flowing:

- Evil involves the power to induce fear or, in some extreme cases, to terrorize.
- Evil is used to control or manipulate other people's emotions.
- It is evil to cause physical pain.
- It is evil to manipulate reality. This can happen in many circumstances, such as politics and intimate relationships. There are many ways that people lie, blame others for their own actions, or otherwise distort the truth.
- Evil people often prey on the most vulnerable—the poor, the frail, the elderly, the uneducated, children, and women.
- Evil people like to exert control over others. This can include a wife batterer, a corrupt politician, or a professor who craves power over his students.

- Evil is witnessed in its power to destroy. This can mean arson, rape, murder, or a suicide bomb. It is also evil to destroy a person's confidence or happiness, or to do anything to lessen a person's sense of safety or well-being, as in the case of a stalker tormenting his victim.
- Moral decay is always a characteristic of evil.
- Evil hates to come in contact with goodness.
- Evil acts include the need to dominate, as seen in sadistic acts such as rape and pedophilia.

VILLAIN BASICS

Villains are characters readers love to hate; they are on a dark path, which is also a collision course with the protagonist. Villains will always be strangely compelling because in all of us still lives the child who long ago met the Big Bad Wolf, Captain Hook, and Dracula. This child is living in the adult, wired in our brains, stirred by primal instincts and fears, and still frightened by nightmares. We write for this child, this younger self, as well as for the shadow, the darker part in each of us that we often hide from the world.

A villain fits in the subset of antagonists, meaning that his role in the story is that he will oppose the protagonist's goals and will cause her to change. The main difference between a villain and an antagonist is that the villain's presence in the story will always cause fear and apprehension in the reader. If the reader is not afraid of him, then the character is not a good villain. Fear in humans is much more complex and unsettling than it is in animals. It has many degrees and can be linked with other emotions that are activated while reading. A villain's role in the story is to stir these emotions to the boiling point.

The other factors that separate villains from antagonists are their primary traits and their levels of morality. An antagonist might be a person with all or mostly positive primary traits; in fact, he can be the nicest guy in town, but he has a role in the story to thwart the protagonist. A villain is never the nicest guy in town, never has primary traits that most people would want to emulate, almost always has purely selfish motives, and typically has moral standards that are criminal and abhorrent.

But just because a villain has the job of wreaking havoc in the story world, it doesn't mean you, the writer, have a license simply to create a character who is evil to the bone without much thought about how he got that way or why he cannot relate to people in typically normal ways. If you find that you've created a one-dimensional villain—such as a villain who's a killing machine with no motivation—then it's likely you've written a melodrama. All characters are a meld of traits and quirks; the most intriguing heroes might have a bit of villain in them, and the most captivating villains have a certain amount of heroism in them. But a hero succeeds because of his values and best traits, while a villain might be undone or destroyed because of his worst traits.

CHARACTERISTICS OF VILLAINS

Villains are characters whose wickedness, selfishness, and intensity will always strike dread in the reader. Although villains are sometimes sympathetic, or somewhat sympathetic, most often their motives make them twisted, cruel, and seemingly unstoppable. These hellions can go about their black-hearted tasks masked or unmasked, but they are most chilling when they walk among us or live across the street. W.H. Auden says, "Evil is unspectacular and always human and shares our bed and eats at our table." This device was one that suspense author Agatha Christie used often, as her villains turned out to be denizens of the upper class or pillars of society. When villains are our business leaders, civic leaders, preachers, and the like, they are doubly fascinating. When you create neighbors, family members, or those who share our beds as villains, you've upped the fright factor because of their dangerous proximity.

A villain can be sympathetic or unsympathetic (we'll go into this a little later in chapter nine), but the reader will rarely, if ever, cheer on the villain's goals in the story because these goals are immoral. Here are qualities that are often shared by villains (not all will apply to every villain, but if your villain has only a few these aspects, it's likely that you've created an antagonist, not a villain):

- Villains are consistently bad; their badness is not a random or one-time event.
- Villains have some defining trauma or situation in their backgrounds that started them down a dark path.

- Villains are often alpha males (or females), meaning they tend to be people others defer to.
- Villains have aberrant moral codes and justifications for crimes and murder, such as following the laws of the jungle or tribe, or

BEGIN WITH THE NAME

Plants, animals, objects, places, and people all have names. Naming people and things in your story has a practical purpose because it appeals to the reader's logic and memory. In fiction, we name characters to differentiate them, to suggest their age, social standing, and personality, to make them solid and distinctive, and to signal to readers that the person is worth noting. Generally, the more complicated your character is, the more distinct his or her name should be, keeping in mind that names evoke responses in readers and ignite their imaginations. All fiction writers should collect names in a notebook, starting with the standard method of gathering names by perusing phone books, obituaries, and baby name books.

Take care with creating your characters' names, especially your villain's name, and be careful not to choose a name that works against type. Generally, you wouldn't choose a name for a villain that suggests a softie, nor would you give a good guy a name that has a dark connotation. The best names are suggestive, reflect the genre type, and reflect an era. In J.K. Rowling's Harry Potter series, Voldemort's name is so feared that few people speak it out loud; they instead call him He-Who-Must-Not-Be-Named. Your villain's name should reflect menace, coldness, and strength. Use hard consonants and sounds to suggest menace or other frightening characteristics, like Stark, the villain in Stephen King's *The Dark Half*. Conversely, good guys will have names that suggest goodness or strength, such as J.R.R. Tolkien's Bilbo, Frodo, Sam, Merry, and Pippin.

You are also wise to use names that are suggestive; for example, Romeo suggests romance, Holly Golightly suggests a light-hearted nature, and Scarlett O'Hara suggests a flamboyant beauty. In Dean Koontz's *Forever Odd*, the villainess is named Datura, which reflects her kinkiness, coldness, and cruelty. However, Koontz cleverly has chosen a name with layers of meaning, something fiction writers are always striving for. Datura is a flowering plant that is also called devil's trumpet and angel's trumpet, and there are many myths associated it with it in cultures worldwide. (For more on Koontz's Datura character, see chapter ten.)

twisted notions of honor and justice, such as those espoused by people involved in organized crime.

- Villains often have secrets that they try desperately to conceal.
- Villains are complicated and multi-dimensional.
- Villains are intelligent, because it takes brains to plan crimes and elude capture.
- Villains are typically not afraid of confrontation.
- Villains are out to destroy heroes.
- Villains make choices that are immoral.
- Villains often have a blindness, denial, or lack of awareness of their own darknesses.
- Villains are motivated by either malice or lack of malice to achieve their ends.
- With their acts, villains try to diminish or extinguish goodness, innocence, or spirituality in others.
- Villains hide their operations and crimes, and they absolutely hate to be revealed.
- Villains often have some aspect of narcissism built into their personality makeup.
- Villains are often concerned with their public images, and they carefully orchestrate what people know about them.
- Villains are extremely unpredictable.
- Villains often cannot handle criticism or threats to their power.
- Villains often scapegoat others to protect themselves.
- Villains sacrifice victims to achieve their ends.
- Villains can ignore their victims' humanity.

- Villains can be attractive, charming, and elegant (these characteristics make the villains chillingly effective).

TACTICS OF VILLAINS

Villains don't just walk the walk and talk the talk, they dare to perform the worst acts in order to make the most gains. These acts can include blackmail, torture, theft, and murder. We might want to label them *homo sapiens extremus*; they'll use any means to achieve what they want—and what they want, they want desperately. To accomplish his nefarious goals, a villain often:

- takes extreme risks;
- obsesses about details and a plan of attack;
- plans a drawn-out strategy that challenges him and his opponent;
- lies to cover his tracks;
- uses wealth, physical appearance, or sexual wiles to draw lovers or underlings into his web;
- finds some way to justify hurting others, usually claiming the victim has gotten in his way;
- controls others by using guilt and loyalty;
- acts with kindness or generosity to throw others off balance; and
- plays head games, and plays them well.

CREATING A POTENT VILLAIN

To create a villain, you will need to give him a compelling physicality, distinctive thought and speech patterns that set him apart, realistic primary traits, and complicated motives. As you're creating your villain, shape him to be a worthy opponent for your hero, and start imagining scenes where he'll dominate and stir up chaos. If the story warrants it, create a secret for him. As you write, reveal the villain in increments as a growing and complicated threat. Portray him aspiring to goals that are opposed to the hero's goals, and decide whether he'll be destroyed or escape in the end.

What makes a villain mesmerizing and dreadful are some of the same things that make a hero riveting: charisma, depth, and motivation. Here are some tips for shaping your villain:

- Make your villain complicated and complex. For example, a villain who is charming and brilliant is much more interesting than one who merely is sinister or evil.
- Imbue your villain with fascinating qualities, like a specific philosophy and vision. The reader wants to understand how your villain sees life, and this vision will often be vastly different from the reader's, but sometimes the reader shares some aspect of humanity with the villain.
- Understand your villain's brand of logic and how he thinks.
- Give your villain a particular and interesting skill set. Perhaps he's a locksmith, an expert in gems, a master forger, a scholar, a chemist, a psychiatrist, or a computer hacker.
- Imagine your villain as a child and teen. For many criminals in the real world, often their deviant behaviors and crimes began in childhood. Determine if there were circumstances in your villain's childhood that caused trauma. For example, the villain might have joined a gang as a teen, or been influenced by an uncle who was spending time in Sing Sing for forgery.
- Consider where your villain lives. A condo in a sleek high-rise? A remote castle? A bungalow in an ordinary neighborhood? Often, a truly depraved villain needs privacy for his misdeeds, as well as a means to hide his crimes.
- Decide if your villain has underlings, or if he operates as a lone entity. If he has henchmen, will he allow them to live if they know too much or make mistakes?
- Decide what your villain's bag of tricks includes. Does he drug his victims? Does he use a computer to send a series of threatening and disturbing e-mails? Does he forge documents? Does he use blackmail, threats, or extortion?

- Make certain that your villain is more than capable of taking down your protagonist.
- Make certain that the outcome of your villain's struggle is delayed and uncertain until the last possible moment.

UNSYMPATHETIC VILLAINS

Let's talk about villains whom readers will not feel sympathy toward and, in fact, will often find vile, repulsive, and evil. When an unsympathetic villain is in a story, he naturally causes worry and suspense in the reader because it's understood that he's capable of anything, and that he is a potent threat. These folks are the monsters of our nightmares, our worse fears in human skin, our bogeyman and demons.

These villains are not like ordinary people. They have the wiles of a jungle commando, the ruthlessness of a cornered slum rat, the heart of a Nazi.

A terrific example of an unsympathetic villain is Jape Waltzer of Leif Enger's *Peace Like a River*; even his name instills a shiver of fear. The story begins in Minnesota in the 1960s, when Jeremiah Land, a father of three, stops two young thugs from raping a young woman in a high-school locker room. The thugs retaliate against the Land family, and one night when they sneak into the Land's home, sixteen-year-old Davy, the oldest son, shoots the intruders. After Davy is arrested for their murders, he escapes from jail while awaiting his trial and ends up in the Badlands of South Dakota. This is where he hooks up with Jape Waltzer, who is raising Sara, a girl-child who is to be his wife.

The Land family begins looking for Davy, and when eleven-year-old Reuben, the younger son and narrator of the story, finds him, he also meets Jape, and that's when the reader starts learning about the villain's capabilities. Before Reuben even meets Jape in a hideaway in the foothills of the Badlands, Davy instructs him to call Jape "Mr. Waltzer."

Enger's description of this meeting is a helpful example of how to make a first impression on a reader:

> He was of unimposing height, under six feet. A practical build, big up top, one of these men you realize why it's called a chest—you had the feeling he had all the tools he needed in there and all in working

> order and daily use. His hair was dark and tied back in a short bob, and he had a high forehead and two rapscallion eyebrows—upswept, pointed, and mobile.
>
> "Mm," he muttered. Those brows of his scared me—they were like flipped goatees.

The reader soon learns that Jape is expecting the Apocalypse, that his speech is formal and bizarre, that when Reuben seems to be praying over a meal Jape demands that he thank him instead of God, and that his temper and changing moods are enough to give a person whiplash.

Like the best of villains, the more the reader knows about Jape, the more she fears him. Davy claims that when Waltzer is around, "I just listen close." For example, Reuben learns that Jape once taught Sara a grisly lesson when her foot slipped on the clutch while they were trying to dump a car into a lake; because of her action, his fingers were nearly severed. Here is Jape's solution to the injury:

> ... her penalty for the slipped clutch was being forced to watch Jape Waltzer take a hatchet and lay the ruined fingers across a stump. ... Jape rolled his left sleeve to above the elbow. He laid the hatchet blade first in a saucepan into which he'd uncorked whiskey. Sara he stationed with paper sack on a three-legged stool next to the stump. He took the fingers separately with two clean strokes, pausing to blow after the first but not cursing or making utterance. He sweated plenty but it was only sweat, not blood, nor did his hair turn white or his mood turn permanently for the worse.
>
> He did make Sara dispose of the fingers, though. She had to pick them up in her own and drop them in the paper sack. She didn't want to, but Jape told her to get it done before he was finished or there would be punishment. He was busy at that moment with needle and suture. She picked up the canceled digits and threw them sack and all in the crackling stove.

After it's clear that Jape is capable of taking off his own fingers and uses the incident to terrorize and exert control, the reader wonders what else he's capable of. Although Davy is an exceptional young man, it appears he's in over his head when it comes to tangling with Jape, which leaves the reader leaning in, wondering and worrying what Jape will do next.

If you were to read a book, such as *Peace Like a River*, with a convincing and unsympathetic villain, you should be able to understand what makes him tick and his justifications for his misdeeds. You should also be able to understand the author's reasons for crafting a villain of Jape's magnitude. Enger is writing a story that keeps drawing a line between good and evil, portraying it as an endless cosmic battle with Jape falling on the side of evil and Davy and the rest of the Land family on the side of good.

Jape is a religious zealot who bends Scripture to justify his misdeeds and way of thinking, and he sees himself as a sort of biblical patriarch. He is an opportunistic control freak who feels a huge sense of entitlement, lives by his wits, and has no interest in normalcy. Thus, when he wins Sara in a poker game, he feels entitled to her body and soul. He lives on the run and steals or cons what he needs to survive. When he runs into Davy, who is on the lam, he takes in the young man because it's always helpful to have another strong and smart male around to help out.

As a fiction writer, it can be enormously helpful to analyze a character like Jape and make a list, such as the one in the previous paragraph, of all the things you know about him, including the so-called proofs of his logic and philosophy. In a typical character arc for a moral protagonist, the character might overcome his fatal flaw and become braver, stronger, or more lovable. A villain's character arc, on the other hand, often will reveal him as more depraved and criminal. For example, Jape, who clearly is ruthless, as when he chops off his own fingers, goes on to commit murder by the end of the story. In your own story, knowing the limits your villain will travel to achieve his aims (usually done with a lack of concern for the fallout) will help you create a plausible character arc.

PREDATORY VILLAINS

Some stories call for a villain who is immoral and twisted, yet not completely villainous, but who still causes suffering in others. However, this character type would *not* be classified as an antagonist, and he is not sympathetic. The reason for this is that he has several dark traits, such as his harmful behaviors are usually deliberate (with an antagonist this is not necessarily true) and the harm he causes has traumatic consequences to his victims. This villainous type in fiction and life is predatory and slippery, and he can sniff out weaknesses and vulnerability like predators in the wild can find the weakest animal in the herd. They're often especially adept at toying with another character's emotions and insecurities. So the bottom line for this type of character is their deceitfulness, cunning, and ability to manipulate people's emotions.

A predatory villain will generally only harm a single character in the story, although he might have a history of hurting others. A predator might go to great lengths to conceal his activities—so far so that often other characters are unaware of his activities, thus allowing him to live a life of relative normality. Typically, a predator singles out a particularly vulnerable character for his attentions.

A good example of a predator is Duncan in Sue Miller's *Lost in the Forest*. The novel is set in the vineyards of northern California and tells the story of Daisy, who, in the wake of the tragic death of her stepfather, seeks solace in a damaging love affair with Duncan, a much older man. Daisy is a pre-teen when the novel begins, and she is gangly, plain, and lonely, while her older sister, Emily, is petite, lovely, and popular.

A predator like Duncan works best in a story with a vulnerable character, and Daisy, in the midst of her aloneness, is losing her moral compass. Duncan spots her stealing money in her mother's bookstore, and he uses this knowledge against her as he starts messing with her head. Since he is decades older (which is often another characteristic of predators), he has an extreme advantage.

As for Daisy, the reader learns:

> She felt he offered her a new version of herself, one she more and more carried with her into her real life. She felt uplifted, in a sense; she felt an elevation over the daily ugliness of high school. She was less afraid, less shy. ... And she loved the strange sex, which asked so little of her.

In the Reader's Guide section of *Lost in the Forest*, Miller writes:

> I wanted to have Daisy uniquely vulnerable to the events of her family's life. Her shyness, her unattractiveness at the moment of the story, her greater vulnerability to her parents' divorce and the birth of Theo, her greater devastation at John's death—all those mean that she's very fragile, very in need at exactly the moment when her parents, too, are most fragile and in need. ...

So if you're using a predator in your novel, make certain that his victim has a special vulnerability, and that the predator knows how to exploit it. Perhaps, like Daisy, your character is reeling from a loss while trying to navigate the stormy waters of adolescence. Or, perhaps you'll want to create a con man to prey on lonely widows, or a femme fatale to troll the bars for her next mark. Predators care about other people, as far as they can use them.

TECHNIQUES FOR CREATING MENACE

Now that you've been introduced to several villain types, let's amplify a few techniques for creating a villain who brings maximum drama and menace to a story. Some stories will call for a reader's immediate awareness in the first pages of a villain's handiwork and potential for evil, some stories will tease the reader with the villain's capabilities until midway through the book, or in the second half of the story he'll explode on the scene like a tornado. No matter when the reader gets the first up-close glimpse of the villain, his presence in the story must always be a palpable threat ready to be unleashed.

A GROWING THREAT

A technique to add to your repertoire is to reveal your villain's potential by showing the reader a series of actions and plans that build over the course of the story, accelerating to a fevered pitch until the villain is an inescapable and malevolent menace. Because fiction is ever-threatening, you want to unmask your villain bit by bit, until his ultimate capabilities are exposed in all their raw power near the end. Along with this evolving danger, you'll want to give villains an array of quirks, habits, and obsessions and toss with their dreams of power. Villains are not the fictional version of a get-rich-quick scheme. They are often methodical, patient, and richly embroidered creatures, and you want their capabilities to creep up on a reader the way a heavy fog overcomes a coastal town.

A terrific example of a villain who is depicted as a growing threat is Corky Laputa in Dean Koontz's *The Face*. The first hints of his monstrous abilities come in the opening pages, when he sends a series of carefully wrought threats to Channing Manheim, the biggest box-office draw in Hollywood, also called The Face. This odd series of threats sets the story in motion and introduces the protagonist, Ethan Truman, Manheim's security chief and an ex-cop.

The reader slips into the villain's viewpoint in chapter nine for a more intimate glimpse of his destructiveness and madness, which opens with "Corky Laputa thrived in the rain." On a spree in Studio City dressed in a yellow rain gear and latex gloves, he trips along in the rain, like a modern-day Grinch, scattering a powerful chemical defoliant:

> Corky's mission was not merely to cause destruction. Any fool could wreck things. He intended also to spread dissension, distrust, discord and despair.
>
> Tripping along, he sang "Singin' in the Rain" as he tosses out cyanide-laced dog biscuits. When he spots a mailbox with a Jewish surname, he drops envelopes with swastika designs with two messages: DEATH TO ALL DIRTY JEWS and a second page with a photo of stacked bodies of concentration camp victims imprinted with YOU'RE NEXT.

And we learn he also sends these specially targeted hate missives to Catholics, gun owners, and African Americans.

Corky is an English professor, but his true vocation is anarchy, and he lives to stir up chaos and fear wherever he goes. This is Corky's top layer of mischief, the most benign of his acts, but the reader discovers other layers of aberrant behavior and madness. Later, the reader finds him writing racial epithets on a men's restroom stall in a shopping mall, then flooding the restroom because an anarchist must be dedicated to his mission of wreaking havoc, large and small:

> All these and numerous others, working at different levels, some as destructive as runaway freight trains hurtling off the tracks, others quietly chewing like termites at the fabric of civility and reason, were necessary to cause the current order to collapse into ruin.
>
> If somehow Corky could have carried the black plague without risking his own life, he would have enthusiastically passed that disease to everyone he met by way of sneezes, coughs, touches, and kisses. If sometimes all he could do was flush a cherry bomb down a

> public toilet, he would advance chaos by that tiny increment while he awaited opportunities to do greater dangers.

By the time the reader is clued in that Corky would like to spread the Black Plague, suspense about what will happen next has been set in motion.

The best villains are extraordinarily clever and capable. If your villain is bumbling, you might be creating a farce, which will drain suspense from your story. A villain typically only missteps in the final pages of the story he appears in, and those missteps are tied to his traits, such as his belief that he's invincible. For example, Corky manages to slip into the Los Angeles county morgue, where he has enlisted Roman Castavet, a pathologist, to supply him with body parts for his threats to Manheim. After Corky murders Roman, the reader is keenly aware that Corky can infiltrate places where most mere mortals would fear to tread, and that he uses people for his aims, then ruthlessly tosses them aside. The reader is also aware of his heartlessness, especially when he drives an ice pick into the pathologist's back. In your own story, you'll also need to demonstrate your villain's *lack* of conscience, empathy, or morality. If the reader cannot witness these sorts of acts up close when a villain purposely causes harm, the reader cannot believe in the villain's threat to the story world.

In writing your villain, keep in mind that he doesn't stumble into badness; when a villain is in a story, he is implementing a campaign, so make sure that your villain lays equally elaborate plans for his wicked endeavors. For instance, Corky uses a fake ID to enter the building, wears rain gear to hide his face from the building's cameras, and wears latex gloves to avoid leaving prints; he had also practiced the ice pick murder on a CPR dummy at home.

As the bodies of Corky's victims start piling up, the reader also learns that Corky was responsible for the brutal murder of his mother. But, like many villains, he manages to justify his loathsome acts because "anarchy could be a demanding faith." Obviously, Koontz is going out on a limb in creating a character who kills his own mother, but in this vein, you'll want to show (in a flashback or in the front story, depending on the demands of your story) the moment in life when your villain slips the bonds of normal humanity. This is always some immoral act that most of us would likely not even entertain in a fantasy.

And, as if the reader isn't already worried about Corky's capacity for destruction, Corky kills his lover and burns down her house, and he kidnaps a fellow professor and keeps him starved, drugged, and tormented for months in his home.

As you structure your plot, you'll want to create a growing threat, and by the midpoint or two-thirds point in the story, make certain that the reader understands at least some of the villain's intentions and the people who are in his pathway. If the villain's intentions are left to be unraveled only in the final acts, then the story isn't exploiting all its potential for nail-biting suspense. So, while you might not want to expose all your villain's plans, you'll want to at least foreshadow or hint at them. When you have a villain in the story, he needs to establish causality—a sort of trajectory of harm that is tied to his motivation.

IN HIS CLUTCHES

This leads us to another key technique in creating villains that sizzle with menace: throw a sympathetic character or characters into his clutches. In *The Face*, the sympathetic and vulnerable characters in Corky's crosshairs are Manheim's son, Fric, Manheim's head of security, Ethan, and Ethan's cop buddy, Hazard.

Through scenes in the present woven with backstory, the reader comes to care about each of the vulnerable characters. Then, as evidence of Corky's cleverness and madness pile up, the reader worries more and more about the fate of the good guys.

Fric is one of those kids you want to take home with you. Lonely, bright, and engaging, the boy often rattles around alone in the huge mansion staffed by dozens of servants (an aspect that makes him more vulnerable). When Koontz crafts a scene where Fric is hiding in a secret closet and is near death from an asthma attack because he can't quite reach his inhaler, the suspense is as taut as a tightrope. In your own story, taking a cue from Koontz, demonstrate a character's vulnerability in action, not exposition. It's one thing to be told a character is asthmatic; it's quite another to watch him almost choke to death.

In many suspense stories, the plot is actually a race against time; whenever possible, cast more than one sympathetic character into the path of the villain and have time running out. Also, imbue the characters that are going up against the villain with spiritual, physical, and emotional wounds and weaknesses that the reader can relate to, and then set the collision course in motion.

UNPREDICTABLE

Another technique to create a menacing villain is to make him unpredictable and slippery as an eel. One of the villain's primary jobs in a story is to keep the reader guessing and on edge. In *The Face*, it seems that Koontz gives away all Corky's tricks in the first two-thirds of the story. However, in the final chapters of the novel, Koontz explodes a series of surprises and daring exploits.

All novel-length fiction contains a series of surprises—some of them foreshadowed, some of the sprung with the deftness of a conjurer. And the evil machinations of villains are the perfect means to spring surprises. As you write scenes in which your villain is going to act out a particular exploit, consider the worst possible outcome for the protagonist or innocent characters in a scene. Whenever possible, you want to use that dreadful alternative if the plot and the level of violence in the story warrants it.

George R.R. Martin's A Song of Fire and Ice fantasy series is swarming with villains. In fact, it's hard to choose the worst of the lot, as royal families, knights, sailors, soldiers, and commoners act out greed, lust, and depravity. It is a sprawling series, with royal families vying for power of a kingdom that was once held by a single king, while a greater danger is encroaching on the kingdom from the north. In the third book of the series, *A Storm of Swords*, alliances shift and change like the wind. In the north, Robb Stark has declared himself king after his father was murdered. As in old Europe, power is consolidated by marriage, and so he promises to marry a daughter of Walder Frey, Lord of the Crossing.

Frey is an old man now wed to his eighth wife and known for his wiles and ill temper. When Robb falls in love and marries Jeyne, a woman from another family, the Freys withdraw their support for the king of the north. To appease him, Robb's uncle, Edmure, agrees to marry one of Frey's daughters. With an entourage of knights, guards, and soldiers, the Starks travel to the wedding at the Freys' castle near the raging Trident River.

Here is the reader's first glimpse of Walder Frey:

> Gout and brittle bones had taken their toll of old Walder Frey. They found him propped up in his high seat with a cushion beneath him and an ermine robe across his lap. His chair was black oak, its back carved into the semblance of two stout towers joined by an arched bridge, so massive that its embrace turned the old man into a grotesque child. There was something of the vulture about Lord Walder, and rather more of the weasel. His bald head, spotted with age, thrust out from his scrawny shoulders on a long pink neck. Loose skin dangled beneath his receding chin, his eyes were runny and clouded, and his toothless mouth moved constantly, sucking as the empty air as a babe sucks at his mother's breast.

As the scene goes on, Robb apologizes to Frey and the women of his house for marrying Jeyne instead of a Frey, as had been arranged. The reader witnesses how Frey is vulgar, bad-tempered, and randy, and how he might still be holding a grudge. Edmure meets his bride-to-be, and the guests retire to their rooms in the castle.

In the next scene, the wedding is in full swing, and Robb's mother, Catelyn, observes that while Frey was miserly when it came to feeding his guests, ale, mead, and wine are now flowing as fast as the Trident. When it comes time for a bawdy ritual where the bride and groom are escorted to their rooms to consummate the marriage, a fight breaks out. But it's no ordinary drunken brawl. Instead, it turns into a slaughter with a surprise attack by an armed guard, and a longsword is twisted through King Robb's heart. In the frenzy, his knights, guards, and army are mostly wiped out in the surprise attack, his body is desecrated, his mother is stabbed and tossed into the river to mock her family's burial rituals, and his uncle is taken hostage.

Thereafter, the event is known throughout the kingdom as the "Red Wedding," and it seems that madness reigns in the kingdom and civilization is doomed.

While the massacre was sprung as a surprise both on wedding guests and on the reader, Martin had foreshadowed the event in earlier chapters when Robb Stark had married Jeyne. But like the craftiest writers, Martin's foreshadowing also whispers about Frey's black heart, and his actions showed that although old, he was still capable of cunning and revenge. His dastardly plan also shows that a villain's actions always have consequences, because after Robb's death, the playing field in the entire kingdom is drastically altered.

In your own story, you want to spring a series of events that the reader doesn't anticipate but will find, upon looking back, that they make perfect sense for the story. This looking back and recognizing the plausibility of events is aided by foreshadowing—the hinting about the future. In this particular case, the foreshadowing was about Frey's traits and history. Foreshadowing is a device that requires a fine touch, and it is easy to overdo. When you read an author of Martin's caliber, it can be helpful to pay attention to the *proportions* of these literary devices, where and when they're placed in the series, and how they affect outcomes.

EVIL PERSONIFIED: SUPER VILLAINS

Super villains are most often found in comics, graphic novels, thrillers, science fiction, fantasy, horror, and action movies. More often found in pop culture than literary fiction, super villains are drawn to be highly imaginative and dangerous.

Super villains are unsympathetic and unredeemable; they are evil personified, and they will often have multiple victims. A super villain rarely, if ever, shows remorse, compassion, or empathy; Voldemort from J.K. Rowling's Harry Potter series is a good example of a super villain. Super villains require a hero with extreme traits to go up against him. In the television series *24*, Kiefer Sutherland's character Agent Jack Bauer often goes toe-to-toe with super villains, as do the film characters James Bond and Indiana Jones.

In the comic-book world, Batman faces super villains such as the Riddler and the Joker; Superman battles super villain Lex Luthor. Mephisto, a super villain from Marvel Comics, once said, "The greatest joy in doing evil is to be rewarded by the sight of those who suffer its consequence!" The traits that we've ascribed to villains will also apply to super villains, but turn it up a notch to create *homo sapiens extremus diabolical* (although in some genres, they're not strictly human). In terms of common traits, super villains:

- are antisocial in that they are trying to control or destroy some aspect of society.

- are dangerous to anyone who gets in their way, but also to ordinary people who might simply cross their path.
- cause suffering to more than one character.
- are almost always sociopaths (see chapter seven).
- seem unstoppable until the final scenes.
- often use brains rather than brawn to achieve their aims.
- operate in the shadows.
- have complex motivations and backgrounds, and can equally stem from a privileged background or an impoverished one.
- begin their crime sprees early in life, sometimes in adolescence.
- are often vengeful and enjoy retaliations.
- have a purpose for being evil, usually to acquire wealth or power.
- loathe the heroes and personalize their relationships.
- often have secret lairs and access to the accoutrements of crime.
- sometimes have something reptilian or monstrous about their physical appearance.
- have a serious flaw, such as hatred of a certain race, hatred of goodness, or hatred of women.
- are cold-blooded or blasé about killing or hurting others.

Contrasting traits are often part of a writer's game plan with drawing a hero and super villain. For example, a hero might be attractive, a super villain, not so much. Harrison Ford as Indiana Jones brings a kind of boyish charm and sass to the role that contrasts nicely to the dark mannerisms of Paul Freeman's as Rene Belloq, a rival archeologist and one of the super villains in the series.

One pitfall in using an über-powerful villain in a story is that it can be easy to resort to a *deus ex machina* for the hero to win or escape. The modern version of this device is that the hero will suddenly pull a gadget out of his back pocket that allows him to dig his way out of a shallow grave, or a homeless guy will stumble into the burial site and rescue him, or he'll latch onto a low-flying news helicopter that just happens to be overhead when he's stuck atop a burning building. The point is that the hero must save himself, not be rescued by the writer's ploys or contrivances.

If you're writing a super villain, you've got a big challenge. You want him to be a huge threat in the story, and to be equipped with wattage and extra skills or strengths, but somehow he must be somewhat realistically drawn. As a starting place in creating any bad guy, but especially a super villain in a story, you might want to begin by making a list of all the characteristics that annoy you in real-life people. Then make a list of the characteristics that frighten you in real people you've known. Lastly, make a list of frightening aspects of powerful people you don't know, but are familiar with, such as high-ranking politicians, world leaders, corporate executives, and billionaires. With these lists, start imagining the backstory and trajectory of such a character. Was he an orphan who felt picked on in school? Was he always interested in power? Or did he come from fairly normal origins?

Go deeper and imagine the character interacting with others in their daily lives. Too often, writers draw villains and super villains as entities completely set apart from humanity. But the people around them can add to their mystique, depth, and prowess. How will he attract followers or henchmen? By paying well or convincing others of his cause? Will his minions be afraid of him or be constantly trying to curry his favor?

After you've played around with shaping the character, imagine ways that you can bring him to life with freshness and verve. For example, you won't want to give your super villain an echoing, mad laugh—it's been done. Perhaps he can be a dandy, or has a penchant for a certain breed of dog, or only eats specific, exotic foods, or collects rare art. Like villains, super villains must surprise the reader not just with their lust for power and what they'll do to achieve it, but also with their depths and quirks and fascinating mannerisms.

CREATING THE VILLAIN'S LAIR

Another terrifying aspect of a villain can be his lair. While a lair can exist in the midst of a sprawling city or the snug confines of a small town,

WEAPONS AND SKILLS

Villains are resourceful, and besides their natural talents, they often have an array of weapons and skills at their disposal to make them unstoppable. They can also have an enhanced physique, martial arts skills, and a strong tolerance for pain. When you create a villain, it's always important to give him an edge in the battlefield (even if the battlefield is a corporate boardroom). The more you know about the villain's bag of tricks and talents, the easier it is to create a hero who can outsmart him. Here are some ideas of things to arm your villain with:

- Armor
- Robot or other techno-helpers at his disposal
- Technical gadgets à la James Bond
- Poisons
- A staff of slavish servants or henchmen
- An army of lawyers
- Photographic memory
- Armed car
- Gas pellets
- Hand grenades

Or perhaps your villain has a unique skill set that makes *him* a weapon:

- Escape artist
- Computer hacker
- Alchemist abilities
- Natural athlete
- Martial arts expertise
- Uncanny marksman
- Ex-military man who can kill with his hands
- Gifted inventor

often a villain's lair is remote or hidden. Sometimes, when a villain has a particularly evil or criminal agenda, it's necessary that he occupy a sort of chamber of horrors, or a remote outpost. Most often, wherever he lives, it is a place where he is invulnerable and at the top of his powers. A lair might be a place equipped with the latest technology and gadgets, it might include a small arsenal, it might be heavily fortified, or it might be a place to hide loot or torture captives.

Since a character's place of residence is always a great way to reveal his personality, you can especially exploit this fact with a villain. It might be gleaming, sterile, and high-tech, indicating someone who is fastidious. Or it might be more of a blank canvas, proving how the villain is always hiding aspects of himself. It might be an old house inherited from the villain's family, housing ugly secrets and memories.

In Laurie R. King's *The Game*, Mary Russell and Sherlock Holmes meet a worthy adversary, and the details of place, including the villain's lair, are so well researched and vivid that the reader can smell the curry simmering on the peat fire.

The villain is Jimmy, the maharaja of mythical Khanpur, and the novel unfolds near the Tibetan border of India in 1924. A skilled undercover operative for the British government has vanished, and it appears he was last seen in Khanpur. In this excerpt, notice how the maharaja's kingdom makes him conveniently out of reach of the British authorities:

> As the mountains encircled Khanpur itself, so high, warm-red walls, built for military purpose, now gave shelter to a garden, several acres of closely planned and maintained lawn, flower, and tree. Its centre was half an acre of lotus pond with playing fountain and water birds; a trio of tame gazelles in jeweled harnesses tip-toed across the close-trimmed lawn sloping up from the water; bright birds sang in the trees that rose half as high as the three-storey walls. …

Stories require that, at some point, the protagonist and villain intersect, and it works best if there is some kind of intimacy involved. So Mary enters his lair as a guest at the maharaja's opulent fortress. The first night, she observes an obscene feast of endless courses; the following day, she joins him on a wild boar hunt and barely survives to tell the tale. But the maharaja's handsome façade of suave manners, authority, and sophistication begins to crack soon after Mary's arrival, and he becomes ruthless, reckless, and unsportsmanlike.

It soon becomes apparent that something sinister lurks behind his wealth and nobility and the great walls of his lair, and as *The Game* progresses, Mary becomes increasingly suspicious of the maharaja. Along with her traveling companions and an exotic assortment of "guests," Mary is discovering they're actually prisoners of a man whose collections run from the exotic to the macabre. In one chilling scene, the maharaja kills a monkey in his zoo, and the reader begins to wonder if every person, animal, and object exists to amuse or enrage him.

King continually depicts her villain through his possessions. She lavishes almost three pages on his "toy room," a macabre collection inherited from his grandfather that includes mechanical toys, waxworks of human figures, a mechanical tiger that roars, and taxidermy displays of rodents dressed for a formal ball, the Ascot races, and a night club:

> ... their furry bodies graced with strips of costume and feathers perkily jutting from their heads. The fourth case held eight infant piglets, of the pale domesticated kind, gathered in a Victorian conservatory around a laden tea table; something about their attitudes made it seem a cruel parody of society at the time—English society, that is.

Thinking of the example above, imagine the possibilities with your villain's lair. First, you'll want to equip it with some accruements that increase the creep factor in the story. There needs to be something about the place that makes the reader edgy, some aspect of the environment that hints at a being who is abnormal or evil, as with the maharaja's toy room.

Second, the villain will always have the advantage in his lair, just as we all have in our own homes. This advantage could come from the fact that his henchmen are hanging out at his lair, or that he has a hidden exit or safe room. As you plot, this advantage might make the villain cocky or overconfident in his lair, a factor that could lead to his downfall.

Third, when innocent characters (victims or the protagonist) are lured into the villain's lair, their vulnerability increases, as does the tension and suspense in those scenes. Make sure you place your sympathetic characters in places and situations where they're ill at ease, ill-equipped, and off-kilter. You don't want your protagonist walking into an unfamiliar place feeling like he's king of the hill.

Fourth, a villain's lair is a great place for a showdown or a dark-night-of-the-soul moment. The showdown will have extra suspense because the place might appear inescapable, or the reader understands that the villain has an advantage there.

A dark-night-of-the-soul moment is often staged just before the climax, when the protagonist is at his lowest point. In this moment, he feels that all is lost, or he is wondering if the cost of the quest has been worth it. A familiar example of this moment is in the film version of *The Wizard of* Oz. Dorothy, played by Judy Garland, has been dragged to the witch's castle by the flying monkeys, then locked in a tower room. The scene begins when Dorothy and her friends are creeping through the Haunted Forest, passing a sign that says, "I'd turn back if I were you." Then comes the long camera shot of the castle—a lonely, gloomy, impenetrable-looking fortress. With time running out, Dorothy weeps for her Aunt Em and her home in Kansas, and she is terrified as the minutes tick off her fate. In these moments, the reader sees the protagonist exposed and usually weakened by the story's events. If your protagonist is facing these terrible moments in the villain's lair, you'll increase the drama of the scene.

TIGHTEN THE NOOSE

Let's talk about more general techniques that will help you squeeze the maximum wattage from featuring a villain in your story. All fiction writers are faced with the task of revealing how people act when impaled by danger, dilemmas, and general misery. When you have a villain in the story, you've amped up this basic storytelling formula. The tension and suspense that a reader feels comes from worrying how the situation will resolve in the end, and also about how the protagonist will act when pushed against a wall, weakened and stripped raw by the story's events and the villain's torments. As we've seen in the previous examples, if the protagonist ends up in a villain's lair, this situation increases the reader's worry.

However, there are lots of ways to amp up the suspense with a villain in the story. First, don't wait too long in the story to introduce the villain. Even if the reader doesn't meet him in the opening chapters, the reader must witness his handiwork, feel his influence, or become aware of a growing threat.

Second, make certain that the story has a cauldron—a place, family, or situation that is inescapable—so that the villain and protagonist are glued together while the conflict simmers away until it boils over. Another thing to remember is that you should avoid using a coincidence to link your protagonist and villain together. If you have a cauldron in the story, you don't need to rely on coincidence or chance meetings. Now, sometimes it's unavoidable to use a chance meeting in a story, but generally a protagonist interacts with a villain because his career forces this meeting or some other inescapable factor of the cauldron. Thus, a cop or detective would have a likelihood of meeting a villain, as would people in other professions that typically encounter criminals.

However, if a villain is, for example, a stalker or sexual predator, the protagonist might encounter the villain because the villain *chooses* her. If the villain chooses the protagonist or victim in your story, try to establish a rationale for this—perhaps your character fits into a specific physical profile, or she reminds him of his younger sister who died. Or perhaps a sexual predator is watching children who attend a school near his house, and he spots a child who always walks home alone from school. The point here is that, as a writer, you try to reinforce the cauldron—make the collision of villain and protagonist inevitable and plausible.

No matter how the protagonist becomes entangled, make certain that you develop an increasingly personal relationship between the protagonist and villain thereafter. This doesn't mean that they sit down for lunch and a nice chat, but rather that they have opposing desires, and the protagonist is forced to resolve something and to face the flaws that are revealed because of the interactions. As your story builds, the villain needs to increasingly occupy your protagonist's thoughts and emotions. When a villain is in a story, the protagonist cannot go about on his merry way. He needs to be preoccupied, and possibly obsessed, with somehow defeating the villain.

Keep asking yourself what else can go wrong for your protagonist and secondary characters, and then keep escalating the threats. Once you plan the villain's opening salvo, or first proof that he's dangerous, keep asking yourself how else the villain can continue to torment other characters. Will the villain threaten the protagonist's family? Will the villain interfere with his career, put his job at risk? Will he kidnap the protagonist? Kidnap his girlfriend, wife, child? Steal his identity and abscond money from his bank account? Ruin his credit? Slip drugs into his drink? Make a series of threatening phone calls? Slash his tires? Will the authorities believe the protagonist when he tries to explain the villain's growing threat?

While the reader wants to see, feel, and hear the ramifications of the villain's actions on vulnerable characters, be careful that you don't spend too much time on reactions. Yes, pain or threats have ramifications, but after a character is harmed, he should be compelled to his next action. For example, if a villain uses a stun gun on the protagonist, the next time they meet the protagonist will be more wary—he'll try to keep more distance between them, or he'll struggle to disarm the villain straightaway. Or, if your villain kidnaps your protagonist's child, the protagonist might react with a mixture of rational and irrational behavior. Maybe he'll endanger himself by slipping into the villain's lair. Maybe he'll decide to raise money for the ransom demand. Maybe he'll decide not to involve the authorities. The point is, when a protagonist reacts to a villain, it has to be through actions—some logical, some desperate—not simply by rehashing events with other characters or licking his wounds. Pain must cause actions that, in turn, cause more events—the fictional equivalent to dominoes toppling.

Remembering that suspense always has a component of dread in it, consider harming or killing off at least one sympathetic character at or before the midpoint in the story. J.K. Rowling kills off characters throughout her Harry Potter series, sometimes in the opening scenes to depict how Voldemort and his followers dispose of anyone who get in their way, or in climatic scenes to build the horror and danger in the series. Like many stories, the Harry Potter series is about the struggle between good and evil, and when good characters are killed off in the end of a book, naturally readers will buy the next book in the series because they need to know the final outcome of this matchup. If you're not writing the sort of story where murders occur, remember that violence and the threat of violence, as well as threatening losses, always put a reader on edge.

Another technique that works in some stories is to feature the villain's viewpoint from time to time. Mary Higgens Clark used this formula often in her romantic suspense stories. Usually, the reader will not spend as much time in the villain's viewpoint, but the reader likes to know things about the villain that the protagonist doesn't know.

AVOIDING CLICHÉS

A writer walks a fine line between creating a believable and compelling villain who represents a major threat in the story, and one who is based on stereotypes and clichés. One of the reasons that villains are so difficult to write is that they have often been thinly drawn or depicted as clichés throughout the history of storytelling. Even the classic villains from timeless children's tales are typically not assigned motives, or, if they are, their motives tend to lack complexity. For example, in the classic fairy tale *Snow White and the Seven Dwarfs*, the Queen tries to murder Snow White out of jealousy and extreme vanity, but this motive is simplistic. It's likely that the Queen is also trying to hold on to and consolidate her power, and Snow White threatens it. In fact, the protagonist should always somehow threaten the villain. Snow White's youth, beauty, and goodness are a threat. If you can make the protagonist's threat credible, then the relationship between the protagonist and the villain will be more realistic and less clichéd.

Besides our early exposure to fairy tales and Disney movies, many writers have also been exposed to the villains of comic series. With names like Death-Stalker, Bushwacker, Mr. Fear, Shotgun, Mr. Sinister, Malice, and Sabertooth, these villains creep into a story on the devil's own breath. They also aren't a subtle bunch. While most Marvel Comics villains have a backstory, they are often omnipotent, or nearly so. My point here is that unless you're writing about a super villain who will appear in a comic or graphic novel, you might need to erase your influences from comics and fairy tales because contemporary readers long for sophisticated and multifaceted villains.

Other clichés exist in fiction—the evil corporate tycoon who wants to take over an industry; the religious zealot who needs unthinking followers and absolute authority; the blood-thirsty warrior who will kill anyone who opposes him in order to win; the dissolute overlord who demands complete allegiance; the mad scientist who misuses his inventions; the corrupt politician who is lining his pocket.

To avoid your villains becoming clichés, it can be helpful to keep the following points in mind:

- **Villains often express what is best and worst in humanity.** It might seem odd to lump them under "best," but consider how clever, exacting, and determined villains can be. Imagine if they'd channel all that talent into creating orphanages or other good works, instead of pursuing their nefarious goals. A villain's energy, talents, and will are always impressive, no matter if his goals and means of achieving them are horrific.

- **Readers need to understand how a villain justifies his actions.** Because villains are often not sane, this requires the writer to cultivate an understanding of psychology and the criminal mind. Has he held a life-long grudge? Has he been overlooked for a major promotion or spurned by a lover? Is he so delusional that he wants to do whatever it takes to rule his kingdom, or the world? Remember that sometimes villains are in denial about who they really are; they won't necessarily see themselves as crazy, misguided, greedy, or evil.

- **If a villain acts or reacts with extreme violence, it's best to foreshadow it in early scenes.** Earlier, we discussed how foreshadowing helps make surprises plausible in fiction, but I want to stress that when a surprise is a murder or other violent acts, at times you want to prepare the reader for the villain's capabilities. In a suspense or thriller, the reader often first becomes acquainted with the villain's capabilities early in the story because there is typically a corpse and the story will be about tracking down the murderer. Such a story will often feature a villain who might kill again and needs to be stopped, or a villain who is on some kind of crime spree. Introducing his crimes early on is another form of foreshadowing.

- **Show how your villain evolves as the story progresses.** As a character evolves, often his motivations change or become increasingly personal. This might mean that your villain becomes desperate, or that he becomes even more cunning in his actions. Or, perhaps he merely wants to achieve

ROGUE'S GALLERY

When it comes to villains, it seems that there is so little time, and so many bad guys. Villains have existed in literature since the first "once upon a time" was uttered. Why? Because the world is scary, and nothing is scarier than another person out to get us. Here are some examples of these bad-to-the-bone villains:

- Hannibal Lector, *Red Dragon* and *The Silence of the Lambs* by Thomas Harris
- Blue Duck, *Lonesome Dove* by Larry McMurtry
- Gollum, *The Lord of the Rings* by J.R.R. Tolkien
- Henry F. Potter, played by Lionel Barrymore in the film *It's a Wonderful Life*
- Jadis, the White Witch, *The Lion, the Witch and the Wardrobe* by C.S. Lewis
- Procrustes, Greek mythology
- Jack Torrance, *The Shining* by Stephen King
- Anton Chigurh, *No Country for Old Men* by Cormac McCarthy
- Mrs. Danvers, *Rebecca* by Daphne du Maurier
- Dr. No and Auric Goldfinger, James Bond series by Ian Fleming
- Marquise de Merteuil and Vicomte de Valmont, *Les Liaisons Dangereuses* by Pierre Choderlos de Laclos
- Victor Ippolitovich Komarovsky, *Dr. Zhivago* by Boris Pasternak

his ends—perhaps knocking off a bank—in the beginning of a story, but then by the end of the story, he wants to kill the detective who is pursuing him. Or, at first the villain wants to take over a company, but then he wants to kill his rivals.

- **Avoid using capes, cloaks, top hats and all the sort of Snidely Whiplash accoutrements that spell c-l-i-c-h-é.** Beware of always depicting villains with sharp features. Think of how an actor like Jude Law, with his handsome, boyish face, can be equally sinister and compellingly attractive.

Beware, too, of using sinister laughter and angry facial expressions. A villain who is composed and nonplussed, à la Hannibal Lecter, is much more sinister than one who loses it at the least provocation. If your villain has facial scars, you'll need to justify their presence in his backstory, not simply slash them down his cheek because scars make him seem scary.

- **Avoid creating a haughty demeanor or voice, because this too has become a cliché.** The same goes for a diabolical smile, sneers, and a wardrobe of all black. And if you're creating a femme fatale who is really a black widow, she doesn't necessarily need to be a curvaceous brunette. A Southern belle makes a terrific villain, as does a corporate lawyer, a buttoned-up librarian, or a principal of a girl's school who is actually on the lam.

Readers want to both fear and respect your villain. The threat to your hero must be credible and real, because if the threat from the villain isn't terrifying and his actions aren't pressing, the reader loses respect for the hero. Also, don't orchestrate the plot so that the villain screws up so that the protagonist triumphs; the protagonist should somehow outsmart the villain or win because he's more desperate or has more will or desire.

A villain can be a petty crook, a mastermind, a mercenary, or a ninja, but when you include a real bad ass in your story, you must do so with verve and originality. It's likely he'll commit despicable acts and harbor unhealthy obsessions. It's likely that you'll feel uncomfortable imagining just how far he'll go to achieve his sinister goals. If he is a megalomaniacal despot or a bored aristocrat who turned to crime to ease his world-weariness, you must understand his background that shaped him. If you're writing horror or graphic novels, often a villain is seemingly omnipotent or demonic, or he might be a mass-murderer or killer-for-hire. No matter your genre or your villain's makeup, he must always be a person the reader has never met before and would never want to meet in real life. As you construct your plot, remember that the climax in a story that contains a villain will always feature a smackdown and be the only ending possible for what has come before.

CHAPTER SEVEN

Sociopaths: Ice in Their Veins

Imagine—if you can—not having a conscience, none at all, no feelings of guilt or remorse no matter what you do, no limiting sense of concern for the well-being of strangers, friends, or even family members. Imagine no struggles with shame, not a single one in your whole life, no matter what kind of selfish, lazy, harmful, or immoral action you had taken. And pretend that the concept of responsibility is unknown to you, except as a burden others seem to accept without question, like gullible fools.

—MARTHA STOUT, PH.D., *THE SOCIOPATH NEXT DOOR*

Everyone has a bogeyman—the real or imagined person whom he never wants to tangle with. Some are criminals, terrorists, or murderers and earn our darkest dread, but some are creeps who live down the block or sit in the next cubical. They repulse, intrigue, and terrify. As characters in fiction, they can star in the villain role and can be petty criminals, serial killers, or heartless despots destroying the lives of their citizens in their quest for power. In this chapter, we're going to talk about a subset of villains who bring so much chaos into a story that it will always ignite around them: sociopaths. Sociopaths come in all sizes and shapes—they are teenagers, men, women, grandmothers, politicians, cops, and mobsters. There are also children who are without a conscience, and will likely grow up to spread havoc as they go through life.

Properly classified, this type of person possesses an *antisocial personality disorder*, but for our purposes, we're going to refer to them simply as sociopaths. Sociopaths have ice in their veins and, like the Grinch, possess hearts much too small. Coupled with a lack of conscience, and sometimes a propensity for crime, sociopaths make terrific villains in fiction, and the worst-case scenario for a spouse, family

THE CRIMINAL FACTOR

In fiction, a sociopath is often a criminal or serial killer. In real life, a criminal might be a sociopath, but this certainly is not always the case; a typical criminal is a person who is sane but ignores what is right and moral. A criminal might simply like shortcuts or was born into a mob family and has witnessed firsthand the lifestyle and payout. After all, why struggle to gain a four-year degree when you can boost cars, brew up meth, or work as the muscle for a loan shark? It's really simple for many criminals—crime pays more than regular jobs, and modern society offers lots of opportunities for scams, such as hacking into computer systems for credit card numbers.

Since the beginning of humankind, there have been criminals. There have been famous criminals throughout America's history; some have even become folk heroes, like Jesse James, Al Capone, Lucky Luciano, and Butch Cassidy. Then there have been criminals, particularly murders and rapists, who clearly are mentally ill and became infamous, such as Charles Manson, Ed Gein, Jeffrey Dahmer, and the Boston Strangler.

Also, let's clarify that in fiction, not all villains are criminals. In previous chapters, we've noted that villains most often have a strong need for power or control, and they commit sinister acts while possessing less-than-stellar moral values. And while they can be impossible to live or work with, this doesn't always make them criminals.

A villain might be the protagonist's rival for love, a job, or respect, but a key difference that separates a villain from an antagonist is his intentions. Villains always aim to cause harm, while the fallout from an antagonist's actions can be unintended. Examples of villains who aren't criminals include Big Nurse in Ken Kesey's *One Flew Over the Cuckoo's Nest*—you wouldn't want to be hospitalized in her ward, but it's likely that a court of law would not find her villainous actions illegal—and Alec D'Uberville in Thomas Hardy's *Tess of the D'Ubervilles*, who is a villain because he takes advantage of Tess and ruins her reputation, but he also cares about her and her family, which makes him an unusual villain.

member, or enemy in real life. Another factor that makes this type so fascinating is that besides their lack of remorse, they are rarely inclined to stop their harmful behaviors.

PSYCHO, PSYCHOPATH, SOCIOPATH: WHAT'S IN A NAME

Sometimes the terms *psychopath* and *sociopath* are used interchangeably. However, the term used by the psychiatric community is *antisocial personality disorder*. This classification comes from the American Psychiatric Association's *Diagnostic and Statistical Manual of Mental Disorders.* This means that people exhibiting antisocial or asocial traits can be identified by their behaviors or patterns of behaviors that are at odds with society's norms.

Also, sometimes people bandy about the terms *psycho*, *psychopath*, and *psychotic* interchangeably, so let's make another important distinction. A person who is psychotic is not in touch with reality, whereas a sociopath is. People who are psychotic can suffer from delusions, hallucinations, extreme obsessions, and other disturbed states of mind. If they break the law, sometimes a court will determine that they're not guilty by reason of insanity, and they sometimes will be sent to a psychiatric facility instead of prison.

On the other hand, people who display antisocial behaviors are usually rational and often have a complicated strategy and rationalization for their behaviors, legal or not. They know right from wrong and the real from the imagined, but they choose self-serving and sometimes illegal behaviors. It is a character disorder, while *psychosis* means the person has disordered thoughts, impulses, memories, and ability to interpret reality.

The main thing to keep in mind is that people, real or fictional, who possess antisocial personalities are typically narcissistic, amoral, and impulsive, and they chronically engage in antisocial behavior. Thus, if your character, whom everyone knows as a decent guy, kills his wife's lover in a fit of rage, then feels intense remorse as he's hauled off to jail, he would not fit under this classification. So, although a person can engage in acts that appear to be antisocial, like murder, it doesn't mean that he fits the classification of anti-social personality disorder. A lack of conscience and empathy will always be the chief characteristics of a sociopath.

Psychologist and researcher Dr. Robert Hare has spent four decades studying deviant behaviors and has created a checklist of twenty factors that indicate a person's psychopathy. In fact, police departments and organizations often use his list of criteria (some of which is included under "Characteristics of Sociopaths" below) to screen job applicants. His work is a terrific resource for writers.

In the DSM, the criteria for being a sociopath is that the person exhibits chronic behaviors in these areas: exhibiting anti-social behaviors before adulthood; having problems in school or the workplace; engaging in one or more anti-social behaviors; and having problems forming relationships.

Finally, although at times the terms *sociopath* and *psychopath* are used interchangeably, some experts use the term *sociopath* to indicate that the person's personality disorder evolved because of environmental or social forces.

CHARACTERISTICS OF SOCIOPATHS

It cannot be said too often: Sociopaths are dangerous—make that cobra-bite-in-the-jugular dangerous. Experts claim that about 4 percent of the population consists of sociopaths, so your chance of running into one in your lifetime is pretty high. And contrary to most beliefs, they are not all sitting in prison or swashbuckling along on a one-person crime spree. For the record, about 20 percent of the prison population is made up of sociopaths, and they account for about 50 percent of the most serious crimes, such as murder, extortion, and kidnapping. Sociopaths can look like perfect family men and can head up companies or church committees, but make no mistake, they are predators. Whatever role they play, they play for their own gain. And they play to win.

When a sociopath is also a criminal or achieves power, the results are incendiary and tragic, as Ted Bundy's murder sprees prove. The despots from Pol Pot to Hitler who have ruled and ruined countries prove what happens when a sociopathic madman gains power.

Remember that, for the most part, sociopaths will look and act normal, and they can be among the most charming and entertaining people you'll meet. Remember, too, that they are not necessarily involved in criminal activities, and that sometimes they are able to create or find environments where aggressive behaviors, such as a need to control others, are tolerated or even admired (think Gordon Gekko, played by Michael Douglas, in the film *Wall Street*). Here are the chief characteristics of sociopaths (keep in mind, though, that to be classified as a sociopath, a person doesn't need to exhibit all of these behaviors—but he will always be habitually dishonest, grandiose, and parasitic):

- Few or no emotional attachments
- Glibness and superficial charm
- Narcissism or grandiose sense of self
- Need to dominate, control, and conquer
- An unwillingness to take responsibility for illegal or harmful acts, or for the pain caused to others
- Aggressive
- Secretive and possibly paranoid
- Impulsive
- Difficulty controlling behavior
- Lacking in remorse, shame, or guilt
- Unable to honor financial obligations
- Failure to adapt to society's rules and laws
- Tendency to blame others and look for scapegoats
- Inability to learn from mistakes
- Lacking a realistic life plan
- A risk- or thrill-seeker
- Desire to dominate and win
- Promiscuous, or unable to be monogamous
- Tendency to camouflage or masquerade lifestyle

- The belief that they are above the law and that other people are their inferiors

Some sociopaths are covetous and will try to steal, besmirch, ruin, or damage some aspect of the people they envy. This could mean ruining a colleague's reputation because the covetous sociopath knows the colleague is smarter than him. The bottom line is this type of sociopath takes rather than earns, and he believes that destiny hasn't dealt him a fair hand, so he must steal from others who have more.

Sociopaths are generally not the worker bees of the world because they often pursue the quick buck or simply live off other people's hard work or good fortune. If a sociopath rises in a corporation or has a lot of responsibility, it will often be the underlings who shoulder the burden of the actual work that needs to be done.

There are many theories about how sociopathic traits are formed. Sometimes sociopathic or anti-social behaviors seem to stem from early childhood trauma or abuse. Hannibel Lecter's beloved sister being eaten by Nazis comes to mind. Children who torture animals or harm siblings or classmates often grow up to be sociopaths. However, studies have shown that some sociopaths come from normal and loving homes, and that many people who are traumatized in childhood can go on to live normal and productive lives. What is most notable about sociopaths is that brain studies reveal that their brains work somewhat differently than those of the normal population, and that they have difficulties processing emotional information in the cerebral cortex.

MODUS OPERANDI: A SOCIOPATH'S APPROACH TO POWER

From the previous list, it's easy to see why sociopaths make great fictional characters, but you might be wondering why they succeed when their behaviors are so outrageous or deviant. You see, not all sociopaths make their way in life by brute force or by flagrantly ignoring society's rules and laws. Often seductive, flattering, spontaneous, and even generous, a sociopath often woos his victims before he strikes. A sociopath usually possesses buckets of charm and charisma, and he wields these traits skillfully. But it's all about self-gratification, and if you're entrapped in a sociopath's sights, it's because he thinks there is something to be gained by your association.

Another thing to keep in mind is that sociopaths are the chameleons of the human kingdom, and, like a chameleon in a jungle setting, they are difficult to spot. They are in all walks of life—they can be cops or robbers, nurses or death-camp commandants, cafeteria workers or corrupt CEOs. Their displays of deep emotions are part of their cover because acting skills are important to their repertoire. In *The Sociopath Next Door,* psychologist Martha Stout explains:

> Being natural actors, conscienceless people can make full use of social and professional roles, which constitute excellent ready-made masks that other people are loath to look behind. ... We believe promises from such people because we assign to the individual the integrity of the role itself. ...

They often possess a kind of glow or charisma that makes them more charming or interesting than the other people around them. They are more spontaneous, more intense, complex, or even sexier than everyone else. Sociopaths are often able to orchestrate some kind of spooky intimacy with victims—sometimes it's sexual, sometimes it's a close friendship—and the sociopath often infers that he and his victim are alike. It's difficult to spot the sociopath's dark side in many circumstances, but it's blacker than a coal mine at midnight. They can hide their true nature (and often their motives) so effectively because, besides their charm and acting abilities, they are masterful and even artful liars—a bedrock trait of sociopaths.

Once you understand how a sociopath operates and what his key psychological traits are, you can have lots of fun writing this type of character—that is, if your idea of fun is creating a human missile. The point here is that sociopaths are as cold-blooded as reptiles—some can even deceitfully pass a lie-detector test without even breaking a sweat. They also seem to have an innate ability to find and exploit the weaknesses of others, so you'll want to create a particularly vulnerable victim or victims for the sociopath. Perhaps his M.O. is to charm a lonely and elderly woman, clean out her bank account, then move on to his next victim, leaving her heartbroken and destitute.

Whenever you feature betrayal in a story line, the reader will instinctively empathize with the victims, and when a sociopath is on the scene, traitorous and predatory behavior is usually part of the storyline. So, using a sociopath as a villain in your story can bring maximum wattage to this role because he'll leave a tornado's path of ruined lives.

NURTURING YOUR INNER PROFILER

If you're going to write about a sociopath, you'll need to nurture your inner profiler so that your character is depicted with deadly accuracy and with captivating details. A profiler is a professional who uses behavioral evidence to help authorities find criminals and solve crimes. Often, a profiler is called on to examine a series of cases and advise whether there is a link between two or more cases based on the crime scene evidence and the victims. While many attribute this technique to the Behavioral Sciences Unit (BSU) at the FBI Academy at Quantico, Virginia, in reality, profiling has been used since the 1880s in law enforcement, particularly in conjunction with autopsies. Profiling is now widely used and recognized because of the media attention of some profilers and their presence in novels, television series, and movies.

Many of the theories taught by the BSU were based on interviews with thousands of criminals and on examinations of their crime records. Experts also have divided criminals into two broad categories—the organized criminal and the disorganized criminal—and their differences are quite revealing. For example, the organized criminal is of average or above average intelligence, the disorganized criminal is of below average intelligence. The organized criminal is socially competent and controls his mood while committing the crime; the disorganized criminal is socially incompetent and is anxious while committing the crime.

Your first choices when writing about a villain is to figure out if he is a sociopath, and if he's organized or disorganized. Remember that sociopaths are likely to stay eerily calm while they're dispatching victims or wreaking havoc, so it's likely they'll be organized. You'll then need to create a character based on the sort behaviors the character engages in. Your best material can often be filched from headlines or historical accounts, and the villain might often be a composite of different people. For example, Thomas Harris's serial killer character Buffalo Bill in *The Silence of the Lambs* is actually based on three real-life serial killers. Bill's penchant for skinning his victims, his house-of-horrors pit where he stashes his victims, and his trick of trapping victims by using a fake arm cast all came from real killers.

Similarly, when casting a sociopath in a suspense story, you'll need to decide on the evidence and clues you'll use in the story, such as autopsy results, forensic evidence at the crime scene, and witness accounts. All the clues must add up to a highly dangerous criminal who is poised to commit acts most people would not dare imagine.

You'll need to make lots of decisions about your sociopathic character. Will his crimes be personal, are his victims people he knows? Does he want to hear his victims beg for their lives? Or will he have a bigger agenda to destroy some part of civilization? Harris was known to sit in on classes on criminal psychology at the FBI Academy, but most authors don't have that opportunity, so they must find other ways to learn about the dark side.

As you make these decisions about your sociopath, research widely, and find accounts of people who have been victimized by these real-life villains. It seems to me that too often writers are so focused on their villains that they don't think deeply enough about the villains' impacts on their victims. To think like a profiler, you'll need to read books written by profilers, such as *Dark Dreams* by Roy Hazelwood and Stephen G. Michaud. You might also want to follow the career of FBI Agent John Douglas, who has been involved in many high-profile investigations, and whom Thomas Harris modeled his Jack Crawford character after. Douglas has interviewed more than 5,000 criminals and has written a number of books on the topic, including *Mindhunter, Journey Into Darkness* and *The Anatomy of Motive*.

As part of your research, delve into books written by forensic experts and the results of the latest studies on personality disorders and criminal behaviors. You'll find many studies documented in professional journals such as *American Journal of Forensic Psychology*, *Criminal Behavior and Mental Health*, *Journal of Personality Disorders*, and *Journal of Clinical Psychology*, among others. Two extremely helpful books are *Without Conscience* by Robert D. Hare and *Base Instincts: What Makes Killers Kill?* by Jonathan H. Pincus, M.D.

Know the M.O. of your villain, along with the arc and range of his destructive capabilities, and make certain to add a few secondary and contrasting traits that make him memorable and original. This means he might meet his victims in bars, in church, online, or in his classroom. The more decisions you make about his M.O., the easier he will be to bring to life. Is he an imposter? Does he use disguises? Is he sexually insatiable? Does he have above average intelligence? Does he travel around in his quest for victims, or does he have a seemingly normal life with a job and home base?

Decide at which point in his character arc the reader will meet him, and how intimate your portrait will be. For example, is the reader going to meet him as his crime spree is just beginning, or is the reader going to meet him after he's piled up bodies in three states with a task force trying to track him down? Will the reader ever slip into his thoughts, or will the reader only know the thoughts of the people trying to stop him? If the reader is in the villain's viewpoint at times, will you include flashbacks or reveal childhood traumas? (For more on creating a villain's backstory, see chapter nine.)

Remembering that editors are searching for characters who possess that *quintessential something*, think deeply about your villain's secondary and contrasting traits, with a special eye for the quirky, the taboo, and the underreported. Perhaps your sociopath likes Puccini or French cuisine, or perhaps he grows prize-winning orchids. Perhaps he has a secret hide-away, dabbles in the occult, lives in a steel-and-glass high-rise, or collects African masks. Perhaps he has a sexual fetish, is a cross-dresser, or attends mass every morning. Perhaps his upper torso is tattooed, or he sports Elvis sideburns and drives a Harley.

In the psychological thriller film *Sleeping With the Enemy*, the vengeful and spooky husband, Martin Burney, played by Patrick Bergin, has an extreme penchant for order. His compulsivity extends to the exact placement of hand towels on a rack and cupboard contents that are lined up with precision. Not to mention his affection for the haunting notes of Berlioz's *Symphonie Fantastique*. As part of his absolute control over his wife, Laura, played by Julia Roberts, he punishes her if the towels or canned goods are not lined up just right. These behavior details are particularly disturbing and are the sort that you want to emulate in your own characters.

Profilers make their living by slipping inside the minds of the most disturbed among us. This means they travel the darkest landscapes of human experience. Like these pros, your job as a writer is to visit these dark and terrible places, then render characters with not only accuracy, but also nuance and originality. Note also that while we're focused on sociopaths in this chapter, many of these techniques just mentioned for shaping characters are applicable to all villains, particularly to villains who are criminals.

ULTIMATE MAYHEM: KILLERS ON THE LOOSE

Let's now talk about a subgenre that most often features sociopaths so we can focus on the larger picture of crafting the right story line to showcase your sociopath creating mayhem. Then we'll move on to several case studies.

Serial killer novels are a subgenre of suspense and thriller novels, and they often feature sociopathic villains. These novels contain more random and graphic violence and gore than regular genre titles, and they tend to feature an especially bleak worldview. These types of stories sell for a simple reason: Serial killers are fascinating. Readers are fascinated not only with broken bodies and crime scene details, but also with the shattered psyches of the people who commit these crimes. It's like when we drive past a highway wreck and rubberneck, trying to see if anyone strewn among the wreckage is seriously hurt or worse. Similarly, when we read serial killer fiction, we cannot *not* look. We must know all, including the killer's gruesome murder methods and twisted reasoning. And serial killers especially fascinate us in these books because we are usually allowed into the intimate moments and hellish thoughts of the most hated segment of our population. In real life, serial killers are rare; in fiction, they roam the lonely streets of every country, and they are the dark echoes of our worst nightmares.

If you plan on writing about these soulless, depraved characters, think about the following advice. As a writer, you've got endless choices in creating a villain, but when you create a serial killer, you need to verify your facts, especially the forensic evidence, crime procedures, and psychological profiles that give a story the exact ring of truth. Nothing jars a reader, particularly an editor, from your story like an inaccurate detail or misstep. If you're drawn to writing about these characters, make certain that your research is impeccable, and that your insight into madness is so accurate, a shrink would sign off on your character's traits.

It can also be enormously helpful to choose a structure of your story line before you begin writing. Typically, serial killer stories feature a chase plot. The reader enjoys chase stories because they have a natural and timeless configuration. It also falls neatly into the good guy versus bad guy pattern that we've come to know as children and that is most often found in suspense, thriller, and Western genres.

It goes something like this: There is a monster on the loose, killing young blondes, children, prostitutes, size 14 women, you get the idea—fill in the blank with your own segment of the population. And there's a hero—a cop, detective, psychologist, medical examiner, district attorney—who must stop the killer before it's too late and his next victim meets her fate. Now, chase stories have been around since our ancestors were running from a pissed-off mastodon or were chasing down a beast because the whole tribe needed to survive the winter on its bounty. So chase stories have elemental suspense stitched into them (*will he or won't he get caught?*) and, for many writers, are the most logical way to plot.

But because you're interested in catching an editor's eye, maybe you don't need to write a chase story, and you want to use a different approach or structure. You could go against type and find another way into the story. You might try a fresh tactic, as seen in Michael Fredrickson's *A Defense for the Dead*. When Fredrickson's story opens, the serial killer is already dead, but he seems to be manipulating and harming people from the grave. The FBI agents have taken down the killer, whom they call Van Gogh because of his grisly habit of cutting off the ears of his victims. The story becomes increasingly complicated with a drag queen, a scam artist, and a lawyer who seems to be trying to prove the killer's innocence. If the supposed villain is already dead, you can see how this story raises countless questions that demand answers.

Or perhaps you want to use a serial killer in a story to comment on some aspect of society or humanity. An example is Sherman Alexie's *Indian Killer*, which is about a serial killer who scalps his white victims. The story takes the reader into various Seattle neighborhoods, including Skid Row, and also the Spokane reservation. However, this is not a typical crime novel or murder mystery; rather, it is a chilling commentary on the dark side of Native American life. The story also reveals the prevalence of homelessness among Native Americans and disturbing truths about Indian/white relationships, as the killings trigger a wave of violence and racism. Alexie's John Smith character has an unusual motive for murder, and the story riffs on cultural identity, radio talk shows, rage, racism, and the Ghost Dance.

Joyce Carol Oates's *Zombie*, which won the Bram Stoker Award, is a case study in how to hone a tale of terror using a particularly creepy villain. Oates is known for slipping violence, abuse, and mental illness into her darker-than-dark mainstream novels and short stories, and *Zombie* is one of her most gruesome stories. The story is told in the viewpoint of a serial killer who is as savage and depraved as they come. Oates was inspired by a real-life serial killer who found his victims, children and teens, in the affluent suburbs of Detroit when Oates lived there, although when you read it, you might be reminded of Jeffrey Dahmer. So, like Oates, your story might feature the villain's viewpoint and comment on dark themes about contemporary society.

The point is, if you're writing about serial killers, begin by reading widely in this subgenre, paying special attention to the stories that break the mold. If you've drawn a character that is a rip-off of Hannibel Lecter, an editor will immediately spot these similarities. Fiction writers need to keep asking themselves *what if*? What if my serial killer is a woman? What if my serial killer is married and has children? What if my serial killer appears to be a doting parent? What if my serial killer is a cop? What if my serial killer is a scientist? What if my serial killer is filled with self-loathing? Do your homework and make your character as new as a freshly minted dollar bill and as complicated as a maze, yet completely true to form.

CRIMINAL SOCIOPATH CASE STUDIES

Let's look at three sociopaths who have turned their considerable talents to crime, noticing how unforgettable each of them is. As mentioned, sociopaths are not always criminals, but when their exceptional abilities are focused on crime, well, people best run for cover.

POSTER BOY: TOM RIPLEY

If there ever was a poster boy for the criminally inclined, Patricia Highsmith has created him in her character Tom Ripley. While it's impossible to catalogue his many crimes and misdeeds since he stars in *The Talented Mr. Ripley* and four sequels, it can be instructive to analyze his personality, M.O., and history.

First, like many fictional villains, Ripley had a bad beginning. Orphaned as a child when his parents drowned, he was raised by a distant and abusive aunt; he escaped her clutches when he was eighteen and moved to New York. Thus, he displays two common factors that shape villains: trauma and abuse. Ripley also is proof that a villain of this type doesn't need to be a slavering demon. In fact, he can be attractive and blend into the highest social circles, especially when he's a "suave, agreeable, and utterly amoral." We know from real serial killers that many sociopaths are attractive fast-talkers and are adept at luring their victims to their untimely deaths.

The reader meets Ripley in the first book when he's impersonating an Internal Revenue agent. This type of character often possesses at least one unusual talent. In Ripley's case, not only is he a master con artist, he's also an actor who immerses himself so thoroughly in his role that it seems he actually becomes the person he is masquerading as. In this case, Ripley murders Dick Greenleaf, a rich playboy, steals his identity, and then starts living a life of luxury. When Greenleaf's friend Freddie Miles becomes suspicious, Ripley dispatches him without a backward glance, and he returns to New York.

Like many sociopaths who are also criminals, Ripley is involved in a wide range of criminal activities. He is involved with art forgery, fakes a will and other documents, becomes entangled with the Mafia, and is responsible for several murders.

Like many conscienceless sociopathic types, Ripley views people as expendable and often harms, abuses, or murders his victims as a means to an end or to provide pleasure. Like many of his ilk, he's capable of extreme violence. Although Ripley claims to abhor murder, he sometimes beats his victims to death. He also has a twisted code of ethics, and he sometimes tries to reason with his victims before murdering them. He tends to see their deaths as unavoidable. Often, part of this twisted code is to normalize and justify murder and crimes, as Ripley does again and again in the series.

Most sociopaths are snobs, believing that they are somehow set apart from normal life and somehow superior to everyone else. They also believe that they are above the law, and that they're smarter and more sensitive, talented, and deserving than other people in society. One reason that sociopaths are so fascinating is that they are often uncensored in their aims, and they display a delicious perversity. Ripley seems to also manifest a kind of disassociation when he's in the midst of murder and mayhem. Most sociopaths have this kind of reptilian quality; it's not that they are completely aware that they're acts are illegal, they just don't care and they don't feel.

As you create a sociopath in your story, you'll want your reader to believe that no one is safe when the sociopath is in the story, so make certain that the ramifications of your sociopath's acts are far-reaching.

You'll also want to make certain that he blends into society and has some special means to get away with his shenanigans until the last possible moment. With a sociopath (and especially a serial killer), you want to prolong his crime spree to milk the suspense. You might also want to go out on a limb with the character and place him in a position of authority, which means he'll have lots of power. But also give him at least one specialized skill that makes his crimes plausible, keeping in mind that sociopaths are consummate actors and when their lips are moving, they're lying.

ENTITLED: WILLIAM "PECK" WILSON

Following in the mold of the amoral Ripley, William "Peck" Wilson adds a modern twist in *Talk Talk* by T.C. Boyle. He is an identity thief and lives off the stolen identities and credit of his victims. Like most sociopaths, he wreaks havoc on the lives of his victims, but Boyle's story is especially interesting to analyze because it's told from three viewpoints, and the reader is allowed into the mind of the sociopath—and Boyle gets him just right.

The story opens when Dana Halter, a deaf woman who teaches at a high school for the deaf, runs a stop sign while hurrying to a dental appointment. A police officer spots her and pulls her over. After he returns to his patrol car to run her driver's license through the department's computers, her world turns upside down:

> She watched till his face loomed up in the mirror—his mouth drawn tight, his eyes narrowed and deflated—and then turned to face him.
>
> That was when she had her first shock.
>
> He was standing three paces back from the driver's door and he had his weapon drawn and pointed at her and he was saying something about her hands—barking, his face discomposed, furious—and he had to repeat himself, more furious each time, until she understood: *Put your hands where I can see them.*
>
> At first, she'd been too scared to speak, numbly complying, stung by the elemental violence of the moment. He'd jerked her out of the car, the gun still on her, shoved her face into the hot metal and glass of her own vehicle and twisted her arms round behind her to clamp the cuffs over her wrists, the weight of him pressing into her until she felt him forcing her legs apart with the anvil of his knee. His hands were on her then, gripping her ankles first, sliding up her legs to her hips, her abdomen, her armpits, patting, probing. There was the sharp hormonal smell of him, of his contempt and outrage, his hot breath exploding in her ear with the fricatives and plosives of speech. He was brisk, brutal, sparing nothing. There might have been questions, orders, a meliorating softness in his tone, but she couldn't hear and she couldn't see his face—and her hands, her hands were caught like fish on a stringer.
>
> Now, in the patrol car, in the cage of the backseat that was exactly like the cage they put stray dogs in, she felt the way they wanted you to feel: small, helpless, without hope or recourse. Her heart was hammering. She was on the verge of tears. People were staring at her, slowing their cars to get a good look, and there was nothing she could do but turn away in shame and horror and pray that one of her students didn't happen to be passing by—or anybody she knew, her neighbors, the landlord. She slouched down in the seat, dropped her head till her hair shook loose. She'd always wondered why the accused shielded their faces on the courthouse steps, why they tried so hard to hide their identities even when everyone in the world knew who they were, but now she understood, now she felt it for herself.

This frightening incident starts the story on a collision course of a sociopath meeting up with his victim. With this course in place, naturally the reader is going to fret over the outcome. Dana is stopped on a Friday and does not appear in court until Monday afternoon, so she has to spend several terrifying days in jail among criminals and prostitutes and crazy people. Dana's deafness also increases her vulnerability. Once it's determined that she was the victim of identity theft, the reader continues to follow her through the system as she's forced to return to prison before she can be officially released. But her saga doesn't end there. She must pay almost five hundred dollars for her impounded car, she's fired from her job as a teacher for being arrested, and she discovers that her credit is ruined. When she finds out that the man who has stolen her identity lives in Marin County, California, not too far from her home, she decides to confront him, and that's when things really heat up.

The alternating viewpoint structure of *Talk Talk* is also worth noting. The first chapter is from Dana's viewpoint, which creates empathy as the reader feels her panic as her world tumbles out of control. Alternating viewpoint sections in her boyfriend's viewpoint and then Peck Wilson's viewpoint wrap the reader tightly into this drama. And because the reader is allowed inside the criminal's mindset for so much of the book, the reader knows so much more about him than his victims do, and the reader worries about a confrontation, sure that Peck has the upper hand.

What is most startling about Peck is that he feels entitled to his ill-gotten gains and the lives of others. And like most sociopaths, his narcissism is complete. However, unlike many sociopaths, there doesn't seem to be an early childhood trauma that shaped him. Instead, he blames his ex-wife for his troubles. You see, he's been living the good life and owned two restaurants in his twenties. Then his wife spoiled their life together by getting pregnant. And then she compounded her insult by losing interest in having sex with him. Naturally, he was forced to seek satisfaction with other women—who could blame him? The pregnancy starts his life sliding out of control, and after the couple divorces, he begins acts of retribution that eventually land him in jail, where he learns how to be a true criminal.

Taking a cue from Boyle, you might want to create this sort of complicated backstory to place your sociopath on the road to crime. Peck, like many sociopaths, believes he's above the law and above toiling away like normal people. The reader witnesses his attitudes toward his gorgeous Russian girlfriend, a woman who was born to shop. He views her, his stolen goods, and his opulent lifestyle as part of his entitlement. How dare anyone suggest anything else? How dare anyone try to stop him?

The reader also experiences Dana's vulnerability, not only because she's deaf and the deaf are often misunderstood and seen as mentally deficient, but because the more time the reader spends in Peck's head, the more the reader worries that Dana's simply outgunned in this matchup. As the story follows Peck as he trades in a car for a new Mercedes using yet another stolen alias, it's clear that he's ruthless and easily enraged, and his sense of entitlement is absolute. And when Dana and her boyfriend try to track him down, he considers them parasites for daring to disrupt his life.

So let's talk about putting some of these lessons to work in your own story. First, it's always fascinating when an author writes a tale dealing with a contemporary situation; for example, identity theft is a fast-growing and damaging crime and can terrorize its victims. In fact, not too far into Boyle's story, you feel compelled to run a credit check on yourself. Also like Boyle, try to wrap your story around themes. In *Talk Talk*, the themes of identity, privacy, and isolation serve to underline the action and are also emphasized in the subplot about Dana's relationship with her boyfriend.

Second, you might want to borrow Boyle's technique of turning an innocent bystander's world upside down, thrusting her into a world of crime. When you do this, your story is bound to be exciting. Also, make sure the sociopath's antics cause a lot of harm, such as the Kafkaesque horror of Dana's arrest and downfall.

Then, consider how your victim might react. If all the characters simply roll over for the sociopath, you water down the suspense. In this case, Dana turns into a vigilante, and in the cross-country game of cat-and-mouse, it's not always clear who the cat is. Like Boyle, you might want to introduce the villain early, use alternating viewpoints and a fast pace to keep the suspense roiling.

TWISTED: STEPHEN BONNET

Stephen Bonnet is one of the most hated villains in Diana Gabaldon's Outlander series. When an author writes a sweeping series with a large cast of characters, as Gabaldon does, it's essential that the villains are especially memorable and that their actions affect the protagonists in profound ways.

In the fourth book in the series, *Drums of Autumn*, Jamie and Claire Fraser and their nephew, Ian, arrive in the Colonies to establish a new life. Early in the book, the reader learns that the family carries a handful of valuable gemstones with them, and that their future will be built from this precious wealth.

It's instructive to follow Stephen Bonnet's path of destruction in this story and to note the ways Gabaldon uses him in a series, because you can adopt the author's tactics for any villain. First, she introduces the villain with memorable details in the midst of a dramatic situation. The book opens with the sound of drums in Charleston in June 1767, and Claire, Jamie, and Ian are in a crowd as a gallows procession passes. They are there to support one of the accused, Gavin Hayes; Jamie has gotten the man drunk to ease his final moments when the noose tightens. As Hayes is dying, another of the doomed men, Stephen Bonnet, takes advantage of the distraction and sprints away into the crowd and disappears with Redcoats in hot pursuit.

After claiming Hayes's body, the group arrives in a churchyard late at night to bury their friend. All are a bit spooked by the dark and their surroundings. This is when the reader first meets Bonnet, who had stowed away with the corpse in a wagon. Note that like most villains, Bonnet will do anything to save himself, including hiding out with a corpse. Keep this trait in mind when you construct your own villain.

Also remember that fictional characters, particularly protagonists and victims, are typically introduced using sympathy-provoking details in a situation that somehow goes against the common grain. For instance, in *Talk Talk*, the reader meets the protagonist, Dana, as she's been pulled from her car and arrested; the reader cannot help but worry and wonder about what comes next. Here, however, Gabaldon turns the tables a bit and manages to create a sympathetic portrayal of the villain that's rich with physical detail, but still hints at his suspicious traits:

> He was young, about thirty, muscular and powerfully built, his fair hair matted with sweat and stiff with filth. He reeked of prison, and the musky-sharp smell of prolonged fear. Little wonder.

> I got a hand under his arm and helped him to sit up. He grunted and put his hand to his head, squinting in the torchlight.
>
> "Are you all right?" I asked.
>
> "Thankin' ye kindly, ma'am, I will have been better." He had a faint Irish accent and a soft, deep voice. …

The reader next discovers that after Bonnet hid under the gallows cart, he climbed into the wagon. He is introduced with more detail:

> … He rose laboriously to his feet, closed his eyes to get his balance, then opened them. They were a pale green in the torchlight, the color of shallow seas. I saw them flick from face to face, then settle on Jamie. The man bowed, careful of his head.
>
> "Stephen Bonnet. Your servant, sir." He made no move to extend a hand in greeting, nor did Jamie. …
>
> Bonnet was what country people called "well set up," with a tall, powerful frame and a barrel chest, his features heavy-boned but coarsely handsome. A few inches shorter than Jamie, he stood easy, balanced on the balls of his feet, fists half closed in readiness.
>
> No stranger to a fight, judging by the slight crookedness of his nose and a small scar by the corner of his mouth. The small imperfections did nothing to mar the overall impression of animal magnetism; he was the sort of man who attracted women easily.

Bonnet goes on to confess that he'd been guilty of smuggling and piracy. When Jamie asks him if anyone had died because of his ventures, he replies, "None that wer not tryin' to kill me first." With some misgivings, Jamie decides to allow him to go free, but then Bonnet asks for their help to escape since the British soldiers would be looking for him. He's told to help them bury Hayes, and with this encounter, their fates become entwined—another plotting trick you should try to emulate.

Then, since villains are terrific vehicles to insert reversals into story lines, the family's next meeting with Bonnet proves he's a man of surprises and not to be trusted. You see, later, aboard a boat at Wilmington, Bonnet and his pirate companions rob the family of their jewels and Claire's wedding ring, and in this single stroke, the family is reduced from riches to rags.

As the story progresses, the reader learns from Bonnet's backstory that his parents died when he was a child living in Sligo, and he eventually went to sea and turned to crime. So again, the writer creates a backstory that illuminates the front story and makes it plausible.

What can be learned from Gabaldon is how to use a sociopath in a series, and how to weave him in and out of various scenarios so that he unleashes the maximum damage to a number of characters, thus creating suspense. Gabaldon also illustrates how to make the villain's actions cause lasting repercussions. Later, Jamie and Claire's daughter, Brianna, joins them in America and is raped by Bonnet in exchange for Claire's ring; Brianna becomes pregnant and isn't sure if Bonnet or her husband, Roger, is the father, thus entangling her with Bonnet.

SWITCHEROO

Let's look at one more way in which to use a sociopath in a story that might work well for a thriller or psychological suspense novel. This technique involves creating a villain who pulls off the old switcheroo. In this instance, the writer uses a main character who is seemingly sane, innocent, or even laudable, and then gradually unmasks him so that the reader sees the true villain lurking under his innocent guise. After all, criminals and sociopaths are especially frightening when they roam among us, their black hearts concealed. Since they're consummate actors and liars, they are perfectly suited for this role. Agatha Christie often used this situation in her mysteries; in fact, her murderers are often people of stature and breeding. This seeming normalcy heightens the horror when the character turns out to be a bad seed, or perhaps the devil's own henchman.

Such a case is found in Laura Lippman's *Every Secret Thing.* In this suspense novel, the backstory has such weight and horror that it creates a series of events and missteps that haunt and influence the front story. When a backstory has such weight, often an author will choose to depict it in a prologue so that it's given its proper heft in the story. In the case of *Every Secret Thing,* the prologue, occurring seven years earlier, starts the story off with a creepy irony:

> They were barefoot when they were sent home, their dripping feet leaving prints that evaporated almost instantly, as if they had never been there at all. Had it been possible to retrace their literal steps, as so many would try to do in the days that followed, the trail would

> have led from the wading pool area, where the party tables had been staked out with aqua Mylar balloons, past the snack bar, up the stairs, and to the edge of the parking lot. And each print would have been smaller than the last—losing first the toes, then the narrow connector along the arch, the heels, and finally the baby-fat balls of their feet—until there was nothing left.

After this, the narration follows the girls, Alice and Ronnie, as they slip on their shoes and continue home. They'd been attending a birthday party together, but Ronnie had acted up, and they'd been banned from the festivities. The story continues in Alice's viewpoint, which reveals her resentments toward Ronnie's behavior and her resentments in general at being forced to associate with her during the summer months because

ROGUE'S GALLERY

These rogues are all sociopaths and give readers and filmgoers a convincing glimpse into a haunted mind:

- Gregory Anton, played by Charles Boyer in the film *Gaslight*
- Gretchen Lowell, *Heartsick* by Chelsea Cain
- Arsonist, *Blue Smoke* by Nora Roberts
- Tyler Durden, *Fight Club* by Chuck Palahniuk
- Casanova, *Kiss the Girls* by James Patterson
- Annie Wilkes, *Misery* by Stephen King
- Charles Bruno, *Strangers on a Train* by Patricia Highsmith
- Alex DeLarge, *A Clockwork Orange* by Anthony Burgess
- The Jackal, *The Day of the Jackal* by Frederick Forsyth
- The Joker, Batman comic series
- Vincent Vega played by John Travolta and Jules Winnfield played by Samuel L. Jackson in the film *Pulp Fiction*
- Patrick Bateman, *American Psycho* by Bret Easton Ellis
- Mickey and Mallory Knox played by Woody Harrelson and Juliette Lewis *Natural Born Killers*

they're neighbors. The reader learns that Ronnie is volatile and Alice is a good girl; that Alice likes to please and Ronnie explodes; that Alice lives in a house of rules and Ronnie lives in a house where children are not well-supervised.

As the prologue ends, the girls find a baby carriage with a baby in it and no grown-ups around. Ronnie suggests that they need to take care of the baby.

The story then jumps to the present; Alice, who is now eighteen, is being released from a juvenile facility. And that's when things get complicated, especially because another child is missing, and she looks remarkably like the girl who was killed years earlier. Lippman does a great job of withholding information until the last possible moment, casting guilt on the innocent party, and unmasking the true villain in a delicious and slowly unfolding tease. Stories with this sort of story line will always engage and entertain readers, and *Every Secret Thing* can serve as a blueprint for laying out this sort of scenario.

The point here is that if you want your character to fool most of the people most of the time, a sociopath is the perfect person for the role. In fact, fooling others is what a sociopath is all about. And if he's got a crime to hide, it's likely that he'll create a barrage of false clues and will, without breaking a sweat, point a guilty finger at another character.

You know how the old rule of real estate is "location, location, location"? Well, the admonition for writing about sociopaths, and all villains, is research, research, research. As you write, look for the chinks in your character's armor. For example, will his gigantic ego be his downfall? Remember, too, that not every sociopath needs to be an evil genius, but he will be a master manipulator. And typically his game is played for high stakes, with a big risk of imminent ruin—but that doesn't stop him from extracting a huge piece of another character's soul along the way.

There is a whole category of readers who snap up stories that feature sociopathic villains, but they want to travel down freshly paved roads. Similar to readers of horror stories, perhaps we read these books because we want to know the unknowable. Perhaps readers want to feel the flames of hell. Perhaps, as the heat rises, we want to feel safe in our beds when the villain meets his fate.

CHAPTER EIGHT

Matching Wits: Heroes vs. Villains

In the old days, villains had moustaches and kicked the dog. Audiences are smarter today. They don't want their villain to be thrown at them with green limelight on his face. They want an ordinary human being with failings.

—Alfred Hitchcock

There's nothing like a showdown. A one-on-one face-off with two people or two teams that both want, both *need*, to win. It's why millions of people watch the Super Bowl each year, not to mention soccer, basketball, and baseball playoffs and championship games. In fiction, a matchup causes skin-prickling anxiety in the reader, and there can be no bigger drama than when a hero and villain go toe-to-toe. This scene is usually staged near the end of the story, and usually the hero, if not both characters, have been somehow weakened by events that have come before. It's in these final moments that the hero calls on his reserves, his greatness, and his goodness to triumph, or, in the case of a tragedy, fail.

In this chapter, we're going to explore more fully the aspects of pitting a hero against a villain. My aim is to suggest several approaches you might take and why, and also to acquaint you with the archetypal elements of heroes. We've been talking about bad asses in this book, and while a hero can be a bad ass—as in, he can be nontraditional, have an attitude, and strike fear in his enemies—his traits place him on a much higher moral ground than other characters we've discussed so far. We're also going to talk about the alpha factor in characters, since often both heroes and villains are alpha types.

Too often, beginning writers tend to write matchups where the situations are almost laughable or contrived. But if you deepen your understanding of what a hero and villain are supposed to accomplish in a story and know the dynamics between your characters beforehand, it can lead to a more sophisticated and dramatic situation.

HEROES 101

Many stories that feature a villain—especially in thrillers, suspense, science fiction, fantasy, and horror genres—will also feature a hero. A hero is a protagonist, but there are differences between protagonists and heroes, just as there are differences between antagonists and villains. A hero is always the good guy, although he can be a bad ass, as previously mentioned. He is also always the most important person in the story, and he always upholds morality in the story because his actions stem from an altruistic nature.

On the other hand, a villain not only causes the reader to be afraid, but also holds an opposing moral code to the hero. The hero's motives and desires drive the story, while the villain influences and blocks those goals. A hero typically tries to help or save other characters at his own peril, whereas the villain tries to help himself, usually at the expense of other characters. While a story's protagonist always represents human impulses and interests, a hero has mega-initiative and is bound to shake up the story world, alter the course of history, and restore order or balance.

Before we explore the dynamics of this showdown, let's make sure we have a clear understanding of what qualities a hero brings to the table. A hero usually sacrifices himself for others, is often larger than life, is an independent thinker, is highly motivated—even if at first he is reluctant to answer the call to action in the story—and he has qualities other characters and the reader long to emulate and identify with.

A hero often wrestles with inner conflict, and this conflict is often about values. A hero can be humorous, self-deprecating, and witty. He has strength or fortitude that somehow sets him apart from ordinary people. A hero usually succeeds in the story despite his flaws, although those flaws are occasionally his undoing, or at least cause him to stumble. A hero is revealed in brave acts and everyday moments, and he is committed to the story goals. At some point in the story, he must make a formal commitment to the quest.

Let's also not also forget that, at first glance, a hero might appear an unlikely type for the role; he could be an orphan, a hobbit, or a shepherd boy. A final characteristic that sets heroes apart from other main characters is that he serves as a stand-in for the reader and for society, as in days of old when a knight went forth in the name of the monarch. While in this role, the hero battles and meets evil or some disturbing element that we mortals are not brave enough to wrestle with.

ALPHA FOR A REASON

As mentioned in chapter four about dark heroes and bad boys, an alpha male or female brings scads of sizzle into a story. It's time for us to take a deeper look at exactly how an alpha status relates to heroes and villains. Previously, we've been looking at characters that are unlikeable, scary, edgy, or evil. Many of the types we've discussed have problems with self-control, particularly in controlling their emotions. Or, there is often something self-destructive in their makeup, their flaws are magnified, or their backstories are difficult to overcome.

Now, let's think about leading men and women who likely *can* control themselves unless provoked or defending innocents, who rarely show their vulnerabilities, who usually know exactly what they want, and go after it full throttle. If your story needs a kick-ass hero, anti-hero, or heroine, then it's likely that you'll be creating an alpha character. In fact, in case you haven't noticed, the attributes we're discussing in heroes and heroines typically mean that the character is an alpha type.

Stemming from research in both humans and the animal kingdom, alphas are the top of the pride, pack, or family. They exist in wolves, dogs, chimpanzees, lions, and other species. They are generally the largest, strongest, fittest, and sometimes most aggressive of the group. They eat first and best, so they have greater odds of surviving. There is a biological imperative for the alphas to perpetuate the species—their role is dominance, and because they are the toughest and most vigorous, they often are the healthiest males and females for breeding.

Animal groups also often have an alpha pair that mate at least once. The other animals in the group will follow or defer to this male, female, or pair. Not all animal societies are led by males; elephants, for example, are led by females.

In a group hierarchy, two other roles or pairs also exist. There is a beta male or female, which is the contender for the alpha role. He or she is subservient to the alpha, acts as second-in-command, and can be a former alpha that has been dethroned or a future alpha if he challenges him for the lead role. Then there are omega males and females. These are the males and females at the bottom of the social hierarchy, subservient to both alpha and beta males and females.

In the human world, alpha males and females have similar roles to play; in fiction, they appear more often in genre fiction than in mainstream fiction. As in the real world, alphas have authority and command respect without trying. Sometimes it's a quiet authority; sometimes it's more aggressive, as in a character like Conan the Barbarian. In Robert B. Parker's Spenser series, the private investigator Spenser and his sidekick, Hawk, are two alpha types that are both on the same side; if they were enemies, all hell would break loose. An alpha is always a dominant, take-charge type of person—the leader of the pack. James Bond, Rhett Butler, and Tarzan are alpha males.

You might consider casting at least one alpha character in your story to make things interesting. One alpha will steer the story; two alphas in a story can generate a lot of conflict and usually an emotional battlefield. In Janet Evanovich's Stephanie Plum series, Ranger and Joe Morrelli are both alpha types interested in the same woman, which generates lots of tension. If an alpha male and alpha female are pitted together in a romance story, they're going to tangle, and one will likely need to capitulate to resolve their differences. Alternately, in a romance, sometimes the female protagonist is forced to choose between an alpha male or a more sensitive beta male. In Kathleen E. Woodiwiss's historical romance *A Rose in Winter*, the heroine, Erienne, is drawn to an alpha male while still adoring her beta-type husband. In Jane Austen's *Pride and Prejudice*, Mr. Darcy is an alpha type, and his friend Mr. Bingley is a beta type. As illustrated in *Pride and Prejudice*, a beta male can play the role of best friend or sidekick of an alpha.

While there are certainly exceptions, you're more likely to come across non-alpha characters in mainstream fiction, such as Jerry Battle in Chang Rae Lee's *Aloft*, Harriet Mahoney in Elinor Lipman's *Isabel's Bed*, and Paul Iverson in Carolyn Parkhurst's *The Dogs of Babel*. Of course, it's difficult to make cut-and-dry pronouncements about any character type or trait because there are so many exceptions, varieties, and blends of characters in the huge world of storytelling. So we're speaking in generalities here; sometimes an author will blend alpha and beta qualities in the same character. Typically, beta and omega types play secondary characters, or a beta is in the process of transforming to become an alpha type, or a beta's qualities might be at odds with some aspect of the story world.

A beta can be portrayed as the quintessential sensitive male—the father who understands his daughter, the scholar or artist, the cop, psychologist, or clergymen who has gone into his field to help humankind. Or a beta type can be a nerd, a boy-next-door type, or a family man. Typical beta qualities are being laid back, self-aware, complex, and verbal. But don't mistake them for pushovers or wimps. Commander William T. Riker of the television series *Star Trek: The Next Generation* is a good example of a beta while Captain Jean-Luc Picard is an alpha type.

A non-alpha character typically won't get involved in actions that propel an action, fantasy, or romance plot unless his back is up against the wall; however, in the changing face of the romance genre, a beta can sometimes play the male lead. In fact, one of the big debates in romance circles centers around whether a beta type can play the role of the hero. The question asks if, in our changing times where women are often in charge of their own lives, do they still dream about a hero who will kick down the door or save her from marauding pirates in a daring rescue? Or, because women are out making a living and juggling many roles, do they want to come home to a man who will give them a backrub? Many romance readers confess they want to read about alpha males and marry beta males.

But let's look closer at alphas because they're endlessly fascinating. Take the case of Conan, an ultra-alpha male created by Robert E. Howard. Conan is the master of many forms of combat; his ability with the sword is unparalleled and few can match his brute physical strength. He also has a sharp wit and a keen intellect, though most people underestimate him as being a mindless savage because of his appearance and lack of a "civilized" education. When his enemies underestimate him, it often means their downfall, especially if they underestimate his intelligence. Quick to anger and often heedless of authority, Conan has problems following orders, which is typical of alpha males. Conan also has spent much of his life with a price on his head—this, too, is often applied to other alpha characters. Despite the fact that he might seem like a tough guy and a rebel, Conan has his own code of honor. In fact, like many alphas, Conan lives by a strict moral code. And, just as with other alpha heroes, this code is often the basis for his logic and actions, and he has been known to travel vast distances to avenge a wrong.

When an alpha type heads up a story, the reader is constantly reminded that the world is a dangerous and complicated place, and that real heroes are few. The jobs for an alpha type in fiction can be many, but it usually involves action. Thus, an alpha is often a cop or detective, or maybe a Navy SEAL who has trained to problem-solve under dangerous conditions. Often, alpha characters are spies, soldiers, bodyguards, and leaders of corporations or countries. Because alpha characters can be anti-heroes, they might also be pirates, bounty hunters, mercenaries, or assassins.

While alphas make terrific heroes and heroines, they are also naturals in the roles of compelling antagonists, particularly villains. In fact, if you examine many villains, you'll easily find their alpha attributes.

PUTTING ALPHAS TO WORK

When the romance genre rose to amazing popularity in the twentieth century, it often featured an alpha male in the hero role, particularly in the bodice-rippers written in the 1960s and 1970s. The essence of a romance is that the characters are going to be forced to change because of love. Thus, the alpha male in a romance needs taming, gentling, and house-breaking by the heroine. He is somewhat lethal, the sort of guy who could pick up a woman and carry her off to the bedroom, or toss her across a saddle to escape a horde of bandits. So there is a strength combined with a smoldering sexuality, a sense of danger, and, most of all, a challenge to the woman. The romance genre has since diversified with the face of the alpha hero changing to reflect the changing times.

There is also another interesting way to use an alpha type in a story, and this too can generate sizzle. It usually involves a story line where a character (usually a beta type) is living a fairly normal existence, when extraordinary circumstances thrust him into danger or adventure. This character might be involved in a mistaken identity plot, where he is an innocent bystander thrust into danger, but the story always features displacement and innocence. In the story, the character must draw on inner resources or qualities that have been dormant or he didn't imagine he possessed.

For example, it could mean that, under extreme circumstances, a usually mild-mannered man will go to extraordinary lengths to protect his family, his woman, or his town. This character isn't necessarily alpha by nature, but he turns alpha because the need arises. An example of this beta-turned-alpha character type is Atticus Finch, from Harper Lee's *To Kill a Mockingbird,* who stands down angry townspeople and a rabid dog, all to protect his family. Another example is William Wallace, a Scottish commoner who took up his sword and led an uprising against the English in the late thirteenth century. In the film *Braveheart,* which detours from history, Wallace is motivated by revenge after his young wife is murdered. What readers and filmgoers recognize in these stories is that people often have the makings of a hero within themselves.

An alpha character's values are never in question; he will dash into the burning building to save children, protect the weak, and take up the fight, no matter what the odds. A beta character is often more complex and nuanced than an alpha character, and he will generally be more sensitive. He is sometimes quirky, softer, and more laid-back than an alpha. Think Alan Alda playing Hawkeye Pierce in the *M*A*S*H* television series, Val Kilmer playing Doc Holliday in *Tombstone,* or Kathleen Turner playing Joan Wilder in *Romancing the Stone.*

Alpha Females

Like alpha males, alpha females do not sit on the sidelines of life. An alpha female will always have steel in her spine. Powerful, sometimes prickly, and even bitchy, an alpha female, like her male counterpart, brings a lot of spice to the page, especially when she's up against an alpha male. Picture the anti-hero and alpha female Scarlett O'Hara going toe-to-toe with anti-hero and alpha male Rhett Butler in *Gone With the Wind*. Many of the female characters who head up suspense series are alphas, including Sara Paretsky's private investigator V.I. Warshawski, Patricia Cornwell's medical examiner Dr. Kay Scarpetta, and Laurie R. King's Mary Russell. If you spot a woman character doing what is typically considered a man's job, chances are she's an alpha.

While they can be swashbuckling bad asses like Ellen Ripley played by Sigourney Weaver in the *Alien* films, alpha females are not just men in drag; they have different qualities from males. For instance, an alpha female shares her leadership and the spoils of the game, and her strength is used to promote community and stability. She is a woman of substance who combines physical potency and sexuality with seriousness of purpose, as seen in the Viviane Walker character in Rebecca Wells's *Divine Secrets of the Ya-Ya Sisterhood*. She can also be mature and connected to the community and her family, as illustrated by Claire Fraser in Diana Gabaldon's Outlander series.

Catherine the Great of Russia is an example of a real-life alpha female, as is Elizabeth I of England. Helen Mirren playing Inspector Jane Tennison in the television series *Prime Suspect* is a good example of an alpha female, but one who has a touching vulnerability and real flaws. As in real life, fictional alpha females are attractive, intelligent, successful, and usually educated. Contemporary research claims that, in the real world, this group has the hardest time finding a mate, which is where fiction comes in to offer contemporary women a fantasy—men who might sweep them off their feet or are up to the challenge of loving an alpha woman.

Another good place to find alpha females is in science-fiction or fantasy stories. One such alpha heroine who is not afraid to mix it up—in fact, wherever she goes, things get bloody—is the character Tomoe Gozen from the fantasy series by Jessica Amanda Salmonson. The Tomoe Gozen saga, consisting of three novels, is set in a universe where magic and mysticism exist along with monsters, devils, spirits, and gods. The series is based on the real-life Tomoe who traveled with the military, but in Salmonson's character, she's a fully realized female warrior and her adventures take place in Naipon, an alternate universe that is a mythologized version of Japan.

The series begins with Tomoe and her companions in the service of a warlord, Shojiro Shigeno. They are fighting Huan, a wizard, and during the battle Tomoe, is fatally wounded, and her friend Ushii brings her to the castle of the wizard to be healed. It is then that a difficult bargain is struck; Tomoe can live, but she now serves as a samurai to Huan. Using his magical powers, he forces her to turn against her former warlord, Shigeno, in a bloody battle, betraying her honor. She then starts traveling across Japan righting wrongs in search of redemption.

CREATING CREDIBILITY

Now that you have a deeper understanding of heroes and alpha types, you need to put this understanding to work in your stories. Step aside from your own life and try to see your story from a great distance, asking yourself what type of character you need to tell your story. A take-charge type? An intellect? A soldier of fortune? Will your character need to show vulnerability often or rarely? Once you know the sort of person who can handle the duties of the story, commit to whether he'll be heroic or alpha or whatever approach to solving problems in the story the character needs.

When an alpha hero heads a story, he needs to stay true to type. I've read clients' manuscripts where they've featured an alpha male or female falling apart, weeping, or becoming hysterical when the going got tough. Needless to say, when their heroes fell apart, so did their stories. So place this understanding side by side with your plans for the character's arc and make certain that everything is in sync.

Heroes and alphas have more cojones than most of us who are burdened with kids, mortgages, and nine-to-five jobs. We read stories that feature these characters for the vicarious thrills of their ordeals and to watch someone kicking butt and taking names. We admire their spunk, grit, resolve, and daring. And they never let us down.

Heroes and alphas always come with flaws and humanness—a vulgar mouth, arrogance, a penchant for sarcasm, a need to prove himself, an addiction, or a cranky disposition (just make certain it's not a whiney disposition). These flaws are not as crucial to the character makeup as in an anti-hero, who is typically highly flawed, but flaws are intended to make a character believable and increase tension in the story. Another way to humanize heroes and alphas is to make certain they don't amble through the story untouched, unruffled, or invulnerable.

THE CASE OF THE NEMESIS

We all know that conflict powers fiction, but nothing provides quite the level of drama as when a nemesis is in the story because the struggle between a hero and his nemesis will be highly personal. Since a villain is an obstacle character, he is going to force the hero to make a difficult choice or act in ways he would rather avoid, typically because it puts other characters at risk. These decisions or acts can be a huge risk, a leap of faith, a daring rescue, or waging a battle with the odds stacked against him. Usually, this forces the hero into some sort of territory—real or emotional—where he's never been before.

When there is a nemesis relationship in the story, it always increases the conflict and the stakes. The reader understands a nemesis is an opponent who cannot be beaten or overcome, or if the hero manages to triumph, it will be at a great cost. Based on the Greek goddess of the same name, the word *nemesis* means "to give what is due," and a nemesis can be thought of as the spirit of divine retribution. A nemesis character always poses the greatest threat to the protagonist or hero. In a sense, this relationship is intimate, since the struggle between the characters is so intense and because the villain often aims at the hero's vulnerabilities. There will always be a battle, and this battle will ultimately be for supremacy. While this battle doesn't necessarily represent the forces of good meeting evil, it always represents vastly different perspectives clashing.

Black Jack Randall and Jamie Fraser, from Diana Gabaldon's Outlander series, show the potency of this sort of matchup. The series begins in 1945 in the Scottish Highlands when Claire Beauchamp Randall visits an ancient circle of standing stones and slips back in time to the 1700s. Struggling to understand what has happened to her, she meets Jonathan, or "Black Jack" Randall, an English officer who immediately starts assaulting her.

She's rescued by Jamie Fraser, a Scotsman, but by this time, the reader has learned Randall is likely the ancestor of Claire's husband, Frank. The family legacy had not mentioned that he was heartless, sadistic, and as creepy as any villain that has ever graced the pages of a novel.

Claire, wandering around in 1940s garb, is immediately suspect as being a spy at worst or interloper at best, and to save her from the English, a quick wedding is arranged between Claire and Fraser. The reader learns that Fraser and Randall share a certain history, and the brutal scars on Fraser's back are from Randall's flogging. Thus, the author deliberately establishes a shared history between Fraser and Randall. Because Randall's in the English military and represents English rule, Fraser's doubly vulnerable to Randall's authority because of the political climate of the times.

The story rollicks through a series of adventures and in a terrible reversal Fraser is captured by the English and is sentenced to hang. As Claire and Fraser's clansmen attempt a rescue him, they learn that Randall is stationed at the prison where Fraser's being held. During the bungled rescue attempt, Claire is allowed to go free when Fraser promises himself to Randall. He is then tortured, cut, burned, beaten, raped, and hideously damaged by the villainous Randall.

After Fraser is finally rescued, he tells Claire:

> "He wanted me to crawl and beg, and by Christ, I did so. I told ye once, Sassenach, ye can break anyone if you're willing to hurt them enough. Well, he was willing. He made me crawl, and he made me beg; he made me do worse things than that, and before the end he made me want verra badly to be dead."

He goes on to explain that he wishes there were some way to heal what was broken and violated within him, and that there is a small, private place within each of us that should be inviolate:

> "You don't show that bit of yourself to anyone, usually, unless sometimes to someone that ye love greatly." …
>
> "Now, it's like … like my own fortress has been blown up with gunpowder—there's nothing left of it but ashes and a smoking rooftree, and the little naked thing that lived there once is out in the open, squeaking and whimpering in fear, tryin' to hide itself under a blade of grass or a bit o' leaf, but … but not … makin' m-much of a job of it." His voice broke, and he turned his head so that his face was hidden in my skirt. Helpless, I could do nothing but stroke his hair.

> He suddenly raised his head, face strained as though it would break apart along the seams of the bones. "I've been close to death a few times, Claire, but I've never really *wanted* to die. This time I did. I ..." His voice cracked and he stopped speaking, clutching my knee hard.

As you can see, the villain's handiwork was enormously damaging. Still in danger, Claire and Fraser manage to cross the Channel to France, where one of Fraser's uncles is the abbot of Abbey of Ste. Anne de Beaupre. But instead of healing, Fraser's condition deteriorates, as he is plagued by nightmares, unable to eat, and weakened in body and spirit. It is during this stay that the reader hears more of the details of Fraser's torture, and of the perversity and depravity of Randall's bloodlust.

Writers can take several cues from Gabaldon, including creating a highly personal situation between the hero and his nemesis. Often, stories will depict the hero falling into his nemesis's clutches. During this capture, it usually seems like all is lost. When a hero fights a nemesis, he might be temporarily defeated, but he is never completely broken. The hero always retains some untarnished part of himself; in Fraser's case, it was his love for Claire. You also want the effects of the struggle to have lasting repercussions, particularly if you're writing a series. Later in the Outlander series, both Fraser's wife and daughter are raped, and his retribution for these violations is fierce and terrible. The torments he underwent in the prison forever haunt him, and the severe trauma causes a lifetime of painful memories and nightmares.

Fraser is also unusually vulnerable because of his deep love for Claire, and because of his personal history with his nemesis. While the hero can outrun and outgun and outsmart most men of his time, once he has been brought to his knees by both love and torture, the reader will always be intimately involved in his fate.

THE MATCHUP

The mightier the hero is, the mightier the villain should be. You see, two of the chief factors that create a hero are his sacrifices for the cause and the villain he's up against. Also note that when I say matchup, I am urging you to place the characters on the stage, separately or together, as often as possible so that the reader can get the full measure of each. If your plot warrants it, this means you won't be creating a shadowy villain who lurks at the story's corners as a mere glimpse of a cape, or that the reader only knows him by the handiwork and destruction he leaves behind. For maximum wattage, bring him into the story before the midpoint, not only fully fleshed, but also as the only person who can cause your hero the most punishment.

As we've discussed, a villain always wants to gain something in the story, and he doesn't care who he brings down to obtain this end; if there is a body count as the result of his quest, so be it. A hero, on the other hand, also has goals, but he's often reacting to the villain or situation, and he places his humanity and other people's welfare first.

Now, sometimes this means that these two characters will be opposites, but sometimes they will be quite similar. For example, if you have an elegant protagonist, you might want an elegant villain. Likewise, if you have a devious villain, you will likely need a cunning hero. Or, if you create a ruthless and ambitious villain, you might want an equally determined and dogged hero. For example, in Thomas Harris's *The Silence of the Lambs*, rookie FBI agent Clarice Starling is brave, smart, ambitious, and methodical. She matches wits with Hannibal Lecter—who is brilliant, devious, secretive, and driven by his inner demons—and Buffalo Bill, a serial killer who is cunning, methodical, and diabolical. Interestingly, in Harris's tale, all three characters were scarred by childhood losses and longings, but Starling channels her energies into helping humankind, while the villains give in to their dark madness and hideous drives.

So keep in mind that it's often effective to create a hero and villain who somehow mirror or echo each other when it comes to capabilities, skills, and drives. However, no matter what their similarities are, your villain should always possess a darker, deeper shadow and values that twist far away from the hero's values. You might want to create an extra dollop of drama by giving both characters similar backgrounds. For example, if your Scotland Yard detective is also a lord, and he brings down another character of his social set, the arrest of the villain will be doubly humiliating and shocking since they travel in the same social circles.

It also can be interesting to feature heroes and villains of opposite backgrounds. For example, if your hero grew up in a hard scrabble situation in a small Nevada mining town and is now a Los Angeles chief detective, the reader's sympathies will increase if he's thrown against a murderous villain who grew up in old money and attended Harvard.

In addition, your hero and villain can have vastly different values. When creating your cast, think about the potential contrasts and similarities, and keep in mind that for every heroic quality and strength the protagonist possesses, the villain possesses its counter quality, or, in some cases, possesses the very same strengths. Here's a quick look at just a few of the potential dueling traits (again, remember that there are no real absolutes here).

VILLAIN	HERO
selfish with debased motives	selfless and ethical
gives in to temptation and falls in his character arc	fights temptations and rises in his character arc
power hungry, greedy, or tyrannical	motivated to help humankind even though at times he's cynical
ambitious, justifies his actions	proactive, accepts responsibility
weakened or destroyed by journey or quest	somehow reborn by the journey or quest (although he, too, can be physically, emotionally, or spiritually weakened)
wants to gain power, control people, and accumulate wealth	tries to bring about justice, perhaps by rescuing or freeing a person, family, place, company, or country from physical harm, tyranny, or corruption
higher nature is shut down	higher nature is awakened by the story's events

A CAVEAT ON MATCHUPS

While it appears from lists such as this one that your hero and villain are equal in strengths and skills, in the story, it should appear more complicated. If possible, in each scene, they should appear unequal—with one having the upper hand. Imagine this: Two wrestlers or boxers step out

EXAMPLES OF MATCHUPS

Here are examples of matchups between heroes and villains that illustrate some of the points just described. You will notice that the villains listed here are not only worthy of the heroes, but they have far-reaching plans that they'll go to any lengths to achieve, and they play to win. Notice, too, how in these matchups, the hero has everything to lose—his life, his reputation, his family, his future, his livelihood. And the hero and the villain are equally committed and just don't quit.

- Hansel and Gretel vs. the witch and stepmother
- Peter Pan vs. Captain Hook, *Peter Pan* by J.M. Barrie
- Willie Keith vs. Captain Queeg, *The Caine Mutiny* by Herman Wouk
- The Fantastic Four (especially Reed Richards vs. Dr. Doom), Marvel Comics
- Spider-Man vs. The Green Goblin, Marvel Comics
- Superman vs. Lex Luther, DC Comics
- Sherlock Holmes vs. Professor Moriarty, by Sir Arthur Conan Doyle
- Rosalind Leigh vs. Olive Martin, *The Sculptress* by Minette Walters
- Tally White vs. the Harvester, *Body Parts* by Vicki Stiefel
- Llewelyn Moss vs. Anton Chigurh, *No Country for Old Men* by Cormac McCarthy
- Sam Bowden vs. Max Cady, *Cape Fear* by John D. MacDonald

into the ring. Both are of equal height, weight, and musculature. Now imagine this: two fighters appear on the stage and one is six inches taller, has a much longer reach, and outweighs his opponent by a good thirty pounds. That matchup, where things don't appear quite so equal, naturally causes more interest, tension, and suspense.

So, put this to work in your story—while you, the creator, know that the hero and villain are fairly equal, within scenes and as the story progresses, it should look like the villain has the upper hand and has outfoxed the hero. A story typically begins with a hero *reacting* to the villain's plots and plans—and worthy villains have lots of plots and plans—and then as the story progresses, the hero constructs goals and plans of his own. Once in a while, you can depict your hero winning a round, but not too often. He needs to appear to be weakening in some way as the story progresses, particularly right before the climax. The matchup needs to be carefully orchestrated in order to maximize the tension.

As already mentioned, in many stories, for every quality that the hero possesses, the villain has a counterquality. However, you might want to think of this mirroring as more of a doppelgänger effect. *Doppelgänger* is a German word meaning "doublegoer" or "doublewalker" and is a look-alike or counterpart. It also can be a ghostly image, such as when you have that eerie feeling that you've glimpsed something on the edge of your vision or in a mirror, but didn't quite see it. In several literary traditions, a doppelgänger is an omen of bad luck or something that foreshadows death. Thinking about this doppelgänger effect in both characters can bring about interesting story lines.

In a similar vein, imagine how you can bring qualities of good and evil into your story without painting one character in inky black and the other in pure white. Imagine, too, how the villain can haunt the hero, as with the doppelgänger effect. Also, consider that when your hero and villain have qualities that strictly mirror each other, or are antithetical, you might be creating stereotypes. For example, if your hero loves justice and your villain sneers at all aspects of the law, then you need to go deeper; when you go with traits that are extreme opposites, you might be creating a soap opera. So as you're creating your hero and villain, try to insert some surprising differences between them, along with small tics, unusual interests, and passions as hidden depths that will be revealed slowly over the course of the story. Also be thinking of possible reasons for them to hide some of their motivations and traits from the world.

Most of Ian Fleming's James Bond novels depict the exceptionally talented 007 as vastly different from the super villains, such as Dr. No or Auric Goldfinger (more on super villains later in the chapter). But if you look closer at the villains in the series, you'll find brilliance, initiative, cunning, and blind ambition—qualities that could be laudable in a better man.

Also keep in mind that when the hero has a particular righteous cause or motivation, this somehow tips the scales in his favor when the villain appears especially unstoppable. For example, think of the dynamics in the film *The Fugitive* where the hero, Dr. Richard Kimble, played by Harrison Ford, is falsely accused of killing his wife and must find the real killer, the villain, Dr. Charles Nichols, played by Jeroen Krabbé. Both are doctors, and both are highly motivated and capable. But Nichols has made an alliance with the devil in the form of a pharmaceutical company and is motivated by greed, while Kimble is motivated by a need for justice—always a powerful factor in a story.

In the film *Gladiator*, the hero, Maximus Decimus Meridius, played by Russell Crowe, is a general and becomes a balls-to-the-wall gladiator after his betrayal and captivity by the villain, Commodus, played by Joaquin Phoenix, who had Maximus's wife and son murdered after killing his own father, the emperor, in order to take over the Roman Empire. A showdown is inevitable, and the two are well matched but vastly different in outlook, morality, and ambition.

It's not always possible to make the villain the antithesis of the hero, and stories where they're vastly different can certainly work. The trick, then, is to make the villain's backstory compelling and make the hero's stake in stopping him personal. Stories in which this scenario plays out include The Lord of the Rings trilogy by J.R.R. Tolkien, where Sauron, the villain, is a dark force trying to take over Middle Earth. While there are many heroes in the tale, the chief heroes are two hobbits, Frodo and Sam. Tolkien has chosen unlikely types to go up against the villain—a device that causes lots of tension and suspense. And once they've taken on the great quest to save Middle-earth and their losses and heartbreaks start taking a toll, the quest becomes so personal that they cannot possibly back down.

HARRY POTTER VERSUS LORD VOLDEMORT: A CLASSIC MATCHUP

Now let's look at one of the most famous matchups in contemporary fiction, because analyzing the intricacy of the relationship might give you ideas on how to make your own matchups more elaborate. The standard wisdom for writing fiction is that if you have a character representing good in the story, then you need one representing evil. Or, innocence must be offset by cynicism or depravity. To effectively feature these classic matchups or opposites, be sure to create freshly wrought archetypes or situations that make the reader deeply experience how the nemesis relationship became so personal and tangled.

There are many reasons for the success of the Harry Potter series by J.K. Rowling—a major one is the imagination of the author that built such an intricate magical world. She has also created a hero who begins the series as an underdog and a beta type but becomes more alpha as the series progresses. She gives him an interesting blend of flaws, weaknesses, and strengths while besetting him with a series of antagonists and villains to match wits with. In fact, in every book in the series, there are several antagonists who turn up the heat. The series also has one of the most famous nemesis relationships in modern literature, between Harry Potter and Lord Voldemort.

Rowling has clearly placed each character on the side of good and evil, but she also has given Voldemort and Harry many similarities to increase the wattage of their rivalry. For example, their wands are "brothers" because each contains a feather from the same phoenix. Their wands having similar origins is crucial to events in the series, as when they meet and duel using them in *Harry Potter and the Goblet of Fire*. Also, because a nemesis always makes things personal, in this same climatic scene, Voldemort uses some of Harry's blood to regain his body (he had not had a human body for some years prior to this).

Both Voldemort and Harry are orphans, both attended Hogwarts, both speak Parseltongue (they can communicate with snakes). They have an unusual shared history since Voldemort killed Harry's parents and tried to kill him when he was a baby. In fact, Harry's famous scar on his forehead came from Voldemort's attempted curse on him, which rebounded onto Voldemort. Because Harry's mother sacrificed herself to save Harry, a special magic attaches itself to Harry, making him formidable. This early meeting between Harry and Voldemort makes Harry famous in the wizarding world as "the Boy Who Lived," and it is responsible for Voldemort's downfall at that time in his life.

In *Harry Potter and the Order of the Phoenix*, Rowling again increases the friction between Harry and Voldemort because Harry starts having glimpses into the dark wizard's mind and thoughts. Using this to his advantage, Voldemort implants a false suggestion in Harry, sending him off to rescue his godfather. Harry and his friends are ambushed by

Voldemort's minions, and Harry and Voldemort clash again, but Harry is rescued. Stricken by the death of his godfather, Harry can barely take in the information that there is a prophecy about him: He must kill or be killed by Voldemort.

The sixth book in the series, *Harry Potter and the Half-Blood Prince,* finds Harry further ensnared with Voldemort because the prophecy is now common knowledge, and Harry is called "the Chosen One" because of it. During this school year, Dumbledore, the headmaster and his mentor, starts helping him learn more about Voldemort's history, particularly his weaknesses. These insights flesh out the backstory of the whole series and are the setup for the final book, where Harry will confront Voldemort.

It's interesting to note that while usually we tend to think of an evil character as the nemesis of a good character, in this case, Harry is actually Voldemort's nemesis also since Harry is the person most likely to demand retribution for his many crimes and to stop his murdering rampage and lust for power. Perhaps the biggest difference between these two rivals is that Harry has the power to love, and Voldemort only has the power to destroy.

DOUBLE TROUBLE

Another interesting factor in the Harry Potter series is that Rowling has given Harry a second nemesis in Draco Malfoy, another Hogwarts student. Malfoy is from a venerable old wizarding family, but his family leans toward the Dark Arts and Malfoy's father is part of Voldemort's inner circle.

Malfoy is, in every way, Harry's chief rival, foil, and shadow image. While Harry has soft features, green eyes, and dark hair, Malfoy has sharp features, blond hair, and cold, gray eyes. Malfoy is a bully who likes to have others do his dirty work for him; Harry champions underdogs, takes risks, and shows courage beyond his years. Like Harry, Malfoy is a talented and cunning wizard. Both boys play on their house's Quidditch team, but Malfoy has won his place on the team because his father bought the team high-powered brooms, while Harry won his place through skills and hard work.

Malfoy and Harry meet in the first book of the series, *Harry Potter and the Sorcerer's Stone.* Malfoy at first tries to befriend Harry, and the reader soon learns he's wealthy, spoiled, and the ultimate snob. When Malfoy and Harry meet again later, Harry rejects his friendship, mostly because they have vastly different values and worldviews. This rejection has lasting results throughout the series. Take note that Rowling creates an event—or, in this case, a snub—that establishes the origins of a nemesis relationship.

Malfoy's chief roles in the series are to undermine Harry at every turn, try to turn others against him, and aid Voldemort's followers in Harry's downfall. But things get really serious as Malfoy becomes more than Harry's nemesis at school, as Rowling transforms him into a growing and dangerous threat by showing him directly aiding Voldemort to take down Harry and murder Dumbledore.

By having two nemeses in the series, Rowling is able to pile on the danger and conflict, reveal Harry's many finer qualities as well as his less-than-noble ones, and give him a complicated set of circumstances and obstacles to respond to.

ENDING YOUR MATCHUP

Endings are more than the reader's worst dreads and fears coming to fruition—they contain a fillip, often a surprise, and an extra dose of genius. In general, the villain rarely shows weakness until the climax, because to do so kills the suspense, although it's permissible to reveal cracks in his armor. Because the villain appears to be superior, more cunning, and more motivated than the hero, the ending, which reverses these facts, has a big job to accomplish.

Follow these general rules of the game when you write the final scenes:

- Do not introduce any new characters. Generally, the characters who are involved in the ending have appeared more than once in the story, and the reader has a sense of their primary traits.
- Do not start new subplots or bring in a lot of new information that cannot be resolved.
- Do not orchestrate the cavalry arriving to save the day. A hero usually saves himself. Heroes can receive some help, but they are not bailed out in the ending—they do their own heavy lifting.

By the time your hero reaches the end of the story, he should be somehow changed. These changes can be for the better or for the worse. He

ROGUE'S GALLERY

ALPHA HEROES

- Augustus McCrae and Woodrow Call, *Lonesome Dove* by Larry McMurtry
- Tarzan, *Tarzan of the Apes*, by Edgar Rice Burroughs
- Kinsey Millhone, series by Sue Grafton
- Buffy Summers, *Buffy the Vampire Slayer* television series
- Travis McGee, series by John D. MacDonald
- General Maximus, played by Russel Crown in the film *Gladiator*
- The Lone Ranger, *The Lone Ranger* television series
- Luke Skywalker, played by Mark Hamill in the Star Wars films
- Lucky Jack Aubrey, series by Patrick O'Brian
- Ayla and Jondular, The Clan of the Cave Bear series by Jean M. Auel
- The Bride, played by Uma Thurman in the Kill Bill film trilogy
- Miranda Priestly, *The Devil Wears Prada* by Lauren Weisberger
- Robert Langdon, *The Da Vinci Code* by Dan Brown
- Harry Bosch, series by Michael Connelly

ALPHA NEMESES

- The Wicked Witch of the West, *The Wonderful Wizard of Oz* by L. Frank Baum
- Lex Luther, Superman comics
- Jack Merridew, *Lord of the Flies* by William Golding
- Smaug, *The Hobbit* by J.R.R. Tolkien
- Melkor/Morgoth, The Lord of the Rings trilogy and *The Silmarillion* by J.R.R. Tolkien
- Darth Vader, Star Wars films

might be stronger or wiser, but also broken, dispirited, more resolved, more wary, or more frightened than he was in the beginning of the story because the events have shaped him like steel in a forge. One of the main responsibilities of the ending is to show these changes in a dramatic scene, to provide proof of tempered steel.

A climax scene with the villain will often be a final test for the hero, and the growth that the reader has been witnessing as he handles smaller conflicts along the way will be in evidence. In fact, his growth or character arc means that he usually has a new set of skills to work with in the ending. Depending on the villain's character arc, he also might have new skills to work with. But a villain's arc never means that he's mending his evil ways.

Avoid giving the villain melodramatic flourishes in the climatic scenes. If your ending scene is graphically violent, you need to be able to justify it. If this is the first violence in the story, the reader will be thrown off guard.

Now, it's true that sometimes endings contain surprises or revelations, but these are always foreshadowed in previous chapters, and they are always a logical and sensible conclusion to plot events.

Sometimes in the ending, the hero realizes that he'll never know the whole truth of a situation, or that a clear-cut solution or resolution isn't possible. Perhaps the cop will arrest the bad guy, but he knows that tomorrow another thug will replace him to lead the drug cartel or porn ring. Some stories require this sort of grim reality, and sometimes resolution isn't a tidy killing off of the bad guys and promotion of the good guys. After all, life is complicated, justice is not always fair, the rich and powerful sometimes get away with their crimes, and a victory is often bittersweet.

But if your ending is somehow ambiguous, the reader often needs a sense of hope or a sense that something good has been gained. Perhaps the hero will keep searching for answers, for criminals, for missing and exploited children. Even a weary acceptance that he'll keep trudging along in his role as protector of the weak is a resolution to the story. The trick to writing a realistic ending is that the main issues of the story have been showcased and shown to be intolerable (such as a child pornography ring or a mass murderer on the loose), and the ending proves the premise of the story. It might be that crime never pays, that good can triumph with the support of moral people, or that justice is blind.

When it comes to writing endings, use caution. Violence goes a long way, as do fiery confrontations, shoot-outs, demolitions, and the like. An ending that includes the villain's demise must be in sync with the level of threat and the genre. For example, if you're writing a thriller, then it's likely that the villain will be killed, and that other characters have been bumped off as the story progressed. If you're writing a suspense story, there also might be a body count, but it's likely the villain will be captured and brought to justice. Avoid using coincidences, car chases, bombs exploding, and acts of nature to end the story. Instead, the reader wants a face-off, the literary equivalent of the shoot-out at the O.K. Corral. Not all villains need to be killed to end the story, but some punishment or justice must occur. Avoid making villains simply disappear or escape.

Once you've got the ending nailed down, don't linger. Create the ending for the maximum emotional impact, then slip off the stage. As you exit, leave the reader with a final note—an anecdote, a dialogue exchange, a glimpse backward, a poignant image. If you're writing a legal thriller or a densely complicated tale, or if the ending was especially surprising or abrupt, you might want to insert a brief epilogue that settles the score, explains the ramifications of the plot, or shows a future that is not mentioned in the ending.

The point of featuring a hero in a story is that he will accomplish acts, take risks, make sacrifices, and venture into places most of us would fear. He also faces villains who would send most of us cowering under our beds, because, as Christopher Vogler says in *The Writer's Journey*, "Villains and enemies are usually dedicated to the death, destruction and defeat of the hero."

Strive to create villains who exist beyond archetypes and stereotypes. Remember that villains are driven by the same emotions and forces that you and I feel: lust, pride, envy, love, greed, ambition, hate, worry. In general, whenever possible, introduce your story's villain in motion or in an action scene. It's not as effective to merely mention his existence—bring him onto the stage.

CHAPTER NINE

Sympathy for the Devil

Our deeds determine us, as much as we determine our deeds; and until we know what has been or will be the peculiar combination of outward with inward facts which constitute a man's critical actions, it will be better not to think ourselves wise about his character.

—George Eliot

It cannot be said too often: Antagonists—and villains, in particular—are complicated, three-dimensional, and robustly knowable people. After all, it is the process of *learning* about fascinating characters in terrible difficulties that draws readers in. Readers especially want to learn about what makes a bad ass tick.

Let's delve into why sympathy is often mentioned with fictional characters, what it really means, and how it applies to bad asses, particularly to villains. Since this chapter is about creating sympathy, I want you to think of sympathy as a much broader concept than the typical definition. In this context, sympathy doesn't necessarily stem from likeability, but, rather, from readers recognizing characters' basic human qualities, aspirations, and sensibilities. Just to note, empathy for characters means that the reader feels like he's identified with or is experiencing a character's goals, emotions, or way of thinking. Empathy, whereby the reader and character are emotionally entwined, is most often associated with protagonists and sometimes with antagonists, but rarely with villains.

So we're going to explore how to reveal the souls and psyches of villains and other complicated types so that they're unmistakable.

Many of the techniques outlined in this chapter can also work with antagonists and anti-heroes, including dark heroes and bad boys. So, although the term *villain* will often appear in the discussion here, consider how these techniques might be applied to other unconventional main characters who require a special degree of intricacy.

There are a number of lessons I want you to take away from this chapter; most of them evolve from having a very intimate knowledge of your characters. Every writer has his own way "in" to the story. Some plan, some dream, some piece a story together like a puzzle as bits of inspiration slip into consciousness. For most writers, plot and conflict are so entwined with characters that one cannot be known without the other.

However, if you're the sort of writer who likes to plan and outline, you might want to begin writing a novel by getting to know your characters within the framework of your plot. Characters without a plot idea are lifeless sketches since each character must fit the particular needs of the story. So it rarely works to merely create characters without imagining the world they'll inhabit and the problems they'll encounter. Once you have even a hazy knowledge of your plot, you can begin to create a cast.

Start by making major choices for your main characters since it will be easier to plot if you first decide on the dominant traits and morality of your main players. As you outline your protagonist's traits and major actions in the story, you'll also make crucial distinctions about him, such as if he's likeable or unlikeable, heroic or ordinary. As your protagonist takes shape, your antagonist—especially if your story calls for a villain—will likely be forming alongside him.

If you're featuring a villain in your story, your essential choice is whether he will be sympathetic (as in someone the reader comes to know and can discern his humanity) or unsympathetic (as in someone whose humanity eludes the reader). The other crucial distinction in creating a villain is deciding whether he's villainous at heart, or if *circumstances* have turned him into a villain. Once these bigger considerations are out of the way, the more intimate details about his backstory and front story can be shaped.

While it sounds antithetical to describe a bad guy as sympathetic, when you create any type of bad ass, you need to look deep into his troubled soul and explore his motivations, desires, and past for the roots of his deformed psyche. He might long for power, acceptance, or fame; perhaps these are desires similar to the protagonist's. While in some stories a stock villain—a person who simply is evil, the type that the reader loves to hate—might be needed, in most stories, when a villain has primal, understandable human drives, the story has more depth and resonance.

While a villain may be sympathetically drawn because you've created him as multi-dimensional and included his backstory, his *goals* won't necessarily be ones that the reader identifies with because those goals are going to be harmful, immoral, illegal, or even evil. (Remember that with anti-heroes or other bad asses, their goals are also sometimes difficult for readers to identify with.) If a villain's sympathetically drawn, it doesn't mean that when he thunders after a victim with a chainsaw, the reader is thinking, *Oh, I bet he doesn't* really *mean to hurt him.* A guy with a chainsaw, unless he's chopping up firewood, will always be dangerous, and the reader needs to believe in his dangerousness. What sympathy provides is understanding.

Creating a sympathetic villain also doesn't mean creating a character who's weak or ineffective, although there is often something rather pitiful about a villain. This pity is typically stirred because the villain doesn't have full access to his humanity, or because he has somehow shut himself off from others or reality.

Sympathy means you'll want to *humanize* a villain so that the reader might come away with a haunting understanding of his twisted soul. A reader doesn't need to like your character, but when he can understand a character, the story has deeper power. Conversely, this also works well with creating protagonists and heroes. If the reader believes in a protagonist's (especially a hero's) *flaws*, he'll believe in the story. If the reader believes in the antagonist's or villain's *humanity*, he'll believe in the story.

Also, sometimes the reader might believe that there is a tiny spark of decency buried within a villain that makes him worth redeeming. In some stories, this spark gets snuffed out when the villain whacks his next victim, sometimes this spark simmers throughout the story, and sometimes it never exists.

FIRST COMES KNOWLEDGE

In many amateur writers' manuscripts, the story suffers from not so much a lack of imagination, but a lack of nuance, emotional range, and detailed knowledge of the human psyche. The results are story people who are merely caricatures.

While you can draw from your own life experiences, writing fiction in which a villain—especially one who is psychologically damaged, such as a sociopath—appears is firmly grounded in research into human psychology, mental illness, and how the brain and emotions evolve through different stages of development.

In writing your villain, you'll want to talk with experts and read articles on abnormal psychology and the latest psychological research. You'll also want to know the basic characteristics of specific criminal types; you'll want to know if they are capable of empathy, or if their lack of empathy sets them apart from the rest of humanity, as we explored in chapter seven about sociopaths. If your story type warrants it, you'll also need an understanding of the criminal justice system, realizing that watching *CSI* and television shows of that ilk doesn't qualify as research.

In real life, most of us prefer to lump people into categories. There's our nice neighbor and our cranky neighbor. Our reliable friends and our flighty ones. The awesome ex-boyfriend and the psycho ex-boyfriend. The wonderful boss and the awful boss. Sometimes these judgments and classifications have validity. If your friend is late nine times out of ten, you'd be silly to expect her to show up on time the next time you meet. If your neighbor throws wild parties every weekend with people vomiting on the lawn and music blaring until three in the morning, it wouldn't make sense to classify this neighbor as thoughtful. So classifying people is simply expedient. But as a fiction writer, you need to be careful about classifications and generalizations.

Because we sometimes paint people with these broad strokes, we might wander through life ignoring all the shadings people possess, discounting their more complicated traits and nuanced reasons for acting as they do. Humans long to bring order to the world—to categorize, judge, and sort people based on a few incidents or missteps. This habit often takes hold during our childhood and adolescence. A teacher gave you a D on a report you slaved over, so he now gets lumped into the "bad" teacher file. A neighbor yells at you for walking on his lawn, so he gets filed under "crank." A friend stands you up, so she is categorized under "flake." Meanwhile, you forget that the teacher is often a fascinating lecturer, that the neighbor sometimes gave you rides to school in bad weather, and that your friend listened to you for hours when you lamented ad nauseum about breaking up with your sophomore-year sweetheart. It's likely that although you're an adult now, you might still hang on to these tendencies of classification and simplification. As you create your characters, you must go deeper and defy the urge to typecast. Otherwise, your characters will likely be thinly drawn, and thus be unsympathetic.

It's also important to realize that good people break our hearts, break their promises, disappoint us, and betray us. Good people can be insensitive or selfish; even the best of us are not always tolerant, patient, and kind. This business of being good while walking through life is enormously difficult. Each day, people and events get on our nerves and strain our patience. A story can be especially dramatic when a decent person missteps, but even more so when a bad person does.

Knowledge of human nature and psychology is essential to fiction writers because we live in a sophisticated age. Your readers might regularly tune in to Dr. Phil or Oprah, read various self-help and inspirational books, and listen to psychologists on talk radio. They've heard theories about why serial killers go on killing sprees, why meth is so addictive, and why intimacy is so difficult for many people. In fact, we're bombarded with information in our society, and much of it strives for an understanding of why people do what they do.

So, while in real life you might quickly classify or lump people into various types, if you're writing a villain in your story, with a few exceptions, he cannot be simplistic. If your villain is a *type* rather than a fully-fleshed person, he can be trite and anemic, a marionette twitching when you pull his strings. You need a source code for his actions, and you need to know how you want your reader to react. Do his actions stem from human weakness, mental illness, misguided principles, or rationalization? Is your villain broken, cynical, or amoral? Is he a poseur? Is he conflicted? Is there pathos at his center?

As a fiction writer, you're aware that you're writing for a sophisticated audience that expects depth, knowledge, and intimacy when reading fiction. Readers don't always need to identify with your characters, but they do want consistency and to meet story people they've never met before. Respect this, and deliver stories brimming with an assorted cast that has complicated reasons for doing what they do.

Think of the villains in Alfred Hitchcock's films as you ponder the lessons in this chapter. It was Hitchcock who said that the better the villain is, the better the movie is. Some of his villains were urbane, some were con men, thieves, and traitors. Sometimes a villain was a married man who'd grown tired of his wife and turned murderous. But most of them had some depth and some humanity, and often they left us wondering about how they came to be. Hitchcock's films also teach writers that the more screen time or pages you lavish on the villain or any character, the more complexity is necessary since readers and filmgoers want to follow rounded characters.

When a villain is in the story, the reader generally will be filled with dread and horror. But you want to engage both the reader's intellect and his emotions. Shakespeare's plays feature complicated characters, most of whom are not simply good or evil. A more contemporary example of a compelling villain is Mitch Leary, played by John Malkovich, in the film *In the Line of Fire*. It's an assassin-on-the-loose thriller, but in this case, Leary is an ex-CIA operative who has suffered a breakdown. He also feels betrayed by this organization and wants payback. Malkovich embodies the complicated and wily Leary, and he seems both believable and menacing in the role.

INTIMACY: SLEEPING WITH THE ENEMY

In real life, people become known to us when we spend lots of time with them, listen to their childhood stories, and witness how they handle themselves in a variety of situations. As most married people will attest, true knowledge of a person comes after you've lived together and shared a bed.

I'm talking about both literal and broader interpretations of sleeping with people, so bear with me. For instance, maybe in your childhood, you shared a bedroom with a sibling, and his snores, breathing, rustling, and habits became the rhythms of your night and created a deep understanding of the person. Perhaps you attended summer camp and felt like you knew your bunkmates intimately by the end of your two weeks together. This type of intimate knowledge can come from sharing a marriage bed or living with a lover or roommate. Spending nights in such close proximity lets you know a person in ways you'll never know co-workers or neighbors. We are all vulnerable and exposed in our sleep, and sharing this particular space makes for a fascinating breadth of knowledge.

In creating your bad ass characters, especially your villains, imagine this level of intimacy. If you can imagine this sort of depth, your villain will be humanized, or perhaps even seem ordinary. An ordinary person with a capacity to harm others is much scarier than an invincible, ten-foot robot that is typecast complete with a maniacal laugh.

Let's think about this: When you sleep with someone, you know what he or she is like the first thing in the morning—bleary eyed and foggy or instantly alert; what he or she wears or doesn't wear while sleeping; and if he or she suffers from nightmares or insomnia. In this level of intimacy, you know if a person hogs the blankets, sleeps in a fetal position, or prefers the windows open year-round. Now, start asking yourself how you can bring this level of knowledge into your story and characters.

You might be wondering how the style of pajamas a character wears makes a difference in your story. The point isn't whether a character wears pajamas or sleeps nude. It likely doesn't matter much if he's a tea drinker or starts the day with a double espresso. The point is to imagine your character with the same depth that you can with your husband, wife, roommate, sister, or brother in a variety of situations.

As with the people you have shared intimate space with, you should be able to make a long list of your characters' preferences, mannerisms, and habits. Know the sort of mess they leave in the bathroom after a shower; in more intimate relationships, know the smell and quality of their skin, the texture of their hair, what parts of their bodies are like—the nape of the neck, the inner elbow, the crooked toes, the hidden mole. Once you know these small and penetrating details, you will have the level of knowledge that helps you understand how and why their minds work. You should also know what sort of routines they follow, and what habits and interests make them tick. And most of all, know their drenching sorrows or wounds, exactly how they feel when they're scared, and what they do when they're afraid.

Keeping this level of intimacy in mind, imagine your bad ass in a variety of circumstances. Imagine him when he's trying to appear charming and normal at a cocktail party or at tea with his godmother. Imagine him when he cannot find a parking space, when he's forced to wait in a long line, when a sales clerk is inept or impertinent with him, or when he must perform a task he's sure is beneath him. Imagine him thwarted at big and small goals, imagine him longing to brag about his exploits but needing to keep quiet, and, most of all, imagine him when his best-laid and most intricate plans go awry.

After all, even villains are going to be depicted under stress and possibly not always at the heights of their power. Perhaps your character will need to rely on underlings who are incompetent, will juggle a family or job along with criminal activities, or will act against his best judgment. Always keep in mind that the events of the story often also exhaust the villain and push him to the limits of endurance, tolerance, and patience. There is nothing that steals credibility in a story like characters who never tire or sleep or eat or pause to nurse a wound.

SHAPING THE BACKSTORY

If you've ever visited a natural history museum where the skeleton of a dinosaur or another huge mammal was reconstructed, you might have imagined the extreme care and delicacy that was involved in assembling the beast. Keep this delicate task in mind as you place the pieces of your villain, bone by bone, into place. You'll be fabricating a range of skills and talents, along with insecurities, flawed thinking, and misplaced motives. It will require the daintiest tools in your repertoire, your most finely honed awareness of human nature.

When it comes to villains, there are deep considerations on how to make him not only a compelling threat, but also a compelling person. In shaping your villain, here are some questions you need to consider:

- What is his "regular" or "normal" world before the story begins?
- What does he do on a normal day?

- Did he come from an intact family or a divorced family? Would he consider his childhood happy, difficult, or best forgotten?
- Did he have a large extended family? If so, how important were these influences?
- Was his family financially stable? If not, how does this affect him now?
- Is he a loner? If not, who are his peers?
- Is he capable of intimacy?
- What was his biggest disappointment? What did he do about it?
- Has he suffered from physical, emotional, or sexual abuse? If so, how are you going to demonstrate the repercussions of this in his present actions?
- Is there a history of addiction, such as alcoholism, in his family? If so, how has he been affected?
- Is he considered the black sheep of the family? If not, what role is he assigned?
- Is there a history of mental illness in his family? If so, what are his coping methods and personality traits as a result?
- Does he have a personal or family secret that is rarely mentioned?
- Was there a tragedy in his family, such as the death of a child, that is rarely mentioned?
- Is there a particular trauma from the past that is going to influence his front story?
- If the trauma were severe, does he suffer from Post Traumatic Stress Disorder? If so, how does it manifest in his actions and daily life?
- Does he have a history of committing juvenile crimes, such as violence against animals?
- Has he ever been incarcerated?

- Has he ever had obsessive fantasies or been a stalker?
- What items does he have in his wallet, safe-deposit box, or hiding place that he doesn't want people to know about?

These questions aren't necessarily appropriate to every member of your cast, but some of these factors might shape your villain's situation.

A VILLAIN'S ORIGINS

If people come from a fragile or troubled family, research proves that they're often at risk to go on to create the same problems or patterns as adults. As children in a dysfunctional home, they often learn these cardinal rules: don't trust; don't talk; don't feel. This means that if a parent is a raging alcoholic, has a propensity for violence, or is involved in criminal activities, the kids will often cover it up and something within them will shut down.

Now, some kids will act out (family therapists have labeled these kids *scapegoats*), and some will act heroic to keep the family system afloat. The scapegoat kid typically reflects the extreme stress felt in the family and is often seen as the problem in the family, but it's usually a parent's drinking or abuse that is the real problem. Often, the first strategy for the children is to move away as soon as possible and somehow distance themselves from their families of origin.

If your villain or other character comes from a dysfunctional family, you'll want to research the various roles played by family members and reflect on how all that has happened in childhood will play out. Has the character lost access to his emotions? Does he trust anyone? Has he recreated a dysfunctional situation, or has he risen above his background?

It cannot be said often enough that the protagonist's backstory, or events that happened before the story begins, haunts the front story with the pain and insistence of a migraine. However, it must also be noted that the villain's backstory has an equal, or mostly likely a greater, influence over all the story's events.

It is rare that bad people just happen. Family members and professionals attest that some children seem simply to be born bad or with a propensity for violence or dishonesty. Or, sometimes genetic factors are pointed out—for example, a child of a sociopathic parent is more likely to be a sociopath than the rest of the population. Or, with children who have learning disorders or Attention Deficit Disorder, if they are not treated and monitored properly, they can eventually take on destructive behaviors.

There is also a possibility that a villain had a fairly normal childhood, but then something happened to turn him to the dark side. Perhaps he became involved with drugs or addictions, which, in turn, led him to crime or an outsider's lifestyle. Or perhaps a tragedy struck later and has shaped your villain, such as his beloved wife or child was killed by a drunk driver and he becomes an avenger. Perhaps a woman is brutally raped, a child is exploited by a pedophile, a teen joins a gang, or a computer geek stumbles onto an online get-rich-quick scheme. Or, at an impressionable age, a villain might meet an influential person, such as a hardened criminal, who turned him away from normalcy. If a villain starts out with a fairly normal upbringing but then turns toward crime or evil, it's essential that you know the turning point and the motivation that transformed him into such a tormenting presence.

And before you start worrying that all this knowledge of backstory and the like will bog down your story, remember that, as the writer, you'll always know more about your characters than what ends up on the page. Depending on the story line, you must decide how much information your reader needs to know so that your characters' actions have a proper context. Thus, as the creator of your characters, you'll know everything about them, even when the information is not explicit in the story.

LEGACY OF TRAUMA

In the overall prison population, many of the convicts were exposed to some kind of trauma or abuse in childhood. The same is true for fictional villains, so it is your job to research exactly how traumas affect and motivate people as they go through life.

Sometimes a villain's backstory won't necessarily be traumatic, but it will still color his adult perceptions. But most characters in fiction are somehow scarred by loss, and this is especially true for villains. I like to think of this as the "runt of the litter" approach. If you've ever seen a litter of puppies or kittens and noticed how the runt is left behind and cannot feed as often as the others, your sympathy for the smaller

A LITTLE LIGHT READING

Here are some resources for getting under the skin of villains and other troubled characters:

- *The Sociopath Next Door* by Martha Stout, Ph.D.
- *Breathing Life Into Your Characters* by Rachel Ballon, Ph.D.
- *The Criminal Mind* by Katherine Ramsland, Ph.D.
- *Emotional Intelligence* by Daniel Goleman
- *Bad Boys, Bad Men: Confronting Antisocial Personality Disorder* by Donald W. Black, M.D.
- *Certifiably Insane* by Arthur W. Bahr
- *The Mad, the Bad, and the Innocent: The Criminal Mind on Trial—Tales of a Forensic Psychologist* by Barbara R. Kirwin, Ph.D.
- *Journal of the American Academy of Psychiatry and the Law*
- *American Journal of Forensic Psychology*

littermate is activated. But sometimes the runt grows up with a fierce sense of entitlement. The degree of trauma in the villain's backstory will directly relate to the degree of villainy in the front story. The more powerful your villain is, the more important it is that you give him a compelling reason for his adult viewpoints and actions.

SYMPATHY STRATEGIES

Let's talk about some of the ways you can make your villains sympathetic—keeping in mind, of course, that sympathetic is not synonymous with likeable. As with creating a character arc for all types of story people, one way to make a villain sympathetic is to show that he's capable of change. This doesn't mean he'll change his evil ways by the story's end; it's more likely that you will show he was once not so twisted, or that you will reveal the loss or trauma that changed him. Some aspect of change is always a bedrock of sympathetic fictional characters, even villains.

Here is a list of sympathy strategies more specific to villains, but keep in mind that all the strategies center around the knowledge that the reader sympathizes with characters going through trials and feeling emotions that he understands:

- Make certain that there is nothing illogical about the villain's actions, as if you are pulling the strings behind the scene.
- Avoid coincidences that bring the villain together with the protagonist to make things happen in the story.
- Beware of giving the villain a backstory that is so horrific or downtrodden that it's supposed to excuse creepy or illegal behavior. While a villain's backstory can start him on the road to crime, it must be realistically drawn and also involve him making bad choices.
- Since sympathy for all characters happens when the reader watches them struggle, especially with conflict or an uphill battle, don't allow the villain to breeze through the story without stirring a hair or breaking a sweat. His struggle to defeat the hero, for example, might cause wonder or begrudging admiration in the reader.
- If you're writing a villain who is up against an ordinary person, make sure the villain has some ordinariness as well. When invincible types are in the story, it kills sympathy.
- Remember that, as with good guys, the reader's sympathy is ignited for villains when he witnesses the villain experience vulnerability, anguish, and embarrassment.
- For most stories, make certain that the villain is too evil to live (even if that means a life sentence in prison).
- Give the villain an opportunity to make a choice, even if that choice is the wrong one.
- Show a crack in the villain's armor, such as willfulness, arrogance, or excessive pride.
- Depict the villain interacting with other characters, perhaps even showing his deep feelings for a loved one, or kindness or empathy toward a vulnerable character.

- Stop thinking about your villain as a character, and instead think of him as a person.

These are basic strategies, but you can come up with your own plans to create a realistic and believable villain. For inspiration, read other authors' works, and make a note when an author implants a revelation about a character's humanity that you weren't expecting.

Remember, you have fiction's basic toolbox—exposition, dialogue, action, gestures, mannerisms, setting—at your disposal to create believability and sympathy. When you find stories in which you particularly believe in the characters, dissect the author's methods. Based on your reading, you might want to use a narrator to stand apart from the story and comment on the story milieu, or on the motives or backstories of characters. If the reader comes to trust the narrator, he comes to understand the characters, including the villain under discussion.

If you want to create depth in a villain, you can also use indirect means. Perhaps a secondary character can offer opinions about the villain, or he can be revealed through newspaper accounts, a trial transcript, a psychologist's therapy sessions, or police investigation notes.

Or, perhaps you'll want to place the reader squarely in the villain's thoughts so he can experience this inner world. In real life, we often long to know exactly what a partner, spouse, or child is thinking. In fiction, we have the opportunity to slip into a character's mind. And this experience can be especially delicious when the character is a villain because the reader understands the rarity of this experience. If the villain is friendless, tortured, egomaniacal, or unable to control murderous impulses, the reader will experience these sensations and feel the chilling reality of this troubled soul. Or, conversely, you might want to shape a villain who is self-deprecating or ruthlessly honest about his own motives, or make his bravado rather admirable.

EMPATHY

When a villain is on stage in a story, you want to elicit a whole range of complicated emotions in the reader. The reader should be fascinated by the villain, worried about his capabilities, and in some way feel that he has met this nightmarish creature. But a story works best when the reader also understands a villain and can see beneath the actions that brand him.

What can be especially emotion-provoking in the reader is when this understanding is also laced with empathy for how a villain came to be. Sometimes, you might want to cause the reader's sympathies to yo-yo—for a moment, he feels sympathy or empathy with the villain, then when the scoundrel pulls off a caper or harms a vulnerable character, these feelings will shut down, only to be activated again when another piece of the villain's backstory shows a deprived childhood.

Author Thomas Harris is perhaps best known for his complex villain Hannibal ("The Cannibal") Lecter, but in his novel *Red Dragon*, he thrusts the reader deep into characters' hearts, vulnerabilities, and souls so that the reader's emotional involvement is complicated and erratic.

The villain in question in *Red Dragon* is Francis Dolarhyde, and he seems to have a benign occupation—processing film in a lab. The lab handles photos snapped at family vacations and birthday parties—records of everyday life that he's never part of. You see, he was born with a cleft lip and palate and rejected by his mother. He was raised by his grandmother, not out of the goodness of her heart, but out of a grudge between mother and daughter. His grandmother, a cold-hearted monster, wanted to keep him close as a pawn in a high-stakes game only she could win.

The story begins when Will Graham, who had been nearly killed by Hannibal Lecter during his capture, is coerced out of early retirement by the FBI's Jack Crawford to help solve two murders. Happily married and a stepfather, Graham reluctantly agrees to work on the case. Much of the opening chapters detail how Graham begins his investigation and starts uncovering small clues. He has never been the same since his dustup with Lecter, and his fragility in the story creates an extra dose of tension.

Serial killers often have a safe place to have their private chamber of horrors, as is the case with Dolarhyde, who lives in a house where the nearest neighbor is a half-mile away:

> Dolarhyde always made an inspection tour of the house as soon as he got home; there had been an abortive burglary attempt some years before. He flicked on the lights in each room and looked around. A visitor would not think he lived alone. His grandparents' clothes still hung in the closets, his grandmother's brushes were on her dresser

> with combings of hair in them. Her teeth were in a glass on the bedside table. The water had long since evaporated. His grandmother had been dead for ten years.

From this description, the reader follows him through an evening alone, including when he watches a home movie of his murder victims. The film is spliced with shots of him sexually aroused, raping his victim, then a final shot of an entire family arranged in a tableau with Dolarhyde capering naked and blood smeared among them.

I don't know about you, but a person as depraved and whacked-out as Dolarhyde doesn't exactly draw tears of sympathy. Especially after another scene where he's alone with a ledger of souvenirs from his victims and newspaper clippings of his crimes, after his feelings of allegiance toward Hannibal Lecter are revealed, and after he kidnaps tabloid reporter Freddy Lounds, forces him to recant something he wrote about

ROGUE'S GALLERY

I strongly recommend reading George R.R. Martin's fantasy series because many of his villains are fully drawn and fascinating, and his characters occupy unique moral territories with shifting alliances, motivations, and goodness. Here is a small sampling of other multi-dimensional villains:

- Hannibal Lecter, *The Silence of the Lambs* by Thomas Harris
- Martin Michael Plunkett, *Killer on the Road* by James Ellroy
- The Wolverine, *The Big Nowhere* by James Ellroy
- Albert, *The Color Purple* by Alice Walker
- Jack Merridew, *Lord of the Flies* by William Golding
- Tyler Durden, *Fight Club* by Chuck Palahniuk
- Flint Marko (Sandman), played by Thomas Haden Church in the film *Spider-Man 3*
- Doctor Otto Octavius (Doctor Octopus), played by Alfred Molina in the film *Spider-Man 2*
- Henry, Francis, Charles, and Camilla, *The Secret History* by Donna Tartt

him, bites off his lips, sets him on fire, and rolls him into the front door of the newspaper office.

By the time Lounds is screaming in agony, the reader has witnessed Dolarhyde's bottomless rage, often a feature of killers. But then to complicate matters, Harris also reveals that Dolarhyde is driven by a desperate loneliness, and that people who are physically deformed will always be outsiders and will always be scorned. The reader has witnessed how, because he's had reconstructive surgery, he has a speech impediment, and fellow employees make fun of him.

Harris tosses another hand grenade into the story when Dolarhyde falls in love with Reba McClane, one of his co-workers. Reba is blind, spunky, likeable, and interesting. Now he has a reason to control his violent urges, but can he?

In reading *Red Dragon*, the reader is worried about Graham and his fragile recovery, especially after Lecter attempts to send Dolarhyde Grahams's address and his family is forced to flee their home. But when Reba becomes intimate with Dolarhyde and enters his house, the place where his grandmother treated him so shabbily, the reader's skin is prickling with worry and anticipation. Then, apparently in a move to save Reba, Dolarhyde shoots himself and sets the house on fire, which brings the reader back to empathy with Dolarhyde. Or does it?

Recovering from her ordeal, Reba is tormented and doubting herself. Graham tells her:

> "... There was plenty wrong with Dolarhyde, but there's nothing wrong with you. You said he was kind and thoughtful to you. I believe it. That's what you brought out in him. At the end, he couldn't kill you and he couldn't watch you die. People who study this kind of thing say he was trying to stop. Why? Because you helped him. That probably saved some lives. You didn't draw a freak. You drew a man with a freak on his back. ..."

Harris, a master grenade launcher, tosses in a final round because Dolarhyde isn't dead after all—the body found in the house was one of his victims.

Just as we're utterly horrified by Dolarhyde, especially when we learn that he considers his massacres his life's work, Harris starts weaving in his backstory and lobbing missiles until we're so caught up in the drama, that, while we're not rooting for Dolarhyde, we're experiencing conflicting feelings about what is left of his tarnished humanness. We understand that people suffering from such severe psychosis cannot see reality in the way that we can. We can imagine Dolarhyde as a much different person if his mother hadn't rejected him, if his grandmother hadn't been so cruel, if his reconstructive surgery had been more successful, if somewhere during his lonely childhood someone would have loved him or at least intervened when he first started showing signs of deviant behavior.

In a similar fashion, if you can create a villain that makes the reader understand him with this depth, you'll have succeeded in humanizing him and creating intricate emotions in your reader.

The forces that shape villains in fiction and in real life can rarely be undone. Thus, when you're creating sympathy for a villain, you're doing so because of his situation and backstory. Not only do readers want to walk along in your protagonist's clothes, they want a close-up meeting with the villain, a meeting so physical and fully wrought that the character's smell, posture, and menacing or seemingly benign presence will take over their senses. Readers want a glimpse or, better yet, a tour of the inner workings of someone drastically different from them.

CHAPTER TEN

Bitches: Dangerous Women

Women do not have any macho tradition to uphold. We are socialized to be nurturing and nice. Beneath these feelings, however, has always been an icy rage. When you ask a woman to focus her imagination toward murder, she treats it as fresh turf and brings to it an enthusiasm that may not be naturally shared by a man, exposed as he has been to violent moments his entire life.

—Sue Grafton

Let's talk about dangerous women who break the rules.

Eve.
Jezebel.
Lady Macbeth.
Lady Chatterely.
Hester Prynne.
Emma Bovary.

Society has always feared women who defy conventions because civilization depended on women to birth and rear children, and to focus on their family's well-being while remaining sexually monogamous. So the criticism and disdain heaped on women who step outside the bounds of civilization has always been much harsher than for men who do the same. We need women to hold down the home front and wake in the night to care for her fevered child, to provide comfort and succor and dinner on the table, and, these days, often to provide a second paycheck so a family can survive. When women don't stick to home and hearth, and especially when women are amoral or lawbreakers, many people become anxious, and thus society has always tried to keep women in line.

This uneasy terrain where traditional notions about femininity meet the reality of women's lives can be fertile territory for creating female characters, especially characters who are rule-breakers. Let's borrow a familiar term from the lexicon and call these characters bitches. For our purposes, a bitch might be an unlikeable protagonist, an antagonist, an anti-hero, or a villain. The point of using a bitch in a story is that she somehow defies traditional gender expectations, roles, and sensibilities to increase tension and introduce intriguing themes. She is often empowered by anger, a need to survive, or self-fulfillment. She is typically dangerous to at least one vulnerable character in the story, and she can also be self-destructive or dangerous to herself.

This chapter is designed to increase your understanding of how you can create female characters who exist beyond archetypes and who are intricate and beguiling. If a bitch is cast in a story—particularly if she is cast as an anti-hero or villain, or in a role that is typical of males (a private detective, for instance)—she needs to be completely female, not be a feminized version of male types.

After all, we've been reading about bitches since we were children and we encountered the biblical story of the conniving Delilah who emasculates Samson, the mythology around the terrifying and vengeful Medea, and the many scary females in Grimm's fairy tales. Because the bitch character is atypical, she creates a special fascination and tension in the reader, along with an age-old appeal from reading myths and fairy tales with witches, jealous stepsisters, and wicked stepmothers in the cast. You see, when a female bad ass is on the page, the contradictions of an angel or mother figure masking a demon or a woman with unusual powers makes for potent storytelling.

ROOTED IN HISTORY

In previous centuries, often when a writer magnified a female character's assertiveness, ambition, or sexuality, or endowed her with any kind of potency, the character was automatically considered a bitch. These days, a potent female in a story can be many things; she might be a bitch or she might not, but she will likely cause tension. You see, although times have changed, they haven't changed all that much, because in most arenas, when a woman holds power, she's often considered a threat. Perhaps powerful women will always frighten a certain segment of the population. No matter what your feelings about the subject are, it's helpful to know that this uneasiness about female potency can be exploited.

Throughout history, there has always been a gender divide, and it was reflected in storytelling. This divide meant there were perceived to be vast differences between the sexes, and it also granted males more power in most arenas. Another aspect of the divide was that since women weren't as endowed with testosterone, and weren't part of war and other violent pursuits, and since they bear children, it was believed that they didn't behave or think like men. They didn't cheat, scheme, or murder. Instead, they submitted, went along for the good of the family or group, and controlled their anger, even if this meant they often weren't in control of their own lives or fate.

Statistics throughout history also show that women are more likely to be the victims, not the perpetrators of violence. Thus, when women turn the tables, the natural order of things is upset and balance needs to be restored. Often, this has meant in real life and in fiction that the bitch must be punished. For example, when one of the first black widows of drama, Clytemnestra, wife of Agamemnon, takes a lover and kills her husband, she is punished. However, if we look closer at the myth, we discover that Agamemnon sacrificed their daughter Iphigenia, and that when he returned from the Trojan War, he brought home another woman, Cassandra. In some versions of the myth, Clytemnestra was murdered by her son to avenge his father's death. The point here is that while the male sacrificed his own daughter and brought home a second wife, it is the female of the story who is often seen as unnatural and scheming.

In most dramatic forms, bitches have been depicted as somehow despicable, sordid creatures who need to be brought to justice or tamed to serve as a lesson to other women who might break the rules. This meant that Lady Macbeth, one of Shakespeare's most frightening female characters, is assumed to have committed suicide, and Gustave Flaubert's Madame Bovary, who has affairs and acquires debt, kills herself at the end of the novel. Let's not forget that despite its tragic ending, when *Madame Bovary* was published, Flaubert was accused of obscenity and the book was put on trial.

Since the 1960s, traditional roles for women have been changing. Marriage is no longer a relationship where men pursue careers and women stay home caring for the house and children, financially and emotionally dependent on their husbands. This sweeping shift of gender roles brought enormous alterations to the landscape that is America, and it has also stretched into other countries.

Women now occupy political offices, boardrooms, and executive suites. They fly to outer space and make breakthrough medical and scientific discoveries. Yet there is something in many of us that still expects women to be different than men, to be kinder, sweeter, gentler, and more nurturing. Socialization still finds women bound to their families. Interested in communication and friendship, and unburdened by high levels of testosterone, they react differently to stress, competition, and power. And because we still expect women to be the gentler sex, they are perceived to be less likely to commit crimes, to sleep around, or to harm others by contrivance or violence.

And because of all these expectations about how women should act, fiction writers naturally have weighed in on the reality of being female and have either voiced the status quo or exploded notions of the so-called gentler sex. In fact, writing about women who flaunt rules, question convention, or seek independence has long been fertile territory for fiction writers. And then if a writer takes things a step further and create a conniving or immoral woman, the results are combustible.

A bitch character can have special potency in a story and can reflect a more truthful or complex version of the female experience. In your own reading, look for characters that unsettle our notions of femininity. Also examine the themes of the stories; sometimes gender-based themes are subtle, but in many stories, they exist below the surface.

BEYOND TYPECASTING

If you examine literature going back through the centuries, generally female characters were cast in several basic roles or archetypes, such as the young, desirable, virginal maiden (Snow White, Sleeping Beauty, Juliet) and the waif who is a vulnerable character and can sometimes be a damsel in distress (Little Red Riding Hood, Jane Eyre). Like the maiden, the waif type is often pure, naive, or gullible, and her lack of experience sends her toward trouble and maturity. The mature and traditional mother figure who is typically asexual (Mrs. March of Louisa May Alcott's *Little Women* and Mary Poppins of P.L. Travers' children's books) is another archetype, and her primary traits are that she's nurturing and dependable. The crone archetype is an older character used in the story for her wisdom and authority (Miss Marple of Agatha Christie's cozy series). With these archetypes, women's roles in the story were closely linked to their age, fertility, and desirability. In fact, if you can draw the sharpest difference between depicting male and female characters, the physical attractiveness of the female has always been more important than for males. That's not to say that attractive males characters aren't necessary to storytelling, but, rather, women are more often categorized by their desirability and sexuality than men are.

When it comes to bitches throughout history, there are also basic types or archetypes. There's the femme fatale, a beauty—in fact, a hottie—who manipulates men's emotions for money or twisted motives and is always sexually confident (Catherine Tramell played by Sharon Stone in the film *Basic Instinct*, Matty Walker played by Kathleen Turner in the film *Body Heat*, Phyllis Dietrichson played by Barbara Stanwyck in the film *Double Indemnity*). There's the flip side of the crone archetype—an older woman who is withered and is often bitter, twisted, and loveless (Miss Havisham in Charles Dickens's *Great Expectations*, Nurse Ratched in *One Flew Over the Cuckoo's Nest*). Another bitch role is the con woman or female criminal (Lily and Myra played by Anjelica Huston and Annette Bening in the film *The Grifters*, Eve played by Anne Baxter in the film *All About Eve*). Another archetype is the adulteress, a true danger to home and hearth (Hester Prynne in Nathaniel Hawthorne's *The Scarlet Letter*, Anna Karenina in Leo Tolstoy's *Anna Karenina*, Madame Bovary in Flaubert's *Madame Bovary*). Then there is the witch archetype, who is sometimes depicted as a crone, sometimes not, but she is always after power, uses enchantments, and operates from her shadow side misusing her abilities and knowledge (the witches in Shakespeare's *Macbeth*).

Bitch prototypes have always existed in myths, fairy tales, and theater (Jezebel in the Bible, the Gorgons, the stepmother in *Hansel and Gretel*, and the jealous fairy, Maleficent, in *Sleeping Beauty*). These types brought with them clear-cut character arcs that usually include a downfall since, as mentioned, bad women are punished for their badness. When American cinema came along, this structure was reinforced, particularly in noir films, and when stars like Barbara Stanwyck, Joan Crawford, and Bette Davis played a skank, they were reviled.

While filmgoers and readers will always naturally react to archetypes, reality has never been so simply drawn, particularly in contemporary times. For one thing, most readers realize that society and families have been in tumult for decades, and fiction writers might want to explore this tumult. Families are not a trove of domesticity, but instead are places of high drama, especially since these days families, along with many institutions, are more fragile than they have ever been. Many taboos, such as sex before marriage, have been dismantled, and women are usually in the midst of this dismantling.

Also consider that there has always been a natural fascination with bad women in real life, such as Lizzie Borden, Bonnie Parker, Ma Barker, Imelda Marcos, and even Martha Stewart, who was jailed for lying about her stock trading. This fascination comes from our expectations because when a woman is conniving or murderous, it throws off what society perceives as the natural order of things.

While we're all familiar with both benign and bitch types, it's a fairly limited repertoire; you might want to create a much more nuanced bitch, or any type of female character, with more delicate shadings for your story.

DEFINING A BITCH

If you're interested in breaking the mold with your character, there is no single criterion for a bitch. However, you might want to consider making several of her dominant traits negative or what society has typically not expected of females. For example, her traits might include being manipulating, selfish, cunning, power-seeking, or vengeful. Or, perhaps your bitch character cannot connect to others emotionally, or she is sexually insatiable. Or maybe she's simply a nonconformist who is opinionated, mouthy, aggressive, ambitious, or confident.

The juxtaposition of what women are *supposed* to be—sweet, feminine, compliant, and vulnerable—and what they are truly capable of being—tough, athletic, powerful, and violent—creates a natural friction that can yield fascinating results in fiction. With this in mind, you might want to brew a blend of traits that hold contradictions or create conflict. Perhaps your character is ambitious, yet is living at a time in history or in a culture where women have few options to express their ambitions.

Another aspect that cannot be ignored is that today, women's lives are shaped similarly to men's lives—most women leave the house each morning for their nine-to-five jobs, they explore the world independently, and they experience sex outside of marriage. So, because women face the same pressures and experiences of men, they might not fit into the archetypes of storytelling and instead might be feeling the disquiet of our times. Like men, they might feel sexual restlessness. Or they might be searching for their authentic self, questioning what fulfillment means for them. Or their main conflicts might be within, or they feel isolated or adrift in their roles. Or, if they're working mothers, the double demands of job and family might lead them to act out.

As an author in today's society, you have much more latitude than writers of previous generations when it comes to writing female characters, and you can write stories, especially endings, that don't provide easy answers and don't punish women for flouting convention. Perhaps your bitch character is not a clear-cut bad ass to focus the reader's anger on. Perhaps she can raise much more complicated truths or issues, and thus create a much more interesting story.

Your characters can confront moral dilemmas and hot-button issues; form complex relationships; question their unfolding identities; be tempted by sin or crime; be delighted by ordinary or forbidden pleasures; or struggle with illness, aging, fidelity, and power. In other words, your characters can face universal themes and issues.

When writing a female character who is a bad ass, you must decide if you want the reader to question preconceived assumptions about women, or if you want the reader to fear or admire her. Perhaps you want to write about especially spunky women because you admire this trait. But then maybe your aim is that the reader asks how she dare be so uppity or bold. This might require that she's particularly abrasive, or that the story is set in previous centuries when such behavior was typically frowned on.

Do you want your reader to be appalled when your bitch character dares not to follow the rules? Or do you want the reader to be silently applauding from the sidelines? If your character has children, you need to make clear decisions about how she sees her place as a mother, even if that means she's ambivalent about motherhood. As we discussed in the previous chapter, sympathy for characters comes from knowledge. So if your bitch leaves her child, as happens in the film *Kramer vs. Kramer*, the reader must understand why she takes this drastic step. Or if, after leaving her marriage and finding a new love, your character places her child in danger, as Anna Dunlap does in Sue Miller's *The Good Mother*, the reader must clearly understand her motivations for leaving and feel empathy for her new life.

On the other hand, in genres from chick lit to thrillers, sometimes the reader is also *cheering* for a bitchy (meaning she has at least several supposedly negative traits) character. Some readers are thinking *good for her, she's broken the rules, she's shattered the glass ceiling, she's enjoying great sex, she's taking risks—it's about time!* The bottom line is that you need to make choices about how sympathetic your character is. Consider using tightly woven themes that will likely somehow comment on some aspect of society.

WALKING A FINE LINE

Women in real life, myth, fiction, and film have often found themselves in a double bind because traits that are considered admirable in men are often considered unattractive in women. For example, initiative and curiosity is rewarded in men, but in the cases of Eve and Pandora, it's seen as the fall of humankind. If a man is assertive, he's manly; if a woman is assertive, she's shrill.

Now, there have been assertive, intelligent, lively females in fiction, such as Jo March in *Little Women*, Clarice Starling in *The Silence of the Lambs*, Idgie Threadgoode in Fannie Flagg's *Fried Green Tomatoes at the Whistle Stop Café*, and Anne Shirley in L.M. Montgomery's *Anne of Green Gables*. The reason these women are not seen as bitches is because their motivations and values—such as honor, justice, and love of family—justify their means and ambitions. Bitches, on the other hand, cannot always claim noble motivations or goals, and they typically are instead focused on their own goals.

Creating a bitch will require genuine insights into human nature and understanding the differences between the sexes. Women and men might not be from Mars and Venus, but their differences make the world go round. The suggestion here is that you create deeply complicated and highly motivated female characters that will surprise readers, and just maybe terrify them.

So, yes, thrill and fascinate readers with a female bad ass, but don't forget plausibility and human nature. For instance, while it has been long thought that a woman who goes wrong is a great menace to society, in reality, men are still most often the criminals and killers. In fact, in the United States, only about 8.5 percent of the convicts are women. If your bitch is a killer, you should research how women commit murder, who they murder, and how and why they get caught.

Luckily, these days, there are lots of resources available for writers. One good source is libraries at universities that teach criminal justice courses. There, you'll find books, journals, and periodicals that are good resources, such as: *Applied Psychology in Criminal Justice, Boalt Journal of Criminal Law, Crime Magazine: An Encyclopedia of Crime, FBI Law Enforcement Bulletin,* and *Journal of Criminal Justice and Popular Culture.* Online, you might want to check out www.copseek.com, which is a police and law enforcement search directory, and www.refdesk.com under crime and law enforcement.

If your story features a female murderer, try to find fresh motivations and methods of mayhem. Or perhaps the murder method is ordinary, but her victims could be found under strange or creepy circumstances—something that proves the mindset of the murderer is especially vengeful, such as defiling the corpse. It's also important to know how far a bitch will go to achieve her aims. Will she sleep with her best friend's husband, or poison her ex's beloved Golden Retriever to get revenge?

While your character might possess a lethal sting, consider exactly what you mean to imply about female rage and bad behavior. As already mentioned, in the old days, when a woman went bad, she was usually punished.

In the film *Psycho*, Janet Leigh playing Marion Crane embezzles from her boss; for her crime, she was ultimately murdered in a grisly shower scene by a ... well, a psycho. The world has changed even since this film was made, and so have our notions of justice. Before you craft your plot, decide if your bitch will go unpunished, and if her crimes will be justified.

WRITING THE FEMALE ANTI-HERO

If your female character is an anti-hero, you have a lot of latitude to create a female who is wrapped in conflict. Especially when creating the female equivalent to bad boys, don't be afraid to give her attitude and swagger, and don't let her apologize for who she is. A bitch anti-hero doesn't always bother to be nice, because she'd rather be real; she is often after power, and she refuses to be a victim. An anti-hero will only follow society's rules when they suits her, and it's more likely that she defies society's expectations and rules. A female anti-hero typically puts her own needs first and won't feel guilty about it. She is often competitive—whether she's competing for a man or with a man for power or position. Sometimes mouthy and full of rage, but always intense, a bitch anti-hero wants something—perhaps to track down a criminal or leave her marriage—and her methods are not always palatable.

Like a male anti-hero, there is often pathos at her core, she has a complicated emotional life, and she'll likely defy conventions in order to get what she wants. As you create your female anti-hero, you need to make decisions about her level of heroism and morality. Remaining true to type, anti-heroes are always of questionable moral character. Depending on where they land on the morality spectrum, you might create an anti-hero as adventuresome, courageous, and, if she's more on the dark side of life, somehow deviant and a true bad ass. Remember that the chief reason we use anti-heroes in a story is for their complexity and moral ambiguity, and because the reader can relate to their realism. When it comes to anti-heroes, we love to hate them and hate to love them because, after all, we should know better.

MORALITY AND MOTIVATION

Like other characters we've been exploring, you need to understand the *why* of your female anti-hero and just how far she'll range to achieve

FEEL THE PAIN

When you write fiction, it is somehow an outgrowth of everything you have lived woven with a big dose of imagination. If you've raised children, you're familiar with depths of love, frustration, and pain that go along with it. You know from personal experience that sometimes winners lose, and that life doles out heartbreak, unfairness, and hard luck. But many writers, particularly women, don't have experience with violence unless they served in the military or a police force, or have studied martial arts. Unless we have taken up boxing, most of us get through our lives without punching or being punched. While growing up, it's more likely that males have experienced more physical pain in sports and have resolved differences with their fists, while typically girls do not.

So if you're writing about female characters that resort to violence or are injured by violence, you likely need to do your homework. You might want to ask permission to spend a Saturday night in an ER waiting room, noting who comes in with injuries from bar-room brawls and exactly what those injuries look like; listen to their pitiful moans as they await treatment, and note the sheen of perspiration coating their skin.

Violence hurts and traumatizes. When a character starts swinging, someone is going to end up with at the least a black eye, aches and pains, or cracked ribs. Violence also leads to disfigurement, broken bones, ruptured spleens or kidneys, concussions, blood loss, and death. If you have a female character wielding the bat at an assailant or an innocent, know not only her physical strength and motivations, but also the results of her actions.

Similarly, if your character is the victim of violence, research exactly what it feels like the day after your ribs have been cracked, your jaw has been broken, or your arm has been fractured. Will your character take OxyContin or Codeine for the pain? How will she be affected by the medication? Will she need to spend a day or two on the couch recuperating? Too often, fictional characters shake off serious injuries and are back in the fray with few consequences or impairments; too often, writers depict violence, but not a plausible aftermath.

her agenda. An anti-hero is flawed but sympathetic as she ventures into shadier moral territory than a typical protagonist or hero would. Your choice as her creator is *exactly* how far she'll venture toward the dark side, and if her flaws will be her downfall.

Here are some possibilities to consider:

- **Is she going to be a backstabber, liar, thief, or cheat?** These are behaviors often exposed on reality television, and producers love to zoom in with their cameras during these revealing scenes. In the film *Working Girl,* Tess McGill, played by Melanie Griffith, is an anti-hero working the angles to succeed in the corporate world. She's not beyond breaking the rules in the name of self-fulfillment and personal gain, especially if it means leaving the secretarial pool and being recognized for her brains and initiative. But then she's up against the backstabbing antagonist Katharine Parker, played by Sigourney Weaver, who has a lower moral code. Katharine is Tess's boss and not only steals her idea after promising equality, but then tries to ruin her in revenge because Tess stole her man. Likewise, in your own story, an anti-hero can appear more heroic if she's paired with a darker antagonist.

- **Is she a warrior type, particularly an avenging warrior?** Warrior types have been around since the legendary Amazons, and science fiction and fantasy most often feature women warriors. In the television series *Xena: Warrior Princess,* Xena is the ultimate kick-ass chick, and she has a character arc that depicts her moving through many levels of morality. The key to these primal characters is that their intense physicality, passion, tenaciousness, and headstrong approach set them apart from traditional female characters. Warriors play to win no matter what it takes, they value freedom, and they are not dependent on males for their identity or happiness.

  A warrior in the suspense genre, Eva Wylie is a fascinating anti-hero in three novels by Liza Cody. Paranoid and even delusional, she makes a living as a guard and a female wrestler, and she's got attitude. As a warrior type, not only is she not warm and cuddly, she's also scary and a loose cannon. But Cody has also created her as oddly sympathetic, perhaps most notably because of her dysfunctional relationships with her alcoholic mother and unreliable sister. But then again, she's got weird relationships with just about everyone else in the stories, too.

- **Is a troubled backstory key to her identity and actions?** If so, you might want to create a dark heroine who is similar to the male counterpart. The female leads in contemporary suspense fiction can fall under this anti-hero type. They often have issues, but at the same time, they also have a level of humanity that makes them especially intriguing. They're not cheery types. In fact, they are always realists, and they can be cynical and angry. The dark heroine often has something troubling in her past, such as abuse, rape, addiction, or guilt over a case gone wrong. Examples of this type of dark heroine are Jane Perry in Laurel Dewey's *Protector* and Kathy Mallory in Carol O'Connell's suspense series.

- **Is she someone who is after revenge?** There is Velma Kelly in the musical and film *Chicago* who kills her husband when she discovers him in bed with another woman. In this case, the audience sympathizes with Velma, but writers certainly have the option of making revenge less than sympathetic.

- **Is she a conniving sort who can descend into villainy?** You might want to think about how the three female leads in John Updike's *The Witches of Eastwick* are portrayed. The three witches use their powers for petty gains like creating thunderstorms, but then things get really ugly when they join their powers to ruin a younger rival.

- **Do you want to create a more benign anti-hero?** If so, you can't go wrong with a screw-up, klutz type, like the television character Ally McBeal. She is typically a free spirit, is no role model, and might be ditzy. Often, this kind of anti-hero is her own worst enemy, but viewers and readers recognize their own pettiness, self-absorption, jealousies, and insecurities in the character.

- **Do you want to cast her for social commentary?** An anti-hero is perfect to showcase society's ambivalent or unfair attitudes toward women. Good examples are the title characters in the film *Thelma & Louise*. Viewers follow the women, who have had enough of the status quo and oppression, as they take matters into their own hands. In the case of this film, the results are mayhem and tragedy, but, of course, you could choose a much different character arc.

WRITING THE BAD GIRL

Let's talk for a moment about bad girls, the female equivalent to bad boys, who were discussed in chapter four. This type of anti-hero will always skate on thin ice and, like their male counterparts, they will always cause tension and heat. A bad girl exaggerates female characteristics, turns them upside down, or uses her sexuality for various gains. We often expect men, especially young men, to swagger, act out, and cheat, blaming these behaviors on the male nature or testosterone, a biological imperative to spread their seed for dominance. Traditionally, the cads and heartbreakers of fiction have been men. But think about what a female character with a need to seduce, conquer, and dominate might look like.

There are several keys to a bad girl's personality: She cares more for herself than others, she hates the rules or flaunts the rules, and she's never a shrinking violet—she's upfront about her brains, sexuality, and goals, and she wields her sexuality as the most potent weapon in her arsenal. She can be a businesswoman, a movie star, a private investigator, or a call girl. She's often sassy, witty, and sarcastic. She breaks the rules and dares you to try to stop her. She can be a flirt, a slut, or a nymphomaniac. Think Madonna, Britney Spears, Courtney Love, and Paris Hilton in real life, Samantha Jones in the television series *Sex and the City*, Bree Daniels played by Jane Fonda in the film *Klute*, and Lula in Janet Evanovich's Stephanie Plum series.

The key to bad girls is that they own their sexuality, and nobody dictates how they act out their sexuality. Possibly one of the best examples of a bad girl in literature is Daniel Defoe's Moll Flanders of *The Fortunes and Misfortunes of Moll Flanders*. Published in 1722, the book was considered scandalous for its frankness and because of the unrepentant nature of the marauding Moll, who marries, deceives, and cons an assortment of men in her search for wealth. Throughout the story, Moll must live by her wits, beauty, and sexuality to survive. The children she has with her lovers and husbands are mostly pawned off for others to care for. Eventually her crimes land her in prison, where she manages to con the authorities out of hanging her, and she heads back to America, where she inherits a plantation. That is not the end of the story, but the point here is that Moll sold her soul and body for survival with little remorse, making her one of the original bad girls of literature.

If you're planning on writing a bad girl character, it's important not only that you understand her traits, but also that you plan a story line for her that is a romp with a series of setbacks, twists, and near misses. Take the reader on a wild ride with the character, as Defoe does with Moll. You need to throw a lot of temptation in her path and possibly leave a trail of broken hearts and scams behind her. This is the sort of character who is constantly in trouble, gets caught, wiggles out of tight spots, and doesn't always learn from her mistakes. Or if there is something to be learned, it's to be sneakier or more opportunistic.

WRITING THE FEMALE VILLAIN

When a bitch in the form of a villain is on the page, the reader should understand that the character has unleashed the darker parts of her nature. In fact, if you create a female villain who is black-hearted and has an agenda, your other characters best run for cover. When female power is raw, unleashed, and furious, it is a thing to fear. So make certain that your villain character is an alpha female with special talents and loads of ambition, and that her presence in the story just might dismantle the male hierarchy. There's a saying that one bad woman is worth five bad men, meaning that when a woman plots and schemes, the results are often disastrous for whomever she's got in her crosshairs.

For example, there is a tale set in the eighteenth century that is about lust and revenge and has a dangerous woman at its heart, the Marquise de Merteuil. The story is *Les Liaisons Dangereuses* (*Dangerous Liaisons*) by Pierce Choderlos de Laclos, and when it was published in 1782, it was considered scandalous. The novel is written via a series of letters in which the Marquise sets a dangerous game in motion when she makes a wager with her former lover, Vicomte de Valmont. The Marquise challenges Valmont to seduce the virgin Cécile de Volanges before the girl's marriage because she's seeking revenge on another former lover, Cécile's fiancé.

As a counter-challenge, Valmont bets the Marquise that he will be able to bed the chaste and married Madame de Tourvel. Unable to engage Valmont in the game, she employs the services of the young Chevalier

Danceny to despoil Cécile. The game is now set for the sinister aspects of human nature to prey on the two innocent and unsuspecting women.

In the film adaptation of *Dangerous Liasons*, the diabolical Marquise, played by Glenn Close, described the plight of women this way:

> Well I had no choice, did I? I'm a woman. Women are obliged to be far more skillful than men. You can ruin our reputation and our life with a few well-chosen words. So of course I had to invent not only myself but ways of escape no one has ever thought of before. And I've succeeded because I've always known I was born to dominate your sex and avenge my own.

If you're writing a female villain, you might want recall the cunning, potency, and rage of the Marquise, and also make the consequences of her villainy affect a number of people. When you have a villain in your story, your protagonist will of course be in danger, but also try to spread maximum damage to as many characters as possible.

VILLAIN TYPES

While we have already discussed the main archetypes for female characters, let's deepen our discussion of other possible types for a female villain.

AVENGER: An avenging woman bent on retribution and revenge makes a powerful character type. When revenge is the motivation, the character taps into a deep well of rage, and she is often illogical or reckless. This archetype has been around since the sorceress Medea, who, enraged at her husband for dumping her for another woman, killed his new bride and slaughtered their children. In the film *The Wizard of* Oz, the Wicked Witch of the West wants to avenge her sister's death and wrest the ruby slippers from Dorothy's feet, and she will do anything, including commit murder, to maintain her evil power.

CONTROL FREAK: There are still many people who are not comfortable with a woman in charge. And when a woman is in power but cannot properly handle her authority, things can get ugly. Nurse Ratched, from *One Flew Over the Cuckoo's Nest*, who was also mentioned as a crone earlier in this chapter, is a terrific example of a control freak. She is driven by a need for order, power, and efficiency, but her shadow side is that she's actually a sadist with a repressed sexuality.

The Queen of Hearts, from *Alice's Adventures in Wonderland* by Lewis Carroll, is a control freak with too much power—a lethal combination. With her penchant for blood-red roses and decapitation, she's a formidable and corrupt villain. Jadis, the White Witch, from *The Chronicles of Narnia* by C.S. Lewis, is another example of a corrupt monarch who is a threat to all who cross her. When you weave an evil heart, deviousness, and chilling beauty into your character, you've got a villain who will terrify most readers.

DIVA: When a diva appears in a story, she stinks up the place. The key to a diva character is her complete sense of entitlement associated with arrogance, a defensive nature, and a need to protect her emotions. She is often in charge of things, and might be a boss, a queen, or an heiress. Her need for attention and gratification, and to be *numero uno*, can spoil her appreciation of life's simple pleasures and relationships.

Take Miranda Priestly in Lauren Weisberger's *The Devil Wears Prada* as a case study. Miranda is one of the worst bosses, as her personal assistant knows, because she's the one schlepping her Starbucks lattes, fielding phone calls, answering impossible demands, and giving up her own life to please her boss. Miranda is imperious, churlish, demeaning, and cold. She feels entitled and omnipotent, and she doesn't seem to care what anyone thinks of her. She is impossibly glamorous and impossibly demanding.

If you use divas in your story, they somehow must have earned their haughty demeanor. Thus, they wield power, and they have the perks and a salary with a few more zeros than the rest of us. They usually have others dependent on them and are in the public eye. A whiny teenager who will only wear brand names and shop at high-end stores is not a diva; she's spoiled. Real divas cause pain to others and are somehow impossible to deal with.

FEMME FATALE: The femme fatale (French for "fatal lover") is alluring, seductive, and scary as hell, especially when she turns the tables on her conquests. She is known to emotionally enslave her conquests and is typically portrayed as a kind of sexual vampire. It is often believed that her dark appetites can steal the virility and independence of her lovers. A femme fatale is sometimes compared to her male counterpart, Don Juan, but she will sometimes go all the way in the story by killing her conquests, ridding herself of a pesky husband or henchman.

She is often drawn to money and power, and she is the ultimate user. However, remember that this siren uses both her body and brains for seduction (think Cleopatra), and her traits usually include being sly and devious. Rebecca of Daphne de Maurier's novel is a woman who wreaks havoc with her lusts and injures those around her. The story essentially is an unraveling of all her machinations and secrets.

A femme fatale exists in many forms of fiction, but particularly in films and novels with a noir approach, romance novels, and hard-boiled detective stories. In a detective story, a femme fatale often serves as the love interest for the detective, and she often poses a threat. Femme fatales have street smarts and exist as a special threat to traditional female roles and the nuclear family. These types of characters are often after independence, and they use men for their ends.

An example of a femme fatale character is Carmen Sternwood in *The Big Sleep* by Raymond Chandler. Zenia from *The Robber Bride* by Margaret Atwood is another femme fatale who uses seduction, blackmail, and other ploys for her own gains and power.

MOMMY DEAREST: There are many versions of the bad mother in real life and in literature. She can be an overreaching matriarch who manipulates her children, or a controlling mother who so identifies with her children that she's lost herself. When a mother is cruel, indifferent, or inept, the situation can create enormous conflict and danger for her vulnerable children. A mother's cruelty can last a lifetime. Examples of this character type can be found in Pearl Cleage's *What Looks Like Crazy on an Ordinary Day*, where a newborn is abandoned by her young, drug-addicted mother, and in Jane Hamilton's *The Book of Ruth*, where the mother is embittered and abusive to her daughter. Another compelling example can be found in Victoria Redel's *Loverboy*, where a single mother is so obsessed with her son that she loses touch with reality.

POWER BEHIND THE THRONE: Throughout history, women who could not outwardly wield power have often lurked in the background as the real power behind the throne or patriarch. These women are often known for their cunning manipulations. A fabulous example of such a character is Cersei Lannister from George R.R. Martin's epic saga. When the reader first meets the story's protagonist, Cersei, she is involved in an incestuous relationship with her twin brother, and she has three children from this incestuous relationship rather than from her husband, the king. After arranging for her husband's death, the crown cannot pass to her, so she is forced to align with other males to achieve the power she craves. Her son becomes king, despite his sociopathic tendencies and ineptness, and she is Queen Regent. But like many women of this type, she resents the restrictions placed on females.

SLUT OR SEXUAL PREDATOR: Sluts, whores, hoes, prostitutes, bimbos, and whatever else you call women who are sexually free or use their bodies for commerce will always cause seismic waves in a story. Readers are fascinated by the sexuality of characters, and famous sluts like Delilah, Fanny Hill, and Moll Flanders prove it. When a villain is also a sexual predator, the story will naturally fascinate readers and bring up issues about gender differences. For example, in *Disclosure* by Michael Crichton, Meredith Johnson is part corporate vixen, part sexual predator. Throughout the story, Meredith is vicious in her career and sexual pursuits, and she plays for keeps—as the best villains do.

SCORNED WOMAN: A scorned woman somehow so identifies with her role as wife, lover, or girlfriend that she cannot let it go. She'll do anything to hang on to or control a relationship, and she likely has deep fears of being abandoned because of traumatic events in her childhood. If hell hath no fury like a scorned woman, then one the most riveting scorned women is Glenn Close as Alex Forrest in the film *Fatal Attraction*. In Alex, we see a scorned lover turning into the ultimate raging avenger as she goes after her philandering lover, played by Michael Douglas, and his family. The scorned woman's key motivations are rage and revenge; another contemporary example of this character is Uma Thurman as the jilted bride in the *Kill Bill* films.

WRITING THE FEMALE SOCIOPATH

As noted in chapter seven, sociopaths make up about 4 percent of the population, so if you're creating a female sociopath character, she is a rare and frightening creature. She'll likely stir an extra dose of revulsion in the reader because one of the main traits expected in women is empathy.

MAYHEM

Although somewhat overlooked by criminologists, women killers are a fascinating breed. If you plan to use one in your story, you'll want to research their mindset and methods. Here are some fascinating facts about this fearsome group.

Women serial killers tend to have longer killing sprees—about eight years—while men's killing rampages generally last about four years. Women serial killers also often "kill softly," meaning with less violent or more hands-off methods, like using poison or suffocating with a pillow, while men tend to shoot, stab, batter, and mutilate.

Women tend to kill for profit or to rid themselves of a burden, such as unwanted children, while about half the murders by male serial killers are related to a misdirected sex drive. Women typically murder people they know, such as husbands, boyfriends, friends, and family members, while men are more likely to kill strangers. Like their male counterparts, most female serial killers are sociopaths, which means they look sane and blend in with society, but lack a conscience.

However, while female serial killers are relatively rare, female murderers are not. And like serial killers, female murderers usually kill the most vulnerable—babies and children, the weak, and the elderly. According to the U.S. Department of Justice, 70 percent of confirmed cases of child abuse and 65 percent of parental murders of children are committed by mothers.

Criminologists and academics speculate that 15 percent of the approximately 7,000 cases of sudden infant death syndrome (SIDS) reported each year in the U.S. are actually cases of intentional suffocation, usually committed by the mother. This alone accounts for at least 1,000 homicides a year. In fact, because it's so difficult to determine if a baby's death was by suffocation, the actual number of infanticides per year might be much higher.

When women are caught at murder, they often defend themselves by saying that they were suffering from illnesses such as postpartum depression, premenstrual syndrome (PMS), and battered wife syndrome. While these conditions can be a factor, it cannot be ignored that, like men, women have a capacity for violence and murder.

And when the character turns her cold eye to crime or harm, it can make us all feel less safe.

A bitch in a story is bad enough, but when she's also a sociopath, everyone best leave town. Besides having zero empathy or concern for others, a sociopath in fiction is usually a criminal who seduces or exploits others for her gains.

This character type must exhibit the typical symptoms, such as chronic deceitfulness, a lack of remorse, not taking responsibility for her crimes and behaviors, and a general desire to control people and make them jump. Once you've nailed down these behaviors, you can make decisions on how far she'll go with her particular wickedness. You might not want to make her a criminal, but rather a woman who seduces then discards lovers for the fun of it, or a boss who likes to ridicule and control her employees. Just keep in mind that their motivation is to make others suffer.

In *Forever Odd,* Dean Koontz gives the reader the sociopathic villain Datura. With the morals of a vampire and the soul of a starving wolf, she encompasses everything men—and women—fear in women. She's kinky and domineering. She comes with several henchmen, who could also be classified as sex slaves, and she wants the protagonist because of his psychic ability. She's also drawn to unexplainable phenomena, such as haunted houses, because she likes the dark evil that lurks there. She'll do anything for kicks, and she'll hurt anyone who gets in the way of her pleasure and twisted goals.

Another type of sociopathic character is the angel of death. These sorts of characters are ripped from newspaper headlines; most often, they are nurses or women in helping professions who kill their highly vulnerable victims. Access is the key to these types, as are their delusions about how they're actually doing their victims a favor by offering them death. And sometimes these characters just enjoy making life-and-death decisions. Annie Wilkes, who is both a nurse and an obsessed fan in Stephen King's *Misery*, is an example of an angel of death who has left a trail of dead bodies.

A terrific example of a female sociopathic serial killer is Gretchen Lowell from Chelsea Cain's *Heartsick*. Like male sociopathic serial killers, Lowell seems motivated by a terrible blood lust and need for power over her victims. She tortures and dismembers her victims, and she has two hundred murders to her credit. The gender switch in this story brings new blood (pardon the pun) to the sociopath/serial killer thriller. A female sociopathic serial killer is the antithesis of a traditional woman because of her lack of empathy; she is the ultimate scary bitch and predator.

Heartsick opens when Lowell's final victim, Archie Sheridan, is pulled from a medical leave to help solve a new serial murder case that has the earmarks of the former case he worked on. You see, Sheridan is a detective who led a task force trying to track Lowell before he became a victim himself. He barely survived Lowell's tortures, in which she removed his spleen, fed him drain cleaner and hallucinogens, and carved into his flesh. Although she's in prison, he's still haunted and isolated after having left his family, and he's addicted to pain pills for his many ills. As you write your sociopath-centered story, try emulating Cain's tactic of taking the reader into a victim's viewpoint and nightmarish memories.

Also like Cain, you might want to give the story a truly fresh twist. After Lowell held Sheridan captive and tortured him for ten days, she killed him, brought him back to life, then phoned 9-1-1 and surrendered to the authorities. Now that she's in prison, she loves Sheridan's weekly visits, when she metes out information about her many victims since many of the bodies still have not been found.

As you think about your story's plot, you also need to plan actions that showcase the sociopath's essential nature, and she needs to be fundamentally different from normal women. Here are characteristics that Cain gives Lowell, which you can emulate in your own sociopathic and villainous bitch:

- She has a special talent for sadism, which is proven by the number of her victims and her torturing and dismembering them.
- There is a trademark of her madness. In her case, she carves hearts into her captive's chests.
- She loves the notoriety of the murder task force and the press coverage. Many sociopaths seek attention and crave infamy.
- She has memorable physical attributes—she's labeled the "Beauty Killer" and looks both innocent and alluring.
- She has special capabilities, such as her medical expertise.

- She feels superior to most people, especially her victims.
- She's not afraid to abuse and use violence, threats, bullying, and other trademark behaviors of sociopaths.
- She's a chronic liar, and she's good at it.
- She uses her sexuality and other so-called female wiles to get what she wants and lure in her victims.
- She uses her charming and duplicitous nature for maximum damage. For example, Lowell forms a support group for the task force who had been hunting her. Sociopaths sometimes like to comfort or idealize their victims before their true nature is exposed; it's one of their methods of roping in victims.

As you can see, when you create a sociopath of either sex, the character must be true to type, so you need to begin by thoroughly researching this fascinating disorder (see chapter seven for resources on sociopaths).

RESERVOIRS OF EMOTIONS

One method of creating fascinating and possibly evil female characters is to tap into their reservoirs of emotions and uncover the backstory that has created their present-day personas. In real life, women who are depressed or troubled usually turn their anger and self-hatred against themselves. In fiction, you have an opportunity to use your character's emotions to create conflict in the story.

An amazing example of using the backstory and tapping into a deep well of emotions is found in the character of Barbara Covett in Zoë Heller's *Notes on a Scandal*. Barbara is a woman in her sixties who has been teaching for more than thirty years. She is cynical, bitter, and living an empty existence when the lovely Sheba Hart joins the school as the new art teacher. A friendship of sorts develops. But if you thought Linda Tripp was a lousy friend to Monica Lewinsky, she's a pussycat compared to Barbara. You see, the story revolves around Sheba's affair with a fifteen-year-old student, and Barbara's role in Sheba's eventual downfall.

The book is written as a sort of diary or reminiscence as Barbara thinks back on the events that led to Sheba's disgrace. Barbara's observations are perverse, witty, scathing, and wicked. In fact, her musings are a wasp nest of hatred, jabs, and cynicism. And no one is spared from her unflinching cynicism, which adds to the tension in the story. The reader hears her inner thoughts during a lunch with Sheba and another teacher: "*Shut up, shut up* I thought, as she chuntered on. *Shut up, you boring cow. Let Sheba speak.*"

When a viewpoint character as untamed and nasty as Barbara is holding forth, readers don't dare turn their heads to look away until the final page. *Notes on a Scandal* is a cautionary tale, because Barbara needs Sheba in ways that you and I most likely don't need our friends—she needs her for salvation, sustenance, and meaning.

Barbara's backstory directly leads to her complicated reasons for revenge, because Barbara is deeply lonely. She explains that no matter how busy you are with to-do lists and reorganizing the linen closet, or doling out small treats to yourself, there is a point when you question if you can spend the day fending off misery. Here is Barbara's admission, with all its heartbreaking truth:

> People like Sheba think that they know what it's like to be lonely. They cast their minds back to the time they broke up with a boyfriend in 1975 and endured a whole month before meeting someone new. Or the week they spent in a Bavarian steel town when they were fifteen years old, visiting their greasy-haired German pen pal and discovering that her handwriting was the best thing about her. But about the drip, drip of long-haul, no-end-in-sight solitude, they know nothing. They don't know what it is to construct an entire weekend of a visit to the launderette. Or to sit in a darkened flat on Halloween night, because you can't bear to expose your bleak evening to a crowd of jeering trick-or-treaters. Or to have the librarian smile pityingly and say, "Goodness, you're a quick reader!" when you bring back seven books, read from cover to cover, a week after taking them out. They don't know what it is to be so chronically untouched that the accidental brush of a bus conductor's hand on your shoulder sends a jolt of longing straight to your groin. I have sat on park benches and trains and school room chairs, feeling the great store of unused, objectless love sitting in my belly like a stone until I was sure I would cry out and fall, flailing to the ground. About all of this, Sheba and her like have no clue.

Notice not only the depth of this confession, but also how it casts a light on all that happens in a story and is, in a sense, the heart of the story. Heller adds this admission when about 80 percent of the story has unfolded and the reader has watched with horrified fascination as Barbara sets up Sheba for a fall.

If you're interested in creating a character like Barbara whom the reader will come to know intimately and will revile yet be fascinated with, then, like Heller, you might want to slowly unravel her motivations, inner life, and truths. You might also want to provide a convenient milieu for the story, like Heller does, as her story also comments on some of the failings and eroding standards of England's educational system, along with the difficulty of teaching teenagers. Her criticisms of the system seem not only rational, but justified. This means Barbara cannot simply be dismissed as an unreliable narrator, but someone who has a rather keen intellect and front-row seat of a changing world.

Like Heller, you might also want to delve into powerful and difficult human emotions—such as envy and loneliness—and then show how they create potent motivations for wrongdoing. While stories with male lead characters will also delve into emotions and motivations, when a woman character is so cunning and twisted, the reader simply needs to know how she got that way. Again, this goes back to society's expectations of women.

Because Barbara was so intimately involved in the scandal, the reader also relishes his role as voyeur as he learns the details of the affair and watches Sheba's life unraveling. Likewise, you might want to give the reader a front-row seat with a narrator that comments on events and puts her own poisonous spin on things.

ALL IN THE FAMILY

For most of us, the bond of family is inescapable, so when an antagonist is within the family circle, the trouble factor soars and immediate tension and conflict sizzle on the page. Since family is also the cauldron of our growing-up years, all the emotional hurts, rivalries, abuses, and misunderstandings have a way of casting a long shadow over the adult years. The reader instinctively understands the sting of being the less-pretty sister or the

ROGUE'S GALLERY

Here is a list of more female characters that don't play by the rules and would likely scoff at the notion of being the weaker sex:

- Adulteress: Becky Sharp, *Vanity Fair* by William Thackeray
- Antagonist: Sula Peace, *Sula* by Toni Morrison
- Anti-hero: Dolores Claiborne, *Dolores Claiborne* by Stephen King
- Anti-hero: Scarlett O'Hara, *Gone With the Wind* by Margaret Mitchell
- Anti-hero: Murphy Brown, *Murphy Brown* television series
- Femme fatale: Honey Deal, *Up in Honey's Room* by Elmore Leonard
- Femme fatale: Suzanne Stone, *To Die For* by Joyce Maynard
- Mommy dearest: Margaret White, *Carrie* by Stephen King
- Mommy dearest: Mrs. Bennet, *Pride and Prejudice* by Jane Austen
- Slut: Lydia Bennet, *Pride and Prejudice* by Jane Austen
- Sociopath: Peyton Flanders, played by Rebecca De Moyer in the film *The Hand That Rocks the Cradle*
- Sociopath: Cruella De Vil, played by Glenn Close in the film *101 Dalmatians*
- Sociopath: Solana Rojas, *T Is for Tresspass* by Sue Grafton
- Sociopath: Hedra Carlson, played by Jennifer Jason Leigh in the film *Single White Female*
- Warrior: Sarah Connor, played by Linda Hamilton in the film *Terminator 2: Judgment Day*
- Warrior: Princess Leia, played by Carrie Fisher in the Star Wars trilogy
- Warrior: Lindsay Boxer, The Women's Murder Club series by James Patterson
- Warrior: Erin Brockovich, played by Julia Roberts in the film *Erin Brockovich*
- Warrior: Arden Grenfell, *Deathweave* and *Darkloom* by Cary Osborne

less-successful younger sibling or not the favorite son or daughter. When a family dynamic occurs on the page, it brings familiar tangles with it, and the reader will sympathize with the protagonist and fear the antagonist.

In Heather Barbieri's *Snow in July*, a small family is the crucible for the story. The protagonist, Erin Mulcahy, is a recent high-school graduate who lives with her mother and is trying to make decisions about her future. She's been accepted to an art school in the east, but can't decide if she should leave town. The reason for her hesitation boils down to her family, or, more succinctly, to her heroin-addicted sister, Meghan.

The inciting incident occurs when Meghan's five-year-old daughter, Teeny, calls Erin and complains that Meghan is sleeping and won't wake up. Erin and her mother set off in the snowfall to discover the latest realities of Meghan's life. When they reach the dive hotel Meghan is staying in, she has bolted. They find that Teeny is hungry and neglected, and that Teeny's baby sister, Sienna, has been given Nyquil to make her sleep. They bring the children home with them.

In the following scene, Erin gives Teeny a bath and by the time the bath time scene is over, Meghan is clearly established as the antagonist and a first-class bitch. The author uses Meghan's vulnerable daughters as the vehicle to do so:

> Teeny strokes my sleeve. Her knuckles are skinned. She's got a lot of scrapes and cuts, as if her skin is too thin, as if it's being rubbed away. Stuff happens when you're a kid. I mean, I know Meghan never hurts her. But sometimes she doesn't pay enough attention. "That's pretty." Teeny flutters the kimono sleeve, making the printed butterfly fly.
>
> "Thanks. Is this okay?" I hold Teeny as she sticks her toe in. There's no softness between skin and bones. She's all angles, a tinker-toy girl.

As Erin scrubs the dirt from her, the reader discovers that Teeny had lice the last time Erin visited, that Teeny has a new scar on her knee from falling on a bicycle while riding unsupervised, and that Teeny and Meghan recently had been living in California and had hitchhiked back to Montana. And the reader gets to see that Teeny is bright and aware and frightened.

Fiction and memoir often focus on addiction, but the story rarely shines a lens on the people in the addict's proximity. The lies, stealing, broken promises, and broken hearts are best known to people who have been victimized by another person's addiction. Betrayal of trust is always a terrific focus for fiction, and this novel spotlights exactly what that feels like to the person around the betrayer. Like Barbieri, make certain the reader understands the ramifications of betrayal, especially the feelings of impotency and rage.

Snow in July illustrates that an extra depth of emotional entanglement ensues when you add sibling rivalry, old hurts, and disappointments to a story. The story is especially effective because Erin, the good girl, has always been eclipsed by her sister, who has even stolen her boyfriends. Many readers can empathize with her position and also her love-hate relationship with her sister. It is often within a family that our deepest wounds are meted out, where we must examine the facts of our lives to understand ourselves. Besides the setting of family, the abandoned mines and dreariness of Montana lends the book an extra layer of grimness, serves as a central metaphor, and highlights the protagonist's need to escape.

If you're writing a story with a bitch who abuses or neglects her children, like Barbieri, find motivations that the reader can understand. Addiction is perhaps one of the top reasons for child abuse, and it lends a note of believability to the story.

Women are naturally complicated, and bitchy women are endlessly fascinating. After all, it takes a certain kind of courage to step beyond the normal roles and expectations for female behavior. So when you add a bitch to your story's cast, make sure that her backstory explains her current behaviors and her front story is a collision course thundering someone toward doom. But keep in mind that you're no longer constrained in depicting sexually free women or aggressive, ambitious women as bad asses—instead, your bad asses can simply be like women found in every walk of life. You also might not need to mete out punishment or retribution, and, instead, redemption or forgiveness might conclude the plot.

CHAPTER ELEVEN

Monsters, Creatures, and Lost Souls

Fear makes the wolf bigger than he is.

—German proverb

They lurk in the shadows and slither in the dark, always ready to strike.

The monster.

The creature.

The embodied demon of our nightmares.

It appears that every culture throughout the world has some form of creature, beast, or twisted human that makes us feel most vulnerable and alone and terrified. What makes monsters so terrifying is that much is at stake when they appear in a story because they challenge their victim's—and the reader's—sanity and sense of reality. When a monster is on the screen or the page, before the story ends, someone will feel isolated and alone. Along the way, encounters with monsters—including the dead, the undead, the deformed, and creatures not easily categorized—will be emotional high points of a story.

In previous chapters, we've looked at characters who are monstrous and yet might look just like we do. To some readers and moviegoers, characters like Norman Bates and Hannibel Lecter are the ones that make us look over our shoulders on a dark night. They are beasts in human clothing, and they really get under our skin. But then there have always been highly dramatic projections of our fears into characters (human and non-human) who are *others*. In this chapter, we're going to use the convenient term *monster*

to classify these others—types that are as different from normal people as possible. They represent what is uncivilized and abhorrent, and they frequently exist in horror, Gothic fiction, thrillers, techno-thrillers, science fiction, fantasy, and mainstream literature. We're also going to look into character types who are classified as lost souls since they've lost some part of their essential humanity. But first, on to the monsters and creatures from the land of nightmares.

For our purposes, let's adopt Joseph Campbell's definition of monster from *The Power of Myth*, where he says: "By monster I mean some horrendous presence or apparition that explodes all of your standards for harmony, order, and ethical conduct." Since fiction is often about events and characters that disrupt order and then actions to restore it, monsters are especially effective since they plunge the story world into extreme chaos, and characters' survival will always be at stake when they're in the story.

Monsters usually play the villain roles in stories, although they are sometimes anti-heroes, such as lost soul types; portrayed sympathetically, as in Mary Shelley's *Frankenstein*; or extremely sympathetic, such as the loveable ogre from the Shrek films. But typically when a monster is the villain in a story, particularly in the horror genre, you are writing a story that is participatory—one that's trying to elicit extreme or primal emotional reactions in your reader, and those emotions are usually dread, horror, or terror. Thus, your reader will experience marrow-chilling trepidation, heart-thudding fear, and physical reactions that might include cold sweat, chills, and adrenalin coursing through his system.

When a monster is in the story, the creature is usually archetypal, there is always some form of chaos or some force unleashed that makes the story world an aberrant or dangerous place, and it always appears as if there is no escape.

The monster story traps the reader in a pitiless world of fright and punishment where the threat can come from many sources. It can be something that is seemingly benign, such as a flock of birds. It can be a murderous Plymouth, rabid dogs, giant spiders, evil clowns, graveyard haunts and creatures made from graveyard robberies, beings who have lost their humanity (such as vampires and zombies), or creatures that are not of the world, including aliens from distant galaxies. These are usually cautionary tales, and since horror often exists in science fiction and fantasy genres, monsters can also be robots or machines made by man, such as Sonny, a robot in *I, Robot*, or HAL 9000 in *2001: A Space Odyssey*. When a robot or machine breaks the rules and turns on humans, the results can be chilling. The bottom line is that monsters do not need to be supernatural, but they do need to be super potent.

A story with a monster in it also needs a protagonist who is somehow sympathetic or vulnerable (this main character can also be represented by a group that is terrorized by the monster). Keep in mind, though, that this doesn't mean the protagonist needs to be a complete innocent—sometimes the protagonist will have stamina and kickback, and sometimes it will appear that he deserves the troubles he's brought on. The protagonist must also be under a constant state of threat—violated at every turn. In fact, in the darkest horror stories, the protagonist often can't recover from the violation.

ORIGINS

Scholars and academics have many theories about the origins of the literature of monsters. What is clear is that monsters appear in all cultures, they have been around since language first evolved, and they represent humankind's deepest and most disturbing fears. It seems natural that primitive humans would devise monsters to explain the unexplainable, such as nightmares, schizophrenic behaviors, human deformities and oddities, exotic and terrifying animals, and natural phenomena like earthquakes.

People have always whispered about ghosts around the campfire, speculated about what happens after death, tried to make sense of senseless killings by assigning murderers as monsters, and believed in creatures that were not human but interfered with human affairs.

It's easy to imagine that early humans saw oddities, freaks, and frights in the world around them and shaped legends and myths about these things. After all, deformed people and animals, along with dwarfs, giants, and great beasts such as mammoths and apes, as well as sea creatures like whales and octopuses, were all difficult to explain. Myths were also devised to explain fatal illnesses, unexplainable tragedies like sudden infant death syndrome, deformities, and mutations. It's also clear that myths were linked to issues of survival. Since often there were tragic or odd happenings within a household or farm—such as cows that wouldn't give milk, droughts, or crop failures—blame was placed on a whole slew of creatures, such as boggarts, brownies, fairies, ghosts, changelings, elves, jinn, leprechauns, and pixies.

Some legends persist in certain regions, such as the Loch Ness Monster of Scotland, the Abominable Snowman or Yeti of the Himalayas, and Bigfoot of the Pacific Northwest. Some legends seem to be based on a fairly logical fear—the fear of giant and fearsome creatures attacking or eating people. Since the biblical tale of Jonah and the whale, it seems fairly logical that humans would fear being devoured and would devise tales based around these fears.

The Greeks had a particularly vivid mythology that included a welter of monsters, many of them the offspring of their gods, many of them tormentors of humankind, such as Cerberus, centaurs, Cyclops, Greyon, and Minotaur.

Many ancient myths star aberrations of humans, such as the Erinye, which means "angry ones." These three fearsome gals are hag-like creatures with the head of a dog, snakes for hair, and bat wings. In Greek myths, they are called the Furies, and their job is to find and punish guilty people. Homer's *The Odyssey* was also replete with horrors and creatures, such as the aforementioned Cyclops, Scylla, the lotus eaters, the sirens, the cattle of the sun, and interfering gods, such as Poseidon. So monsters are nothing new to the pantheon of storytelling.

Monster stories were passed down in oral and written traditions, told by the humble and the scholarly. One of the earliest monsters in recorded history was Grendel in *Beowulf*, and monstrous visions were found in Milton's epic poem *Paradise Lost*. *The Castle of Otranto*, written by Horace Walpole in 1765, is considered the first Gothic novel, although sometimes Ann Radcliffe's *The Mysteries of Udolpho*, written in 1794 and said to be influenced by Walpole, is credited as the first Gothic horror novel. In the early 1800s, a great flowering of monster stories happened, and storytelling has never been the same. Jacob and Wilhelm Grimm collected hundreds of folktales and horror stories told over the ages in northern Europe into their now famous collection. Around the same time, Mary Shelley's *Frankenstein* started a literary trend, as did Washington Irving's headless horseman in "The Legend of Sleepy Hollow." The flowering, if we want to call the literature of monsters a flowering, continued with Robert Louis Stevenson's *Strange Case of Dr. Jekyll and Mr. Hyde,* Bram Stoker's *Dracula,* Edgar Allan Poe's über-creepy short stories, and Jules Verne's *20,000 Leagues Under the Sea.*

M.R. James's *Ghost Stories of an Antiquary* was published in 1904, and in 1923, the first issue of *Weird Tales* was published. By the 1930s, scary radio shows such as *The Shadow* were broadcast, and in 1938, panic swept across America following the broadcast of Orson Welles's radio dramatization based on H.G. Wells's *The War of the Worlds.* Many people missed the opening explanation and believed it was a real invasion. H.P. Lovecraft began publishing short stories for pulp publications such as *Weird Tales* and influenced generations of horror, science fiction, and fantasy writers. Beginning in the 1930s, J.R.R. Tolkien introduced generations of readers to Middle-earth and the many creatures and monsters that inhabited it. In the 1940s, Ray Bradbury exploded onto the literary scene with spooky stories, many originating from memories of his childhood. In the 1950s, many monsters were in science fiction stories and films, such as *Invasion of the Body Snatchers, The Thing From Another World,* and *Godzilla, King of the Monsters!* Beginning in the 1930s, horror writers were deeply influenced by films, and they remain so today.

The late 1950s included the release of Shirley Jackson's chilling *The Haunting of Hill House* and Robert Bloch's novel *Psycho.* Starting in 1959, Rod Serling's *The Twilight Zone* television series was broadcast into millions of homes. *Rosemary's Baby* by Ira Levin caused a sensation in 1967, as did William Peter Blatty's *The Exorcist* in 1971. Then in 1974, Stephen King's *Carrie* became a bestseller, King became one of the most read authors of all time, and the horror story was forever changed. Once King and other writers of fright tales experienced success, booksellers started promoting this type of story as a distinctive genre.

As the twenty-first century dawned, it was clear that all things monstrous were an important part of contemporary culture and literature. The unknown, the dark, the hideous—we have always told these tales. We have always had a morbid fascination with death, fear, and suffering. Monstrous tales are a way to transform our traumas and wildest fears into a story with the belief, though perhaps not justified, that this form of entertainment makes our fears manageable.

LAYERED IN THEMES

Monster stories will always be about reality turned upside down, sideways, and backward. They exploit our fears of what lies out of our sight range, in another dimension, or beyond the grave. While stirring our primal fears, monster stories will always question the norms that we take for granted, probe the depths of human psychology, and challenge our perceptions of reality, good and evil, and the nature of humankind. If you think back to the origins of monster tales like *Beowulf*, they are usually meant to be thought-provoking, not just a schlock and gore fest. While some monster stories, such as teenage slasher films, are simply created to shock and disgust, the best stories force us to face our assumptions, fears, and desires.

So it seems that to create effective fiction with a monster in a main role, the story must also give the reader something to think about, some deeper issues beyond what appears in the scenes. You do so by weaving in themes or central concepts that cause layers of resonance. And because the characters in a monster tale are stripped bare by fear and desperation, they often can easily *carry* themes about what it means to be human and heroic during trying times.

At its most basic level, monster stories, especially horror fiction, are insightful explorations of so-called reality and how the mind works. Such a story often delves into how most people are emotionally wounded; explores what constitutes natural order and what constitutes morality; and shows us the shadow that lurks within every human and how we project it out into the world—the varying shades of good and evil and how we judge ourselves, each other, and world events. However, woven into almost all monster stories are elements of vulnerability, powerlessness, and loss of control—these elements work side by side with themes to both frighten and suggest a deeper meaning.

In *Danse Macabre*, Stephen King's critical study of horror, he writes that horror fiction "exists on three more or less separate levels, each one a little less fine than the one before it." King writes that the finest emotion is terror, and below it lies horror and revulsion. It is likely that there will always be slasher films and schlocky B movies aimed at a not-too-discriminating audience. These stories are designed for revulsion or the gross-out effect. And there will also be stories written mostly to horrify. But well-crafted horror fiction is more than a splatter-fest; it speaks to our timeless fears, but also of timeless themes.

While some may feel that horror or any story with a monster as the villain is less important than other types of literature, make no mistake that stories created to thrill and chill are also literature and have been written by some of the most talented writers. In a 1997 interview originally published by *Omni Online*, Peter Straub, author of many spine-tingling tales, explained why he was drawn to writing horror:

> And I was conscious that horror had a great literary history. Hawthorne, Henry James, Poe, many others had found a depth and seriousness in it which made horror, to me anyhow, more valid, more interesting and worthy, than the general run of mystery fiction. Horror was not about the invention of clever puzzles. It dealt with profound emotions and real mysteries, not who had left the footprints under the gorse-bush and how the key to the library had wound up in the Colonel's golf bag. Horror could touch people, change them, make them think. While it was certainly entertaining, there was much more to it than mere weightless entertainment.

You can divide stories that frighten the reader into categories based on a primal fear of the reader: fear of monsters, fear of the demonic, fear of Armageddon or human annihilation, and fear of the monstrous from within. Within these broader themes, writers can mine endless ideas, all threatening human safety. For example, Edgar Allan Poe's "The Fall of the House of Usher" has a theme of a cursed family or a tainted bloodline, a theme also handed down from Gothic traditions. Often, this curse seems inescapable, or stories imply that fate is inescapable. Poe in particular weaves his stories with death and burial themes and capitalizes on the reader's fear of death in stories such as "The Premature Burial" and "The Masque of the Red Death."

In horror tales, primal struggles take place, and themes such as the fine line between sanity and madness, lawlessness, corruption, depravity, safety, violation, outcasts, exile, hope, salvation, and redemption, are explored. Along those lines, monster tales explode reality and norms. For instance, Jack Finney's *The Invasion of the Body Snatchers* takes ordinary people and replaces them with identical aliens. This sort of "pod people" theme shatters reality and makes our neighborhoods and homes unsafe, especially when the person replaced is a beloved. Ira Levin's *The Stepford Wives* is another depiction of this theme, and it is also woven with themes of a dangerous rampaging patriarchy coupled with technology. Thus, monster tales can also uncover the emptiness or threats of a patriarchal or bourgeois culture.

Monster stories also often explore religious themes, such as the holy and unholy, and characterizations of Satanic beings, as in *The Exorcist*. Morality is often explored in tales with horror elements, and we often see characters displaying impulses of rage, vengeance, and lust. Oscar Wilde's *The Picture of Dorian Gray* is considered a Gothic classic and introduces themes of immortality, vanity, and selling one's soul.

Other themes seen in these stories are likewise closely aligned with human nature; an example is forbidden knowledge or violating the natural order and the price that must be paid, such as when Dr. Frankenstein is destroyed by the monster he created. In daily life, we often see or experience the results when people overstep, and a monstrous tale can showcase our more human inclinations to covet, to seek personal glory, or to try to conquer death. Stories like *Frankenstein* also comment on loneliness, alienation, and a need for companionship. Doppelgängers, doubles, and the shadow lurking within are explored in stories like *Strange Case of Dr. Jekyll and Mr. Hyde*.

Some tales comment on humankind's insignificance or frailty. Or they uncover a universe that is indifferent or hostile to the humans who dwell in it. For example, H.P. Lovecraft's *At the Mountains of Madness* and *The Shadow Out of Time* and H.G. Wells's *The Island of Doctor Moreau* showcase that humans are not the lords of the earth. Human frailty is also depicted in stories where a disease or plague takes over, or where people are turned into zombies.

The risk of unleashing science or technology, which often ties in with greed, is another common theme, as illustrated in Michael Crichton's *Jurassic Park* and the film *The Fly*, based on George Langelaan's short story. It is no coincidence that the evolution of science and technology goes hand in hand with an explosion of stories that depict these dangers not only to people, but also to our fragile planet. It's also no coincidence that nightmares made in laboratories are frightening, and humankind fears being what can be formed in a Petri dish. Greg Bear's *Blood Music* is about a germaphobe who injects altered noocytes into his body, which then starts transforming the human race. We also fear intelligent machines because, after all, people are replaced by machines in the workplace every day in real life.

Monster tales and ghost stories also ask what happens after death and exploit our fears of death and the dead. The films *The Sixth Sense* and *The Others*, for example, ask where the dead live and how they interact with the living. Ramsey Campbell's *Incarnate* explores a sort of crossover of reality and the dream world, where the dream world is similar to the afterlife.

Many fiction writers begin with the simple question "what if?" With stories featuring monsters, that question is exploited and twisted, designed to make the reader squirm and gasp, but monster stories also question how human values, connections, and emotions play out amid some terrifying scenarios.

CRAFTING A MONSTER

Let's get down to what it takes to create a monster that lives in the reader's imagination or, better yet, nightmares. It takes more than having a knack for the creepy or nasty to create nightmares and the villains who live there. If your villain is a monster, sometimes it possesses human-like qualities, and sometimes it has nothing human in its makeup. If it is a beast or creature, this character cannot seem like an ordinary person wearing animal skins. Your monster character must be somehow extraordinary and seething with quintessential malevolence.

Anthropomorphic creatures are the staple of many Disney cartoon movies, and anthropomorphism is fun—if you're a kid. This trend started with Aesop's fables and gave us the metaphoric characteristics we've become too familiar with, as when a fox is aligned with cunning or tortoise with tenacity. When a monster is rampaging in the story, while you might be tempted to write it with characteristics of a wolf or another animal, instead think of the dehumanization of the character that is crucial for real goosebumps in your reader. Consider these points as you write your monster:

- **Make your monster primal and mighty; don't sanitize the creature.** The exceptions are children's picture books and the monsters that might exist in stories such as Maurice Sendak's *Where the Wild Things Are*. So unless you're writing for tots, forget loveable, huggable beings. Explore the nightmare realms of the imagination and give the reader a being that makes him quake with terror. (More information about writing for younger readers is found in chapter twelve.)

- **Endow your monster with a potent physicality.** In our nightmares and childhood imaginings, the monsters that terrify us aren't necessarily clearly drawn. But when monsters appear in your fiction, you have to make all sorts of decisions about height, size, and skin type. Perhaps the creature is furry or reptilian. You'll decide whether it's a quadruped or biped, and if it's capable of communicating with humans. Will it have extraordinary powers, or strengths and abilities more often found in nature? For example, grizzlies aren't supernatural, but they are capable of enormous destruction. Will it have red eyes, a distinct odor, fangs, or claws? Will it operate alone or in a pack?

  When you're creating a monstrous character, make choices about your degree of monstrosity. Will it display emotions? Is it capable of thought or reason? How far will the monster go to achieve its ends—murder, exploit a person's weaknesses, destroy a town?

- **Consider the fear factor from every angle.** Since a monster's job description is to make people feel afraid, think about what actions and characteristics the monster will have to do this. Will it have supernatural powers or supernatural strength? Is it as tall as a building, like King Kong? Can it fly, like the witch in *The Wizard of Oz*? Can it create fire with a flick of its wrist, and order around its cowering minions?

  Here is an example of a creature that inspires fear. It comes from Ray Bradbury's "A Sound of Thunder," which is about modern-day people traveling back in time to hunt a dinosaur. Note how his description of the creature creates terror and awe:

> It came on great oiled, resilient, striding legs. It towered thirty feet above half of the trees, a great evil god, folding its delicate watchmaker's claws close to its oily reptilian chest. Each lower leg was a piston, a thousand pounds of white bone, sunk in thick ropes of muscle, sheathed over in a gleam of pebbled skin like the mail of a terrible warrior. Each thigh was a ton of meat, ivory, and steel mesh. And from the great breathing cage of the upper body those two delicate arms dangled out front, arms with hands which might pick up and examine men like toys, while the snake neck coiled. And the head itself, a ton of sculptured stone, lifted easily upon the sky. Its mouth gaped, exposing a fence of teeth like daggers. Its eyes rolled, ostrich eggs, empty of all expression save hunger. It closed its mouth in a death grin. It ran, pelvic bones crushing aside trees and bushes, its taloned feet clawing damp earth, leaving prints six inches deep wherever it settled its weight. It ran with a gliding ballet step, far too poised and balanced for its ten tons.

In monster fiction, readers meet what they most dread. As the writer, this requires that you mine new veins of horror and imagination. Every writer needs to find his own way into fresh creative territory, especially when it comes to creating characters or creatures designed to frighten. Perhaps you'll want to ask your friends about their nightmares, think back to your first memories of frights, and read the first scary books of childhood to tap into the most basic fears. You might want to test your ideas out on readers such as your critique group, specifically asking if the characters or creatures you're creating seem freshly drawn. But mostly, when it comes to the monstrous, take risks to create chills in your reader.

- **Know your monster's biology, history of origin, and other essential qualities of the animal group.** If your story features a werewolf, you'll want to know about the characteristics of wolves—how they prey on other animals, how far they range, the social order of the pack. You'll also want to know the history or origins of your creature. This means you'll need to know the exact backstory of your creature, and also the wider understanding of it. If your creature is a werewolf, you'll research folklore and legends to know that these creatures are shapeshifters and turn into a wolf-man, because of a curse and by means of magic. They are associated with the full moon and primal instincts. You also need to learn how werewolves react to wolfsbane and religious objects such as crosses.

Perhaps you'll want to add a few wrinkles to this formula, yet retain the basics about werewolves, such as that they're carnivorous hunters. When you create creatures such as werewolves, imagine their capabilities enhanced by heightened senses, particularly smelling and hearing.

- **Read widely so that you know what type of monster, vampire, or wizard stories have been done to death, as well as what conventions have been overwritten.** Also, when searching for story ideas, you might want to pay attention to stories in the news, scientific discoveries, or disturbing realities of our era. For example, what would the world be like if global warming starts melting the icecaps? Or if experiments done in corporate laboratories or by the military go awry?

- **Beware of clichéd endings, such as the vampire is offed with a silver bullet or crucifix, or the creature tumbles to its death from a cliff face.** Your ending must be the logical conclusion of events that answers the story question set in place in the opening chapters. Endings in monster stories need some element of surprise, and they cannot be vague or ambiguous. Readers need to know the monster's fate, as well as the fate of the humans it has been interacting with. Once the conflict is over and the menace has been beaten back, duck off the page and set the story world back to some kind of order.

  Endings often contain a delicious final burst of action and a twist or a note of irony. For example, in the final moments of Ira Levin's *Rosemary's Baby*, which asks what happens when Satan sires a child, Rosemary, the mother, gives in to the eternal tug of maternal instinct and coos to her baby.

  While there are certainly tragic endings in stories that involve monsters, endings are often happy or offer a mixed message. For example, in the film version of *The Shining*, Jack Torrance freezes to death in the hedgemaze while his wife and son live. In the novel version by Stephen King, the hotel is destroyed so that the malevolent forces cannot possess anyone else.

  In a happy ending, usually the human character somehow quells the monster, escapes, and is far away from the danger. However, some stories have a final shocking note where the reader learns the danger has not been quelled. To examine how a writer can slip in surprises and layers of meaning and insight, read the short stories of Ray Bradbury, particularly "The Man Upstairs" and "The Emissary."

- **Don't splatter blood and gore into your story simply because you can.** The best monster stories disturb our daytime thoughts and nighttime wanderings. They don't make us want to shower afterward. So be proportionate—and, at times, simply suggestive—when it comes to gore. A little blood goes a long way.

MINING THE TERROR

Let's talk more about mining the terror with monsters, which can be some of the most potent bad guys. When a monster is in a story, it is likely that the writer is creating genre fiction. However, a story like *Lord of the Flies*, which has horrific themes and conflict about what happens to a group of school boys when civilization disappears, would not be classified as genre and it wouldn't be classified as a monster tale. You'll also find ghost tales such as Henry James's *The Turn of the Screw* with its Gothic influences don't neatly fall into a category, nor does something like Franz Kafka's *The Metamorphosis*. When a monstrous presence is in a story, the writer's imagination is rampaging, exploring cobwebby corners, and asking "what if?" What if a man becomes a beast? What if a cemetery suddenly becomes filled with its underground inhabitants? What if a spaceship landed with a mission to take over Earth? What if cell phones spread a zombie virus? What if a powerful robot cannot be killed?

Monsters can come from more seemingly mundane aspects of life, as in Stephen King's *The Mist* where a thick fog enfolds a town, or from biological warfare or even the supernatural. As children, most of us come to believe that monsters have a form—the ghost at the window, the monster under the bed, the flitting shadows in a haunted house. As adults, our fears change and are more reality-based, but when we read fiction with monsters, we tap into both the childhood fears of the scary unknown and the adult fears of losing control—because a monster in the story means a huge loss of control. So for most of us, monsters are part of our childhood, and they can be the shadows, the unknown, and the worst of what we dare not imagine.

You have many choices when you use monsters on a rampage, but there are some elements these stories always include: the normal world is disrupted by something unexpected, powerful, and uncontrollable; danger, most often cloaked in evil as the controlling force in the story; and high stakes, such as sanity and survival.

For example, let's look at the movie *The Birds*, which is based on Daphne Du Maurier's short story. Whenever I spot an unusual number of birds flocking, I feel the cold finger of fear on my spine, and I would guess you have the same reaction if you've seen the film. When nature becomes abhorrent, humans feel particularly vulnerable since we are all at the mercy of nature. Here are conventions in this film you can emulate in your monster story:

- The inciting incident is *seemingly benign* and takes place in a pet store in San Francisco and starts the characters on a collision course with fate. Melanie Daniels, played by Tippi Hedren, meets Mitch Brenner, played by Rod Taylor, in a pet shop.

- This leads to Daniels *stepping in the world of danger* when she arrives in Bodega Bay, bringing lovebirds as a surprise gift for Mitch's younger sister Cathy. After she sneaks the birds into the house and is about to leave by boat, she's attacked by a gull, the first unexpected element that *creates tension* and *foreshadows* trouble. Because of her injury, she stays the night and learns chickens aren't eating. That night a bird flies into the house and dies, more foreshadowing.

- The following day in the midst of Cathy's birthday party, birds attack the children, *endangering vulnerable characters*.

- That evening, a flock of swifts swarms down the chimney in a terrifying flurry. Characters are beginning to suspect that *something monstrous has been unleashed*.

- *The stakes and danger increase* the next day when Lydia, Mitch's mother, visits a neighbor to discuss his chickens and discovers his bloodied corpse and his home littered with dead birds. This is the *point of no return* in a horror story—when the danger can no longer be brushed aside or attributed to natural causes.

- As the death is being investigated, Melanie arrives at the school to pick up Cathy. Crows are flocking on the playground. Melanie and the teacher try to lead the children past the birds, but they attack. Afterwards, as often happens in horror stories, there are *disputes among the characters about reality and if the danger is real.*

- In a particularly horrific scene, Melanie, Mitch, and the townspeople in the diner watch in horror and helplessness as a fiery explosion at the gas station sends flames shooting into the air, casting a pall of Armageddon over the small town. By this time, a hysterical women accuses Melanie of bringing on the trouble, *since often in monster tales someone is scapegoated because characters cannot face the truth of what has been unleashed.*

- The schoolteacher Annie is killed by the birds. This is the *midpoint reversal,* and by this time, *the normal world disappears and characters struggle for survival.*

- That night, the Brenners barricade the house, certain another attack will take place. The family and Melanie *barely escape the horrific onslaught* with the birds trying to break through the barricades. They fall into an uneasy sleep.

- Later, Melanie wakes to a sound and climbs up into the attic where she's viciously attacked by still more birds. This is often the moment in the story where *the danger seems inescapable* or the dark-night-of-the-soul occurs.

- Melanie is rescued and they all manage to leave the house, creeping through a landscape of birds that inexplicably allow them to escape, providing *an ending that represents some kind of order restored.*

In your own stories, you can adopt some of these methods. First, the setting, attacks, and theme are unfailingly realistic. The story tiptoed into the danger with that first gull attack and hints about the chickens; likewise, you don't need to immediately plunge the story world into chaos, but can hint that something is amiss, introducing the threat in increments. Sometimes, it is suspected that the characters are fabricating the horror, so often the first incidents can be overlooked by some characters.

While the entire town is in danger in *The Birds*, the drama focused on a few characters. Also, the setting of a small seaside town serves to *isolate* the story, creating a *cauldron of desolation*, and you always want to trap characters, closing off escape and safety.

Like *The Birds*, use violence to prove the danger, but make sure it's not overstated. In the movie, while some characters are killed, most characters survive the attacks, but the *potential* for more death is clear because the townspeople are simply outnumbered.

SCARE TACTICS

The bottom line for all fiction is that the story is a lie the reader can believe in with characters he comes to know and care about. In horror or monster stories, the bottom line is that the reader will believe *and* be afraid. The monster scares him, the monster's powers and agenda scares him, and the characters' vulnerabilities scare him. The best monster stories force the reader to turn the pages with growing dread and prickling anxiety. These tales make the reader feel terrifyingly alone and ask how much control humans have over their fate.

So let's get down to brass tacks on how to achieve fear and believability when crafting tales with monsters:

- **Think bookends, as in the opening and closing.** The threat or some abhorrent element appears fairly early in the story, and the opening paragraphs or scene contain a hook. Generally, most monster stories either start fairly briskly introducing the horror early, or at least hint at or establish a pinprick of foreboding. For example, in opening scenes of the film *The Exorcist*, the family hears a scratching noise from the walls and thinks they might have a rat infestation on their hands. As in *The Exorcist*, the characters might not take the threat seriously at first, but for moviegoers and readers, their neck hairs are starting to prickle.

Sometimes the reader is immediately plunged into the action, as in Stephen King's *The Cell*, where the zombie threat is introduced in an opening scene at an ice cream stand. Sometimes the threat is at least hinted at or an atmosphere of threat is suggested in the opening pages by darkness, rain, or fog. If you want to start with a benign status quo in your first pages, it should still make the reader tingle with the knowledge that not all is as it seems.

Here is the opening to Shirley Jackson's *The Haunting of Hill House*:

> No live organism can continue for long to exist sanely under conditions of absolute reality; even larks and katydids are supposed, by some, to dream. Hill House, not sane, stood by itself against its hills, holding darkness within; it had stood so for eighty years and might stand for eighty more. Within, walls continued upright, bricks met neatly, floors were firm, and doors were sensibly shut; silence lay steadily against the wood and stone of Hill House, and whatever walked there, walked alone.

I don't know about you, but after reading those first sentences I want—no, I *need*—to know what walked alone. Sometimes a tale, such as Mary Shelley's *Frankenstein*, is written as a frame story, so the opening introduces the terrible consequences of the monster's rampage, then the story explores how it all came about and why it came about.

- **Use delay tactics to elevate the tension and suspense.** While the threat appears early, fear of the unknown is delicious and you also must delay the ultimate dustup with the monster. Delay any questions nagging at the reader to create suspense. After all, before Little Red Riding Hood meets the Big Bad Wolf, she must walk alone in the dark woods. The reader must hear her hesitant footsteps and the wind sighing and moaning in the trees, see the deep shadows cast by the giant firs as she draws closer and closer to the wolf's razor-sharp fangs, and feel that the world is eerily off-kilter and dangerous.

- **But don't delay too long.** While delay can be delicious, depending on the length of your story, typically by the end of Act I, the reader must be fully involved with the physical reality and threat of the monster. In most forms of drama Act I concludes with a plot point that pushes characters into a world of danger.

- **Make sure the monster or threat appears to have the upper hand and is unstoppable.** In stories where a monster is on the loose, the humans are all vulnerable, at risk, and trapped in a nightmare that appears as if there is no escape. In Stephen King's *The Cell*, since so many people own and use cell phones, millions of zombies are created attacking the living, so the non-zombie survivors are left to roam, seeking safety. In this story, when hordes of zombies first appear, people reach for their cell phones to dial 9-1-1 to report the havoc, but then a signal sent via the cell phones turns users into zombies, thus creating more hordes out for human flesh. In this story, the main threat is that the survivors appear to be outnumbered.

In every dangerous encounter and around every creepy corner, the reader needs to be reminded of death and the fear of death. Often, the cauldron for your story—the vast ocean if it's a sea monster, or a creepy castle if it's a ghost story—must also give the monster some advantage.

- **Keep in mind that a high ratio of harrowing action scenes keeps the reader on his toes.** Horror is staged one harrowing scene after another until the danger escalates into an explosive, all-out contest. So, yes, make your story as spooky as a haunted house on Halloween during a thunderstorm, but weave the details into action-charged scenes staged up close and personal.

- **Turn up the heat with plot twists, surprises, and reversals throughout the story.** A story with a monster must depict what we rarely or never want to meet in real life. Keep in mind that all writing requires a series of twists and surprises while taking the reader where he doesn't want to go. The reader wants your character to stay home tucked safely in bed, locked away from the sociopathic creep who is murdering women in the small town. So what does the character do? She spots a mysterious light flickering in the woods behind the house and sets out to explore, while the reader is yelling, "Get the heck back into the house and double bolt the door!" And the reader is worried about what might leap out in that gloomy woods, but what if you sent the story heading in an ever more sinister direction? What if the character is in *layers* of trouble, and not only is there a serial killer in her midst, but also something supernatural lurking right behind her?

- **Use the story as a test of character.** Most horror stories require the protagonist or victims of the monster to rise up to an extreme challenge or test of character. As in action stories, characters will manifest bravery and bravado. Because characters are often fueled by desperation and face overwhelming odds, including the unknown and the unexpected, the reader admires them just for surviving. While the characters might long to cut and run or cower under the bed, there are always compelling reasons for why they must fight the monsters. Ethan and Fric, the vulnerable protagonists in Dean Koontz's *The Face*, are good examples of characters that must face down a bad guy and a supernatural threat, and it takes all their courage and wits to do so.

A monster story provides writers with a particular showcase for a character's primary traits. A courageous person will likely act courageously, a coward might wimp out. The point is that this story type is perfect for unveiling characters and making the reader care about the outcome.

- **Make sure the setting is atmospheric.** Following in the Gothic traditions from where it began, monster story settings must crackle with tension and danger, and also create a world the reader can believe in. When a world that we know, with its smells of coffee and toast and bacon, is invaded by a monster, the results are deliciously involving. In horror stories, the world is unsettling and realistic at the same time. Language and sensory details are key to creating an atmosphere of tension and threat. However, the world must be tangible and believable. If the story world feels realistic, then when incredible events or never-before-seen creatures arrive on the scene, the incredible element will be more easily believed.

The more supernatural the tale is, the more the writer is required to create a world shadowed with spooks and roaming dangers. So fill it with dark passageways, bat-filled caves, gloomy skies, early dusks, impenetrable forests, and echoing castles.

Also don't forget to connect mundane details with horrific results—a thunderstorm makes it difficult to track the monster, for example. To balance out the worst parts of monster tales, you need everyday details and breathers in the story to establish credibility and normalcy. If there are no normal moments in a story, no matter what the type of story is, you've got melodrama.

- **Provide the reader with an extra dose of catharsis in the ending.** All fiction endings provide catharsis, but in monster stories, in the end when the monster is driven back or destroyed, the catharsis is enormously relieving. Stories with monsters provide a kind of safety valve from the stresses of everyday life. In the monster, there are so many shadow traits that it is no longer seen as redeemable. Typically, a monster must be destroyed and the protagonists must triumph because of determination, goodness, ingenuity, a tool, or some solely human solution.

Often, the ending shows some hopeful future of safety. In the film *The Birds*, the protagonists escape as the sun rises, a metaphoric image of hope. Also, good endings offer a twist that the reader or viewer didn't see coming. In *The Birds*, the viewer wasn't expecting that vast numbers of birds to allow the characters to escape. In monster stories, while the major conflict is resolved and order is restored, such as the shark being killed in *Jaws*, not everything needs to be tidied up. You want the horror and certain questions to linger a bit. After all, the world holds countless birds, and the oceans are filled with thousands of sharks.

LOST SOULS

So far in this chapter we've been mostly discussing monsters as villains in your stories. Let's talk now about characters that are not easily defined, but certainly have the power to frighten and ignite the reader's imagination. Lost souls are characters that have lost an important aspect, if not all, of their humanity. These types are not easily categorized, but they are anti-heroes or kin to dark heroes. Often misunderstood, they are outcasts, wanderers, and loners alienated from the human race. While they are fascinating, they are somehow repulsive yet sympathetic. Lost souls are often isolated and don't always portray typical emotions and motivations. They are usually intelligent, sensual, and mysterious.

Lost souls can embody loneliness in a story, and they are often the prisoners of circumstances. Some lost souls have cohorts, and often these friends are also outcasts. But generally, they have few or nebulous connections to normal society. Sometimes a lost soul has a broken or damaged spirit, usually because of some tragedy or deep loss, and sometimes these losses lead to revenge. However, unlike monsters, the reader can come to know their hopes, fears, and inner life, and to view them as people rather than as objects of horror.

A lost soul can be deformed, such as Victor Hugo's Quasimodo from *The Hunchback of Notre Dame*. Quasimodo was abandoned as a baby by

SHAPESHIFTING

Much fiction is about transformation—in fact, a person changing because of the tremendous pressure of the story's events is central to many stories. When it comes to shapeshifting, a writer takes this concept and pumps it up with mega steroids and a breath of magic. Shapeshifting refers to the process whereby a person or being changes into a dramatically different physical persona. This can mean the person turns into an animal, a werewolf, or a witch. The change can be temporary or permanent. Usually, the shapeshifting is done to acquire powers, to hide or escape, or to live as an animal. On the other hand, someone can be transformed as a punishment, as in *Beauty and the Beast* or in *Snow White and Rose Red*. Myths, particularly Greek myths, have many tales of transformation, as when Athena transforms Arachne into a spider, and Leda becomes a swan.

A shapeshifting story requires some intricacy and knowledge of the tradition. For example, in the myth of the selkie, a seal can shed its skin to take on human form; she must be careful to hide the skin in a safe place so that she can slip back into the skin and resume life as a seal. However, if a human finds the skin and hides it from the selkie, she can be doomed to a human existence. The film *The Secret of Roan Inish* does a terrific job exposing this aspect of the selkie myth.

his parents because of his hideousness; he then comes to live within the confines of the great cathedral. Through his job as the bell ringer, he becomes deaf, which further isolates him.

Or take the case of vampires. They have existed in folklore and legends for centuries, with their chief characteristic being they live on the life force of others. Made famous by Bram Stoker's *Dracula*, these creatures epitomize outcasts. When Anne Rice came along with *Interview With the Vampire*, she breathed new life into the character type by playing with old norms and making many of her vampires elegant, erudite, and intelligent, even as they are drinking the blood of their victims. Another terrific example of a lost soul character is Joe Pitt from Charlie Huston's *Already Dead*. Huston manages to make his dark tale roil with fresh depictions of the vampire mythos and a world we can only visit in fiction.

ROGUE'S GALLERY

Here are haunting stories where the monsters and monstrous events will stay with you long after the last page is turned or the screen turns black:

BOOKS

- Alien invasion: *Influx* by J.C. Jones
- Creatures: *The Wolfen* by Whitley Strieber
- Haunted family: *Bellefleur* by Joyce Carol Oates
- Haunted house/family: *The Haunting of Hill House* by Shirley Jackson
- Nature as monstrous: *The Nestling* by Charles L. Grant
- Lost soul: *The Green Mile* by Stephen King
- Lost soul: *'Salem's Lot* by Stephen King
- Lost soul: *They Thirst* by Robert R. McCammon
- Lost soul: *I Am Legend* by Richard Matheson
- Lost soul: *Grendel* by John Gardner
- Satanic themes: *The Exorcist* by William Peter Blatty
- Supernatural: *Weaveworld* by Clive Barker

FILMS

- *The Day the Earth Stood Still*
- *Forbidden Planet*
- *Blade Runner*
- *What Ever Happened to Baby Jane?*
- *Hush ... Hush, Sweet Charlotte*
- *Silent Running*
- *Aliens*
- *War of the Worlds*
- *King Kong*
- *Carrie*
- *A Nightmare on Elm Street*
- *An American Werewolf in London*

Another Anne Rice novel, *Cry to Heaven*, depicts lost souls not usually featured in fiction. It is set during the Baroque period, when the Catholic Church did not allow women to perform in the churches, and the stars of the church choirs and opera stages were the *castrati*, men who had been castrated in order to preserve the pure soprano voices that otherwise disappeared with the onset of puberty. The story follows two castrati, Guido Maffeo and Tonio Treschi, the protagonist. Tonio tries to fulfill his desire to become one of the greatest opera singers in Europe while plotting revenge on his brother for having him castrated and exiled from his family. The story opens with a startling scene:

> Guido Maffeo was castrated when he was six years old and sent to stay with the finest singing masters in Naples.
>
> He had known only routine hunger and cruelty among the large peasant brood in which he was born the eleventh child. And all of his life, Guido remembered he was given his first good meal and soft bed by those who made him a eunuch.
>
> It was a beautiful room to which he was taken in the mountain town of Caracena. It had a real floor of smooth stone tiles, and on the wall Guido saw a ticking clock for the first time in his life and was frightened of it. The soft-spoken men who had taken him from his mother's hands asked him to sing for them. And afterwards rewarded him with a red wine full of honey.
>
> These men took off his clothes and put him in a warm bath, but he was so sweetly drowsy by that time he was not afraid of anything. Gentle hands massaged his neck. And slipping back into the water, Guido sensed something marvelous and important was happening to him. Never had anyone paid him so much attention.
>
> He was almost asleep when they lifted him out and strapped him to a table. He felt he was falling for an instant. His head had been placed lower than his feet. But then he was sleeping again, firmly held, and stroked by those silken hands that moved between his legs to give him a wicked little pleasure. When the knife came he opened his eyes, screaming.

Rice's castrati can be examined for their lost soul characteristics, especially noting that they will always be set apart from normal men. *Cry to Heaven* illustrates some of the main traits of lost souls: They are artistic and somehow tortured, they are loners, they are seen as worthy of salvation, they are depicted as sensitive, and, in their protagonist or anti-hero role, they can sometimes be heroic.

TIPS FOR WRITING LOST SOULS

While lost souls will prick the reader's sympathies, this sympathy can come and go, and the characters also might cause revulsion. This revulsion doesn't need to come from their evil nature, because these are types who are caught in inescapable circumstances, so instead, think of them as prisoners of circumstance. Another reason the reader's sympathies for lost souls might come and go is because this character type is often changeable and unpredictable. After all, who knows what a vampire might try next? Lost souls also embody the unknowable, the *other*. Along these lines, since they're typically sympathetic characters, they won't be indiscriminate killers.

Remember how we said that anti-heroes have pathos at their core? Similarly, lost souls have a restless, disconnected, lonely essence, and they're often struggling to attain some humanity. Sometimes they long to be like ordinary people, but sometimes, like many of Anne Rice's characters, they realize this is impossible. Often, they were once normal and can only hide in the shadows or outskirts of human life. Sometimes they're charismatic, alluring, and classy. Sometimes women (or men) fall for them, and sometimes they run screaming.

Unlike monsters, on first meeting them, you might not realize that lost souls are not like regular humans. Thus, they can blend in … but only for a little while. Eventually, they'll need to go home to their crypt, their creepy bondage club, or their small group of outsiders. Or, if they're fairly benign, like Koontz's Odd Thomas, they simply want to be left alone most of the time. But unlike monsters, lost souls can have relationships with other characters instead of merely lurching around in a story wreaking havoc.

Lost souls also have emotions and desires, which makes things more complicated. But regardless of if they have motivations or emotions that the reader can relate to, they must retain an alienness that sets them apart. Lost soul characters work best when the reader can slip into their thoughts and feelings to understand how they see the world.

Which leads to the next point: You probably won't picture these characters at the gym or on a picnic. Their milieu is underground, darkness, shadows, outer space, and other places the reader is not familiar with. But, while you cannot picture these types pumping iron, there might be something sensual or sexual about them that also adds to the mix, and almost always, they're sympathetic.

Stories that have monsters as villains explore our primal fears and acknowledge the nature of humankind that includes violence, lust, and beastliness.

But the best fiction sheds light on some aspect of humanity, opens our minds, and gives our imaginations a workout. When you write to frighten, the story and themes must somehow matter, must somehow explore realms of humanity, loss, and emotion. It is not a gross-out contest between writer and reader; it is part thrill ride, part waking nightmare, part contemplative tale.

So, yes, make your monsters deadly, but also make them fascinating, not merely killing machines. And while you're at it, keep working your craft. Formulate your tastes, analyzing your likes and dislikes. Ask yourself why you're drawn to the dark side, why you think fear is so delicious. What really scares you? Is there something you can harvest there to shape into a story? Watch films, asking yourself about the cinematic techniques you can borrow for your story.

CHAPTER ELEVEN

Bad Guys for Younger Readers

"Has it got any sports in it?"

"Fencing. Fighting. Torture. Poison. True love. Hate. Revenge. Giants. Hunters. Bad men. Good men. Beautifulest ladies. Snakes. Spiders. Beasts of all natures and descriptions. Pain. Death. Brave men. Coward men. Strongest men. Chases. Escapes. Lies. Truths. Passion. Miracles."

"Sounds okay," I said, and I kind of closed my eyes. "I'll do my best to stay awake … but I'm awful sleepy, Daddy."

—WILLIAM GOLDMAN, *THE PRINCESS BRIDE*

Over the years, I've noticed that several types of writers gravitate toward writing for kids. In the first group are teachers, librarians, and parents who have learned firsthand that a children's story can weave magic into, and perhaps alter, the life of a young reader. In the second group are writers who believe that it's easier to write for kids than for adults, so they gravitate toward this age group based on that notion. Nothing could be further from the truth, though, because kids' books require characters that the reader feels intense identification with. They also must explain or reveal something important about human nature and entertain a highly discriminating audience.

If you're writing for children and young adults, it is especially important that you familiarize yourself with the genres, conventions, and age group you're writing for. You'll want to read widely, ask kids what they enjoy reading, and talk to parents, teachers, and librarians. While you might be familiar with classics for kids—*The Wind in the Willows, The Yearling, A Wrinkle in Times*—as well as perennial favorites like the Nancy Drew and the Hardy Boy series, you'll especially want to analyze how kids' books today differ from the classics and the books you read as a kid. Analyze plots, pacing, and voice, and note how the characters are made authentic. This is especially important because both children's and young adult literature is a rapidly changing landscape; we're living in a golden age for young adult literature, with some of the best authors writing for younger readers. Realize, too, that today's kids are coping with more pressures than those of previous generations, so perhaps you'll want to reflect that reality and not shy away from realistic, gritty, or controversial topics.

If you're not a parent, or if your kids are grown, you'll need to observe kids in environments where they feel the most comfortable, such as school, the mall, playgrounds, theme parks, and video arcades. In your observations, note body language, dress, hairstyles, expressions, gestures, and how they navigate the room. And, of course, you'll want to observe how conflict and bad guys are handled. How do kids cope with bullying or gangs demanding loyalty, or an older sibling who picks on them?

Once you've gained an understanding of your reader and have a sense for today's market, then you're ready to craft the story. It's especially important that you create a story with broad appeal and crackling conflict. Many young protagonists wrestle with inner conflict in fictional stories, much of the conflict in stories aimed at younger readers happens because a *situation* has landed the protagonist in a dilemma. Thus the story unfolds in scenes in the moment, many face-to-face with an antagonist or villain, and demonstrates the character arc that results. The situation might be the protagonist dealing with the loss of a parent, abuse, or moving to a new town. Within this situation, you want to show the character struggling with universal themes, such as fitting in with a group, difficulties making or keeping friends, or facing peer pressure.

MAKE THE STORY AGE APPROPRIATE

When writing for kids, start by figuring out your reader's age, and thus the level of reading ability and sophistication your story can include. You'll also want to understand the interests, concerns, and problems that readers in this age group experience. (In this chapter, I am generally not referring to picture books, but rather, books written for kids who are reading on their own—teens and preteens.)

After you identify your reader, factor in that kids often read about kids who are slightly older than themselves. This means that ten-year-olds are likely reading about twelve- or thirteen-year-old protagonists.

Age categories for children's books aren't written in stone because various publishers have established their own categories, and several book categories might lie within broader age groups. Also, not all bookstores classify books in the same way. Some will have a "chapter books" section, while others will have a "middle-grade reader" section, and other stores lump most books for teens under "young adult." While "young adult" readers are broadly categorized as children ages twelve to eighteen, obviously within this broad group there are subgroups of readers. You can imagine that a story aimed at a twelve-year-old will be quite different than one aimed at an eighteen-year-old.

Making decisions about featuring a villain or monster in a kids' story is tricky, so it's important to nail down your audience demographic first because, depending on their age, most children want to feel safe while they engage in the joy ride of fiction. The younger the child is, the stronger the need for safety. Kids want to enjoy the fright factor without feeling personally threatened, feeling shivers but not emotional distress. As for teens, their limited experience means they need fiction as a safe haven to stockpile understanding and adventures without treading into actual danger.

Then there's the issue of how much physical and emotional danger the protagonist can struggle against. The dangers an eight-year-old protagonist faces will obviously be milder than those faced by an eighteen-year-old. It's not that you cannot feature genuine villains or life-threatening struggles in your stories, but the resolution of a kids' story—especially those written for readers under ten or so—must do more than end the conflict and solve the issues raised in the story. The resolutions must also set the story world back in order, even if that order is in a shaky state of things. While the protagonist will usually have undergone a character arc, many stories require that the endings feature a kind of safety zone or breathing room. If you're writing a young adult story, for example, after the climax and resolution, the ending might feature the protagonist hanging out with his friends reflecting a bit on what has happened. Sometimes in a story that is gritty or has realistic themes like homelessness, this resolution might mean the protagonist has found the strength to keep plugging along. So if you're interested in writing about hot-button topics, don't think that you're constrained by needing happy or fluffy resolutions. The point is that in the best kids' stories, the danger has made the reader think, feel, and fear within a built-in buffer zone.

PRETEEN VERSUS TEEN

Let's set up a few perimeters in writing for preteens versus writing for teens. You don't want impressionable readers to bring the horrors from a fiction story into their real lives. They should be able to understand the delineation between the two worlds. This is especially true if you're writing a story set in the real world with cafeteria food, Gap stores, and homework assignments. If something or someone unspeakably terrifying creeps into a world much like our own, the fright can be delicious, but kids must ultimately believe it could never really happen in their town.

Preteens

When you're writing for younger kids, especially those who are reading on their own for the first time, you'll need to decide what level of threat the story needs. Just to recap: Antagonists threaten the protagonist's goals and happiness; villains threaten the protagonist's safety, life, and sanity, and possibly other characters; and super villains threaten the protagonist's life, other characters, and the story world. So a mean science teacher, a playground bully, or a parent with some illness or preoccupation might be enough conflict for your story, and you won't need to stir in a killer to make things scary.

On the other hand, maybe you're writing a rough-and-tumble pirate tale with a truly villainous pirate who enslaves kids or threatens a stroll down the plank to the protagonist. Or maybe you want a witch, monster, or golem in your story who threatens the characters' lives. But since these are fantasy or horror genres, you'll emphasize the fantasy elements of the story to provide the necessary balance. Thus, setting, atmosphere, and sensory details will be important proofs of the alternate fictional universe.

You also might want to use humor or a dash of silliness to deflect the fright factor, as R.L. Stine does in his Goosebump horror series aimed at preteen readers. Another gimmick that Stine uses often in his novellas is that things are not as bad as they seem, or the monster turns out to be a hoax. His stories also introduce themes like if kids are brave and stick together, they can escape danger.

Stine's monsters run the gamut: hamsters, mummies, skeletons, aliens, and a haunted mask, among others. At times, the stakes are high and the protagonists are in danger. Then, sometimes his titles—such as *The Horror at Camp Jellyjam, Let's Get Invisible!*, and *The Abominable Snowman of Pasadena*—hint that the stories are also silly, thus toning down the fright factor.

If you want to write a Goosebumps-type story for preteens, borrow some of Stine's techniques:

- Try the "fish out of water" scenario for kids' stories since there is an automatic empathy for the discomforting situation.
- Have things seem normal at first, but then have them soon go wrong.
- Insert inexplicable happenings that cannot be explained in the normal world.
- Have a good reason to trap the characters so there is no way out or no place to run.
- Use realistic details—from everyday life like sibling teasing, food and meals, vacations, and furniture—to anchor the stories with some plausibility to make the creepy stuff believable.
- Make the villain extremely physical; the reader needs to experience the creature or person through all the senses. For example, give him clammy skin, piercing eyes, a swampy smell, or a slithery walk.

Or, you might also want to borrow from the playbook of Brian Jacques and his highly successful Redwall fantasy-adventure series written for ten- to fourteen-year-old readers. His stories feature potent villains and violence, but the characters are animals, so the reader experiences some distance. Jacques pits the peaceful mice, squirrels, shrews, moles, and otters against animal villains—the rats, weasels, foxes, and stoats. Techniques writers can borrow from the Redwall series include:

- Characters have anthropomorphic responses and motivations, brought to life with realistic dialogue and bowing to conventions about the species' characteristics.
- The whole story world is interwoven with astounding detail, intricacy, and understanding of medieval times sprinkled with everyday life. These parts of life include meals, feasts, gathering berries, drinking elderberry wine at celebrations, the passing of time, and seasons.
- The line between good and evil is clearly drawn, and the whole series is based on morality since the peaceable creatures of Redwall have vowed never to harm another creature except those who seek to destroy them.
- Success is never easy, and complications ensue.
- The villains always fight hard, have a lot at stake, and at first glance seem invincible.
- The story has swashbuckling, mythic, or Tolkien-like features: huge battles, struggles, quests, journeys, and sieges; imprisonment; a warrior who reluctantly assumes his role; prophecies and legacies; and complicated relationships and alliances.
- The story doesn't leave out tragedies, such as deaths of sympathetic characters, because this proves the potency of villains, or the cost of war, the battle for freedom, or justice.
- Villains have names that suggest their less-than-virtuous characteristics, such as Drigg Slopmouth (a stoat), Fangburn (a rat), Clubface (a weasel), and Damug Warfang (a Greatrat).

Teens

There's a lot more than hormones going on with teen readers. We've been talking about the "ring of safety" in writing for kids, but with older teens, you have choices about whether this safety zone exists, or if it's just very thin. Many teen books are about angst and personal discovery, and often the antagonists and villains in the stories have enormous powers in the protagonist's life. Mature and dark themes such as sexual abuse, gangs, rape, illness and mental illness, suicide, and drugs often exist in these stories. Characters aren't drawn in black and white, meaning that sometimes the protagonist can be an anti-hero, and sometimes the conflict can stem from an antagonist, such as a parent who believes he wants what is best for the protagonist. Also, doing the right thing might not be a simple choice, and sometimes even doing the right thing doesn't mean a happy ending.

Some of the themes found in teen fiction include: fitting in with a group or society, being out as a homosexual, needing a family, dealing with death, and dealing with abuse or estrangement. If the story is about abuse, assault, rape, neglect, or other especially difficult issues, the story is often about fighting back, and the ending shows the character coming out the other side and defeating, confronting, or escaping the villain. An example of this type of story is *Mercy's Birds* by Linda Holeman. It's about an impoverished teen girl, Mercy, who could be a poster girl for living in a dysfunctional family, as her mother is depressed and sometimes suicidal, and her Aunt Moo is an alcoholic. When Moo's boyfriend, Barry, threatens Mercy and makes sexual advances, Mercy feels like she doesn't have anyone to turn to. The family needs Barry for his rent money, and, like the best teen stories, things seem to be spinning out of control. Eventually, Mercy finds support from a friend and her boss, and she finds the courage to confront Barry and end the abuse.

As in *Mercy's Birds*, try to capitalize on the fact that many teens feel alone and estranged, or as if other people were born with operating instructions and they were not. Painful and raw emotions are often exposed, as in Darlene Ryan's *Rules for Life*, which is about dealing with the death of a mother and coming to terms with a changing world. In this case, Izzy, the protagonist, is up against two antagonists: her father—to whom she's been extremely close, especially since her mother's death, but who suddenly becomes cold and distant—and his new girlfriend—who becomes her stepmom and is a woman Izzy can't relate to. As in adult fiction, when an antagonist is a family member, the reader will naturally identify with the protagonist and situation. On page one, the reader and Izzy are introduced to a threatening change:

> I knew my father had had sex the minute I walked into the kitchen. It wasn't as though he was smoking a cigarette and basking in the afterglow. It was more subtle than that.
>
> But I knew.
>
> It was his hair. Dad is really particular about his hair. It's strawberry blond, like mine. He spends more money on shampoo and conditioner and gel than I ever would. I just wash mine and twist it up in the back. He goes to a stylist at a salon where you have to make an appointment two weeks in advance. I go to the walk-in place and take whoever has a free chair.
>
> Dad wears his hair sort of long for someone who's forty. And the whole left side was flattened against his head with a few pieces coming out at weird angles, like he'd slept on it funny. Which meant he'd slept somewhere else, because the first thing he would have done here when he got up, was shower and fix his hair.
>
> So I knew he'd had sex. Plus I could see the neck of his tee shirt in the vee of his sweater. It was inside out.

If you're writing about a problem with an antagonist, as in *Rules for Life*, it works best if there is no escape from the antagonist, as is the case when the antagonist is a family member, teacher, classmate, or neighbor.

As you write your story, capitalize on a teen's need or sense of fairness and unfairness. The teen reader will always understand tyrants and bullies because at some point most kids meet or face bullies in their schools and neighborhoods, so this is a natural role for antagonists and villains in your story.

ESPECIALLY VULNERABLE

In the first chapters of this book, we explored how the reader's feelings of vulnerability and primal fears are exploited when we write fiction. Many of the concepts and advice covered in early chapters work when writing for kids, but you'll need to amp up story elements so that there is intense reader involvement. To do so, draw on your childlike feelings and memories of vulnerability when designing antagonists and villains. Remember how you sometimes felt powerless and afraid, or longed for more freedom? Imagine what it would be like to be in a tough spot without a car, credit cards, and other adult resources we often take for granted. And then give the villain and antagonist *proximity* to the protagonist.

Your protagonist will likely feel powerless, afraid, and constrained at times, but keep in mind that kids experience emotions—such as anger, jealousy, loneliness, loss, hate, love, abandonment, and powerlessness—without the buffer that adults possess. When most adults feel intense emotions, they are still able to cope because they know they've felt these emotions before and they will pass. Kids, without years of experience in handling difficult feelings, are often more vulnerable.

Thus, don't use unnecessary danger, horror, or violence merely for the splatter factor; make it proportionate to the protagonist's resources and age, and to the threat in the story. If it's appropriate to your genre, use magic talismans, helpers, or your protagonist's powers as a safety valve in a too-scary story world. Villains can be found in both mainstream fiction, as in *Mercy's Birds*, and genre fiction, like the Redwall series. But no matter what the story type is, give the young protagonist traits, skills, or potency that help defeat the villain. In most kids' books, the ending brings the character and reader safely home after a perilous thrill ride. This generally assures the reader that good triumphs over evil, most people are decent, and brave kids can triumph over monsters and bad guys.

Another way that you can use vulnerability in your writing is to make the threats extremely personal and threatening to the protagonist's world. For example, in Carl Hiaasen's *Flush*, Noah (the protagonist) is visiting his father (the antagonist) in jail on Father's Day. He's been arrested for capsizing a casino ship because he's sure the owner (the villain) is dumping the ship's wastes into the basin where it was docked, meaning the tide sweeps the wastes out into the ocean.

As the story progresses, Noah's father remains unrepentant, and his mother is threatening divorce. Because fiction writers need to strip away a kid's resources, Noah's two best friends are out of town for the duration of the story and can't help him defend himself when the ship owner's son threatens him and beats him up. So the stakes are high and threaten Noah's sense of security, and unfairness and injustice play a big role in the story.

To increase the vulnerability necessary to make kids' fiction work, you often must disable the adults in the story, forcing the young protagonist to face things on his own. In *Flush*, for example, Noah's father's hands are tied because of his legal situation, and his mom is focused on the family survival, not justice.

As another example, in the teen novel *The Candy Darlings* by Christine Walde, the protagonist's mother dies in the inciting incident, and throughout the story the character's father is so overcome with grief that he becomes ineffective and clueless as a parent. The nameless protagonist and her father move to a new town to start over and she attends a private school where she meets the villains, Meredith, Angela, and Laura, as well as Megan Chalmers, the antagonist, who is also a new girl. Megan is the antagonist because she is fearless and mouthy, and she doesn't care about gaining the favor of the popular clique; she also teaches the protagonist to stand up for herself. The villains are popular and beautiful, and they set the standards for the school. At first, the protagonist is befriended by them, but then they turn on her, and she instead becomes friends with the mysterious and rebellious Megan.

Because the popular girls are as mean and conniving as they are pretty, Megan dubs them MAL, a prefix meaning evil. But because of their looks and status, teachers and other adults cannot see their true nature, increasing the protagonist's and Megan's vulnerability. In a climactic scene, MAL sneak up on Megan and the protagonist in a snowy fortress in the woods, binds them with duct tape, and buries them in the snow with only their heads showing. Megan and the protagonist are eventually helped by another outsider and barely survive this ordeal.

Walde mixes fantasy with realism because Megan tells the protagonist horrific stories that sometimes border on pornographic, and the reader can't be sure which parts are true and which aren't. Through a volunteer gig, the girls meet an elderly woman who also spins a fantasy tale. This mix of fantasy and reality works to diffuse the grim truths and difficult issues of the story, as does the candy that Megan and the protagonist eat to cope.

Many young adult books are about trying to be popular or fitting in with a clique, but the difficult lessons most of us learn during adolescence can be particularly potent when the villains in the story are realistic or all-powerful, and when the protagonist is especially vulnerable because adults aren't available for help.

STRATEGIES TO EXERT PRESSURE

Like adult fiction, kids' stories require a structure that exerts pressure on a protagonist and creates danger. But, with a few exceptions, books written for younger readers are shorter than books written for adults, which causes constraints on you as the writer. This means you won't have as many scenes and opportunities to bring your bad guys onto the page and show your protagonist coping with trouble.

In the first act, typically the reader learns just how far the villains will go or what's at stake. For example, in Nancy Farmer's sci-fi futuristic novel *The House of the Scorpion*, the protagonist is Matt. He's a clone of El Patrón, the 140-year-old drug lord of opium, an area called Aztlán that lies between the United States and what was formerly Mexico. In the beginning of the story, Matt doesn't know he's a clone, and it isn't until the middle of the story that he realizes his true purpose, which is to provide body parts for El Patrón. In these middle scenes, Matt confronts this hideous reality first by seeing another clone who has had some of his body parts harvested, and he is so crippled and ruined that his suffering seems unimaginable. Not long after this sighting, El Patrón collapses during a wedding and needs Matt's heart to survive. Matt must escape to Aztlán, but—because fiction requires a series of twists and deepening conflict—after he escapes, he is captured and put into a slave labor camp for orphans, where his survival is again precarious.

As in adult fiction plots, have your story depict a dark-night-of-the-soul—the bleakest moment near the climax when the protagonist is battered by the story events and the situation looks hopeless, as in the burial scene in *The Candy Darlings*.

In *The House of the Scorpion*, Matt and his friend Chacho are tossed into a boneyard, and escape seems impossible. The adults, called Keepers, who run the worker camp, are punishing Matt and Chacho because they led an uprising. Here is how Farmer introduces the dark-night-of-the-soul:

Before them stretched a wide basin that had once been full of living water and was now filled with dead whales. The homes stuck up like a gigantic bowl of thorns.

"This is what we call the boneyard," Jorge said pleasantly.

Matt remembered someone saying, when he first arrived, *You won't get away with your swanky ways here. We've got something called the boneyard, and any troublemaker who goes through it comes out as harmless as a little lamb.*

"Shall I take the tape off now?" one of the Keepers inquired.

"Only from his mouth," said Jorge.

"But that means he won't be able to climb out."

"He tried to kill me!" said Jorge. Matt felt the tape rip off. He flexed his mouth, ran his tongue over his bruised lips. "You think you're thirsty now," Jorge said, smiling. "Wait till tomorrow."

"*He's* the murderer," cried Matt, but he had no time to say anything else. The men swung him up and out. He came down with a crash, and the bones shifted and let him fall though. Down he tumbled, rolling this way and that until he arrived at a plateau of skulls. He hung in the midst of a sea of bones, with the blue sky visible through a fretwork of ribs and vertebrae. He turned his head cautiously. Below was a pit whose dark depths he could only guess at.

Farmer makes matters worse and worse, as when she introduces vampire bats crawling on the boys, when the sun rises in the punishing sky and their thirst becomes unbearable, when a thunderstorm sweeps in and spills hailstones on the boys, and when Chacho gives in to the trauma and despair of their plight. Often, the dark-night-of-the-soul is the most harrowing scene of the story, and, like Farmer, you might want to prolong the danger and, thus, the suspense.

These key moments in the plot provide explosive emotions, reflect the toll of the story's events, show the character confronting a towering hurdle and inner conflict, and make the reader worry. Endings are often based on the character's worst fears or worst possible outcomes. Perhaps your protagonist can concoct a particularly ingenious solution to the story's problem. Also, often in kids' stories, the final battle or scene is staged in front of other characters rather than a one-on-one confrontation. This fulfills kids' fantasies of being the hero to a crowd of applauding admirers.

And almost all fiction written for kids features characters solving the main conflict without help from adults. However, many kids' books feature well-meaning adults to balance out the villains or evil in the story. So, while J.K. Rowling's Harry Potter is helped by Dumbledore and other adults, when push comes to shove, it is often Harry drawing on his will, magical abilities, and hard-won skills to save himself and others while delivering another blow for the good guys.

Finally, like adult novels, stories written for younger readers need themes and a premise to provide resonance and potency. In *The House of the Scorpion*, the themes are about cloning, friendship, and hope. The premise is that every life has value, which is proven by Matt's escape and eventual reversal of fortune.

CREATING A POTENT VILLAIN

As mentioned previously, not all kids' stories need a villain, but when you use one in your story, he needs to have a special potency. D.J. MacHale has written a young adult fantasy series about Bobby Pendragon, a time traveler, and he bases the series on an intriguing dramatic question: What if you discovered that you were not who you thought you were? In the case of Bobby, he learns he's a Traveler, a person who possesses extraordinary abilities and travels to other universes to help struggles and right wrongs, but especially to defend the world against the super villain in the series, Saint Dane.

In the first book of the series, *The Merchant of Death*, MacHale launches the story with a rollicking hook, sympathy for the protagonist, and an engaging, believable voice while weaving in a bit of the status quo, which features Bobby living a seemingly normal and satisfying life in Stony Brook, Connecticut. The reader quickly learns that Bobby's Uncle Press needs his help to rescue people on Denduron, an alternate universe. To reach it, Bobby and Uncle Press hop on a motorcycle and whisk off to an abandoned subway station to enter the flume—the entrance to the alternate world. This is when the reader gets his first glimpse of Saint Dane, the super villain.

Like MacHale, make sure that the villain or antagonist shows up early in the story, or that there is at least a strong sense of his powers or menace hanging over the opening chapters. In the case of the Pendragon series, the stakes are high, because Saint Dane wants to tip the balance of Halla (all the territories of the universe, including Earth and all its time frames, past, present, and future) into chaos and possible annihilation.

In Saint Dane, MacHale has created a potent super villain who adds plenty of menace to each story line. Saint Dane is a shapeshifter, which gives him a supreme advantage and allows him to turn into strange beasts. He also possesses an array of magical powers, such as conjuring objects, bending other people to his will, and reading minds. The author never quite reveals Dane's hand. The reader knows he's evil and that his plans for Halla are destructive, but the reader is only provided glimpses of his schemes because MacHale keeps Bobby and the rest of the cast off-center and reacting. Like many villains, Saint Dane is delusional in that he feels justified in his acts. The reader first meets him as he's disguised as a policeman and, along with Bobby, the reader learns the cruelty he's capable of when he bends the will of a homeless man:

> Suddenly the cop snapped a look to the homeless guy. It was a cold look that made me catch my breath. It stopped the homeless guy in his tracks. The cop stared at him with an intensity I'd never seen. The guy froze, and then began to shake like he had a fever.
>
> The subway horn blared. The train was almost in the station.
>
> The homeless guy looked as if he wanted to get away, but the cop's laserlike focus had him locked in place. Then, something happened that I won't forget as long as I live, though I wish I could. The homeless guy opened his mouth and let out a horrifying, anguished cry. Then he ran. But he didn't run away, he ran for the tracks! The train entered the station in a blur, and this guy was running toward it.
>
> "No! Stop!" I shouted. But it didn't matter. The homeless guy kept running … and jumped in front of the train!

After Saint Dane's victim meets his fate with a sickening thud, Uncle Press confronts Saint Dane, saying that the murder was beneath him.

Saint Dane replies with an innocent shrug, "Just wanted to give the boy a taste of what is in store for him." And after that warning, Saint Dane begins to transform in front of them, until he's nearly seven feet tall, with long hair, pale skin, and icy blue eyes that make Bobby understand the will behind them that could force another person to leap to his death. Then a gun battle erupts between Saint Dane and Uncle Press, and Bobby is running for his life toward the flume and his dangerous future. Once young readers have experienced Saint Dane's power and tricks, they'll be worried about Bobby's chances of survival.

There are many techniques you can learn from MacHale, but especially note how he keeps developing Saint Dane as the series evolves. From the first meeting with him, the reader wonders about his reasons, resources, and mindset. Wisely, MacHale withholds those answers until the last possible moment. As Saint Dane evolves, so does Bobby, which ties in with MacHale's themes of self-empowerment and the gifts each person brings to his life. For example, the author kills off Uncle Press, an especially endearing character, forcing Bobby to become more self-reliant and confident. If you, too, can tie your character's evolution to your theme or premise, younger readers will understand these subtleties.

AGE-APPROPRIATE VILLAINS

One of the most difficult aspects of writing for kids happens when you need to create a threatening villain that your young protagonist is capable of slapping down on his own—no cavalries to the rescue, no well-meaning adults helping out, no fairies swooping in to save the day. The protagonist—who will often be at a disadvantage because of his age, size, and experience—must muddle through on his own or with the help of other characters his age, and his victory must be realistic, even when it has magical elements. Thus, you're often creating protagonists with a special skill or knowledge, or with unusual determination and spunk.

This is often the case where a kid's nerdiness or intellect—such as his love of science, computers, or gadgets—helps save him in the end. An example of this is in Mary Pope Osborne's *Magic Tree House*, a chapter book series where the adventurers Jack, a bookworm, and his sister, Annie, stumble into adventures and misadventures via books found in a magical tree house. The tree house is owned by Morgan le Fay, King Arthur's sister, and the books hold magical powers. In each story, Jack and Annie open a particular book and then are whisked back in time or into the future, or to distant lands or outer space. They tangle with some danger or mystery—a terrifying dragon, a tsunami, mountain gorillas, pirates, a tornado, and dinosaurs, among others. They've also taken part in history during the Civil War, the Revolutionary War, the San Francisco earthquake of 1906, and the sinking of the *Titanic*. By being daring and brave, and by keeping their wits about them, Jack and Annie manage to survive each situation and teach the reader valuable lessons about compassion and common sense.

Just as in adult fiction, a villain in a young adult novel will have an impressive bag of tricks, and he is often clever, sly, and extremely driven or ambitious. Because young readers need lots of empathy for the protagonist, you might want to show the villain enjoying suffering or the fallout from his evil. But again, a little of this sort of fiendish delight goes a long way.

As I mentioned earlier, when unfairness is part of the story line, kids naturally understand the dynamic. Unfairness looms large in the A Series of Unfortunate Events series by Daniel Handler writing as Lemony Snicket, and the series is a terrific example of how children's books use a villain to demonstrate that adults have power over children's lives. The three Baudelaire children are orphaned in the first book in the series when a mysterious fire destroys their home. The clueless Mr. Poe, their parents' banker, entrusts Count Olaf, their nearest relative, with their care. The trouble is that Olaf is an uncaring and scheming scoundrel. He's only interested in the fortune that Violet, the oldest child, will inherit when she's eighteen, and he'll resort to murder to acquire it. This capitalizes on a common theme in kids' books that adults cannot be trusted. It's difficult for the children to prove Olaf's mistreatment, but after they manage to do so, he flees, but never gives up on acquiring their fortune. In books that follow, he finds them and pursues new schemes to steal their inheritance. Additionally, the series has a Gothic, gloomy pall that increases the tension, and Olaf has a creepy cast of minions that add extra problems and dangers.

The whole series is extremely cohesive in terms of voice, Gothic elements, and outlandish story lines. Handler makes clever use of language and irony, as well as the voice of the opinionated narrator, Snicket, who has his own set of problems in following the Baudelaire orphans since his enemies are pursuing him to denounce him. Thus, the author makes Snicket part of the plot. And although the children face treachery, misery, and near-death at every turn, they appear to be the only sane people in a world turned upside down, where most adults are less than sane. The whole series is also interwoven with humor, which brings light-heartedness to the darkness of the plots. The series features a villain who will stop at nothing to acquire the children's fortune, and the series seems to teach that life doles out plenty of hardships, but if a kid has allies and inner resources, hardships help you find yourself and your strengths.

MENACING AND MEMORABLE

Besides being menacing, a good villain should linger in the reader's imagination long after he finishes the story. The first novel in Cornelia Funke's young adult series, Inkheart, introduces Capricorn, a dastardly and memorable villain. Funke delays the introduction of the villain, and instead reveals details through secondhand accounts and in increments. By the time the reader meets Capricorn, he's thoroughly frightened of him. Meggie, the twelve-year-old protagonist, first learns about Capricorn from Dustfinger, a man who existed in a story with him. You see, Meggie's father, Mo, a bookbinder by trade, has a hidden past and an unusual talent: When he reads stories aloud, the characters sometimes escape the boundaries of the story world and join the real world, and his readers sometimes leave the real world and join the story world. This is how Capricorn came to be such a threat to Meggie and her father—he has plans for them and will go to any length to achieve his evil goals.

In the opening scenes, Dustfinger tells Meggie that she had met Capricorn once, but she'd been too young to remember him. He begins by describing how Capricorn loves to watch things suffer, such as a bird being eaten by a cat. He then continues:

> "Capricorn can't bind books like your father," Dustfinger went on. "In fact, he's not much good at anything except terrifying people. But he's a master of that art. It's his whole life. I doubt if he himself has any idea what it's like to be so paralyzed by fear that you feel small and insignificant. But he knows just how to arouse that fear and spread it, in people's homes and their beds, in their heads and their hearts. His men spread fear abroad like the Black Death, they push it under doors and through mailboxes, they paint it on walls and stable doors until it infects everything around it of its own accord, silent and stinking like a plague." Dustfinger was very close to Meggie now. "Capricorn has many men," he said softly. "Most have

> been with him since they were children, and if Capricorn were to order one of them to cut off your nose or one of your ears he'd do it without batting an eyelash. They like to dress in black like crows—only their leader wears a white shirt under his black jacket—and should you ever meet any of them then make yourself small, very small, and hope they don't notice you. Understand?"
>
> Meggie nodded. Her heart was pounding so hard she could scarcely breathe.

This example from Funke illustrates how to create a villain who poses a threat, and who will complicate the protagonist's life and force the protagonist to change because she needs to overcome her fears to escape. Capricorn's evil power is complemented by his cast of minions, dressed in black and toting shotguns, who are murderous, violent, and not afraid of anyone or anything.

HARROWING ON ALL SIDES

With the Inkheart series, Funke has actually written about a group of villains instead of a single villain, and has ranked them according to their danger, depravity, and power. At first, the reader thinks that Capricorn is the main baddy, but as the story progresses, he also meets Capricorn's main henchman, the knife-wielding Basta, and his black-hearted mother, the Magpie. Then there is the Shadow, a villain who doesn't appear until the series climax, but who manages to haunt the story before his arrival with his depravity and powers. In fact, Capricorn is determined to control Meggie and her father because he wants them to summon the Shadow into the real world so that he can be the Shadow's master. Thus, when bad guys are coming at Meggie and her father from all sides, their situation appears especially dire.

Near the end of the story, the Shadow is described this way as Meggie reads out loud to a gathering:

> "He came only when Capricorn called him," she read. "Some times he was red as fire, sometimes gray as the ash to which fire turns all that it devours. He darted out of the earth as fast as flames lick their way up wood. His fingers and even his breath brought death. He rose before his master's feet, soundless, faceless, scenting his way like a hound on the trail and waiting for his master to point to the victim. It was said

> that Capricorn had commanded one of the trolls who understand the whole art of fire and smoke to create the Shadow from the ashes of his victims. No one was sure, for it was also said that Capricorn had ordered those who called the Shadow to life to be killed. All that everyone knew was that he was immortal, invulnerable, and pitiless, like his master."

As Meggie reads, the Shadow begins taking shape, growing taller and taller, amid the stench of ash and sulfur. He is described as having no face, but with "terrible eyes, red as the embers of a hidden fire."

ROGUE'S GALLERY

This list contains not only villains, but also stories that demonstrate characters grappling with difficult antagonists:

- Antagonist: Anna's father, *Wrecked* by E.R. Frank
- Antagonists: Matilda's parents, *Matilda* by Roald Dahl
- Villain: Miss Trunchbull, *Matilda* by Roald Dahl
- Villain: The Grinch, *How the Grinch Stole Christmas!* by Dr. Seuss
- Villains: Aunt Spiker and Aunt Sponge, *James and the Giant Peach* by Roald Dahl
- Villain: The Grand High Witch, *The Witches* by Roald Dahl
- Villain: Judd Travers, *Shiloh* by Phyllis Reynolds Naylor
- Villain: Jadis, the White Witch, *The Lion, the Witch and the Wardrobe* by C.S. Lewis
- Villain: IT, *A Wrinkle in Time* by Madeleine L'Engle
- Villains: Terrorists, *How I Live Now* by Meg Rosoff
- Villains: Louise and Dave O'Hearn, *In the Middle of the Night* by Robert Cormier
- Villain: Stacy's mother's murderer, *The Other Side of Dark* by Joan Lowery Nixon
- Villain: Mike Vamp, *Don't Look Behind You* by Lois Duncan
- Villain: The Cold One, *The Cold One* by Christopher Pike

The Shadow's appearance in the story provides an exciting climax and resolution, but he also appears amid intense actions that the human characters have set into motion. Funke has many techniques to emulate, but one you should especially pay attention to is her language—it is rich and spooky and alive.

When you write a villain into a story, you have an opportunity to take young readers to places where they'd never visit in real life. It's especially important that a villain's lair or the place where he's most powerful be especially vivid and dangerous. Your story might take place within a glittering magical kingdom, amid a small town, or in the protagonist's backyard, but the setting must always help provide the story's emotional ups and downs. In the Inkheart series, things happen in the dark a lot—we're all at a disadvantage in the dark. When Meggie first meets Capricorn in his village, she's taken into a room that's filled with dozens of candles in heavy silver candlesticks, but Meggie notes that instead of casting light, the candles seem to fill the room with shadows.

Young readers are looking for stories, language, and characters that sweep them away into a vivid and sharply drawn world. Since most novels for young readers are intensely character driven, slip deep inside your characters so they feel as real to you as your own children or young friends. Don't write for this age group unless you can see the world through the eyes of a child, or have vivid remembrances of childhood or teenage emotions. Also, when deciding on the potency of your bad guys, remember that one of the jobs for writing for this group is to instill hope and a sense of possibility in readers.

Questions for Bad Guys

The following are questions to pose about various character types, especially antagonists and villains. However, you would be wise to know the answers to these questions for any major player in your story.

- What does he most desire in the story?
- What does he fear most?
- Does he have enemies?
- How is he larger than life, meaning what qualities and actions does he have that linger in the reader's imagination?
- Is he distinctive in appearance and attitude?
- Does he have an interesting career?
- Is he disfigured, or does he have another physical characteristic to make him memorable?
- How far will he go to achieve his goals?

- Have you first introduced him with flair?
- Is he introduced early in the story?
- How does he act when he loses his temper or is enraged?
- Does he use bad language?
- If he were wakened from a sound sleep, how would he act?
- If he were to face an intruder in his home, how would he act?

- Does he lie?
- Has he experienced any great losses in his past?
- If he is somehow repulsive, can this be justified?
- Is he somehow sympathetic or likeable? If so, why?
- Is he somehow flawed, vulnerable, or wounded—mentally, physically, or emotionally?
- Does he have specific crime skills or powers?
- Is his motivation plausible and interesting?
- Is he capable of insights, humor, or irony?
- Is he powerful enough to crush the protagonist?
- Is he included as an adversary in key scenes in all three acts of the story?
- Is he defeated at the end of the story?
- If you saw him walking toward you for the first time, what would your first impression be? Would his true personality be apparent via this first impression?
- What is most noticeable about his appearance? Besides these physical characteristics, is he neat, sloppy, stylish, flamboyant, elegant, or Bohemian?
- How does he move and hold his body? What does his body type, movements, and gestures say about him?
- Does he remind you of a celebrity, a person you know, an animal, or an object?
- What kind of clothes does he wear? Expensive? Conservative? Trendy? Outdated? Do these clothes reflect his personality?
- What is his voice like? Throaty? Sexy? High-pitched? Squeaky? Confident and resonant? Timid and barely audible? Is there laughter in his voice? Does he talk quickly or hesitantly? Does he have a lisp, an accent, or recurring pet phrases?

- What time in history was he born and growing up in? Are these events still relevant in his life? What decade had the most influence on him?
- What games did he play as a child? Did he spend time outdoors? Was his neighborhood safe?
- What is the most important thing in his life? Is it a spouse, child, job, or possession? Is this importance healthy? Does he fear losing it?
- Is he driven, competitive, or obsessive? If not, how will you create his conflict? Do the problems, complications, and challenges of the plot affect him personally?
- How does he react to the secondary characters? How does he act toward children, sick people, elderly people, and animals? How does he treat cab drivers, store clerks, waitresses, and people on the street?
- How is he going to grow and change as the result of the story's events? Will he become weaker before he gets stronger? Will he almost give up? Will he mature?

Index